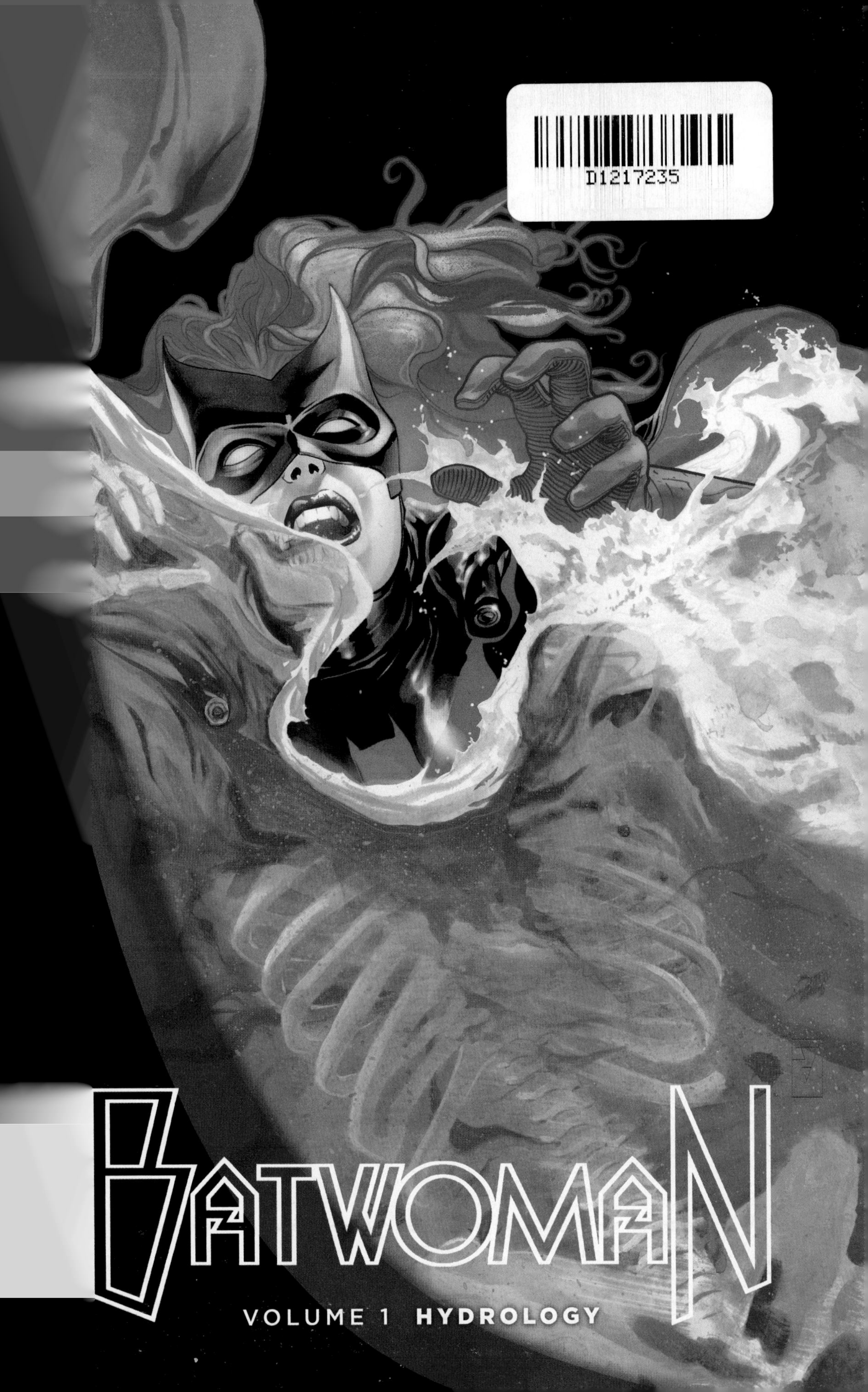

BATWOMAN

VOLUME 1 **HYDROLOGY**

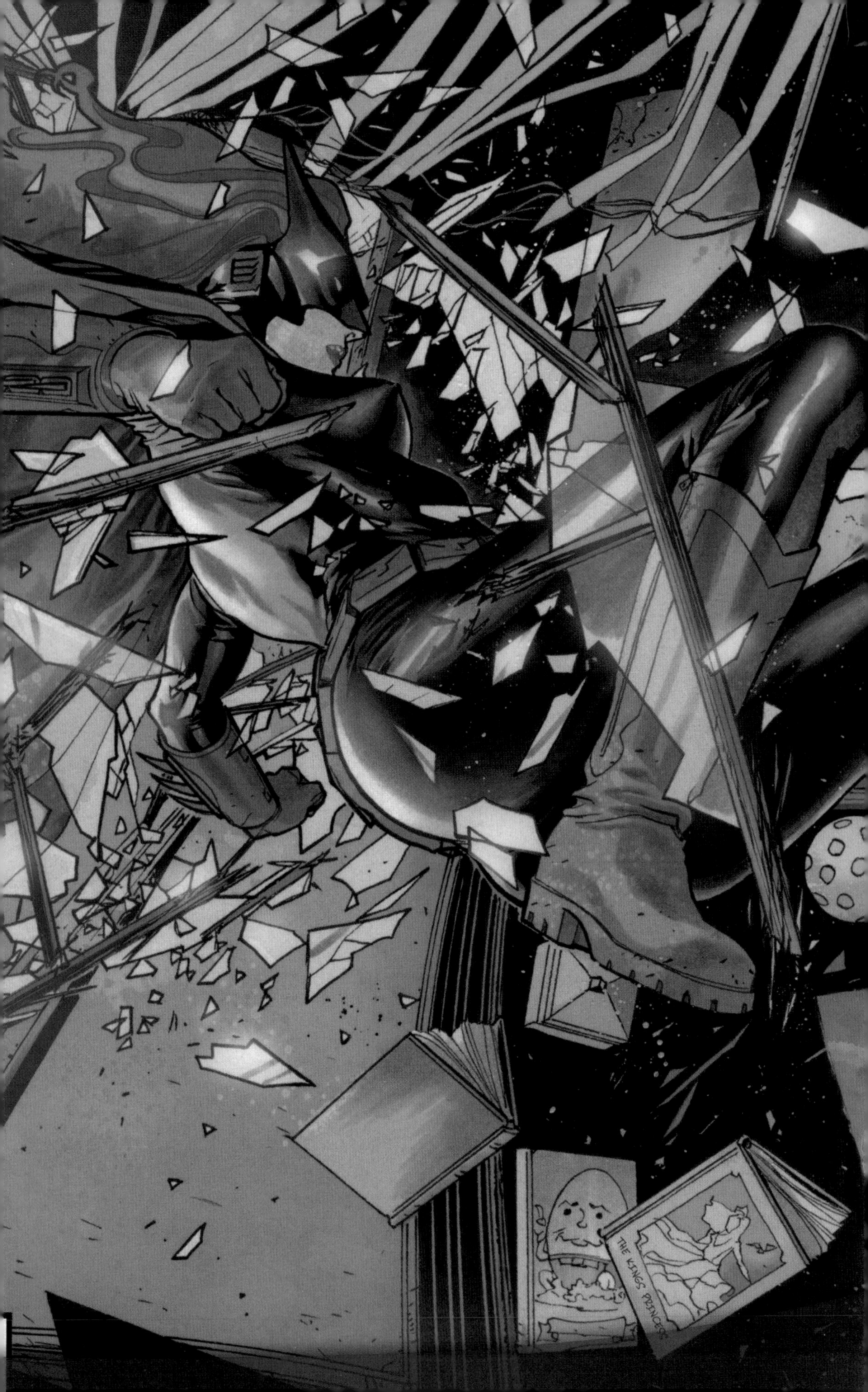
THE KINGS PRINCESS

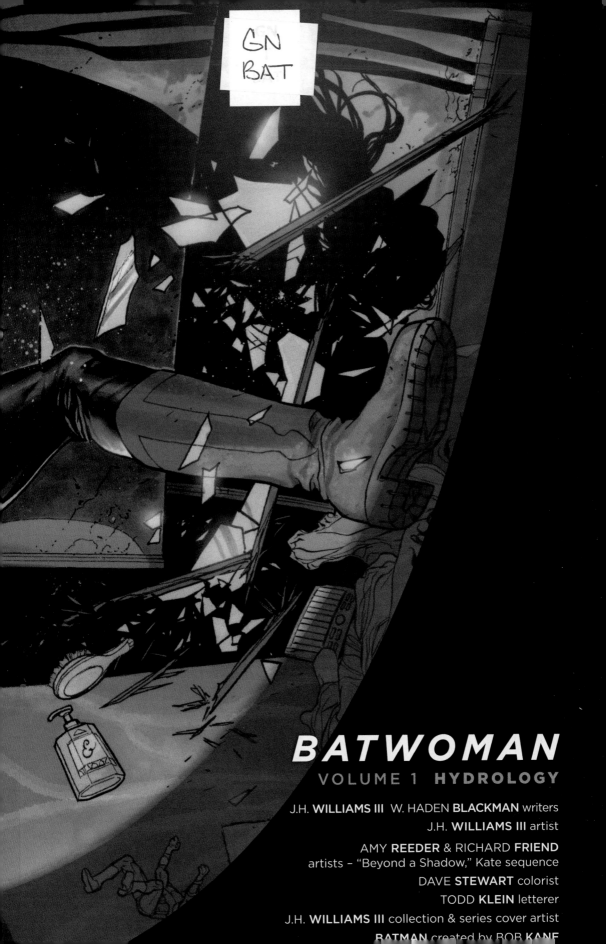

GN
BAT

BATWOMAN
VOLUME 1 *HYDROLOGY*

J.H. **WILLIAMS III** W. HADEN **BLACKMAN** writers

J.H. **WILLIAMS III** artist

AMY **REEDER** & RICHARD **FRIEND**
artists – "Beyond a Shadow," Kate sequence

DAVE **STEWART** colorist

TODD **KLEIN** letterer

J.H. **WILLIAMS III** collection & series cover artist

BATMAN created by BOB **KANE**

MIKE MARTS Editor – Original Series HARVEY RICHARDS JANELLE ASSELIN Associate Editors – Original Series
RICKEY PURDIN Assistant Editor– Original Series PETER HAMBOUSSI Editor
ROBBIN BROSTERMAN Design Director – Books ROBBIE BIEDERMAN Publication Design

BOB HARRAS Senior VP – Editor-in-Chief, DC Comics

DIANE NELSON President DAN DIDIO and JIM LEE Co-Publishers GEOFF JOHNS Chief Creative Officer
JOHN ROOD Executive VP – Sales, Marketing and Business Development
AMY GENKINS Senior VP – Business and Legal Affairs NAIRI GARDINER Senior VP – Finance
JEFF BOISON VP – Publishing Planning MARK CHIARELLO VP – Art Direction and Design
JOHN CUNNINGHAM VP – Marketing TERRI CUNNINGHAM VP – Editorial Administration
ALISON GILL Senior VP – Manufacturing and Operations HANK KANALZ Senior VP – Vertigo and Integrated Publishing
JAY KOGAN VP – Business and Legal Affairs, Publishing JACK MAHAN VP – Business Affairs, Talent
NICK NAPOLITANO VP – Manufacturing Administration SUE POHJA VP – Book Sales
COURTNEY SIMMONS Senior VP – Publicity BOB WAYNE Senior VP – Sales

BATWOMAN VOLUME ONE: HYDROLOGY

DC Comics, 1700 Broadway, New York, NY 10019
A Warner Bros. Entertainment Company.
Printed by RR Donnelley, Salem, VA, USA. 10/4/13. Second Printing.

HC ISBN: 978-1-4012-3465-2
SC ISBN: 978-1-4012-3784-4

SUSTAINABLE FORESTRY INITIATIVE

Certified Chain of Custody
At Least 20% Certified Forest Content
www.sfiprogram.org
SFI-01042
APPLIES TO TEXT STOCK ONLY

Library of Congress Cataloging-in-Publication Data

Williams, J. H., III.
Batwoman volume one : hydrology / J.H. Williams III, W. Haden Blackman.
p. cm.
"Originally published in single magazine form in Batwoman 0-5"—T.p. verso.
ISBN 978-1-4012-3465-2
1. Graphic novels. I. Blackman, W. Haden. II. Title. III. Title: Hydrology.
PN6728.B365W55 2012
741.5'973—dc23
2012002252

T 96312

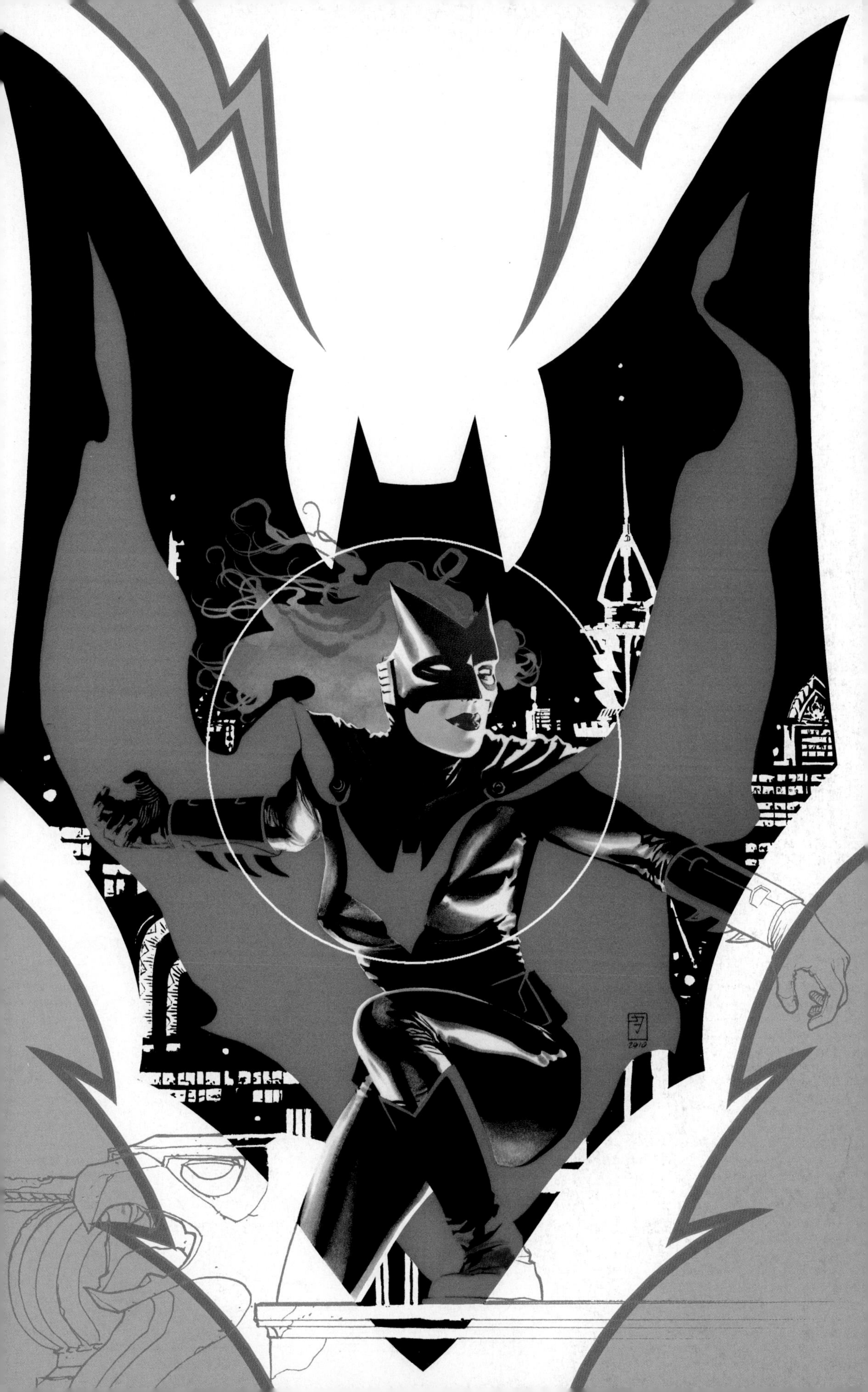

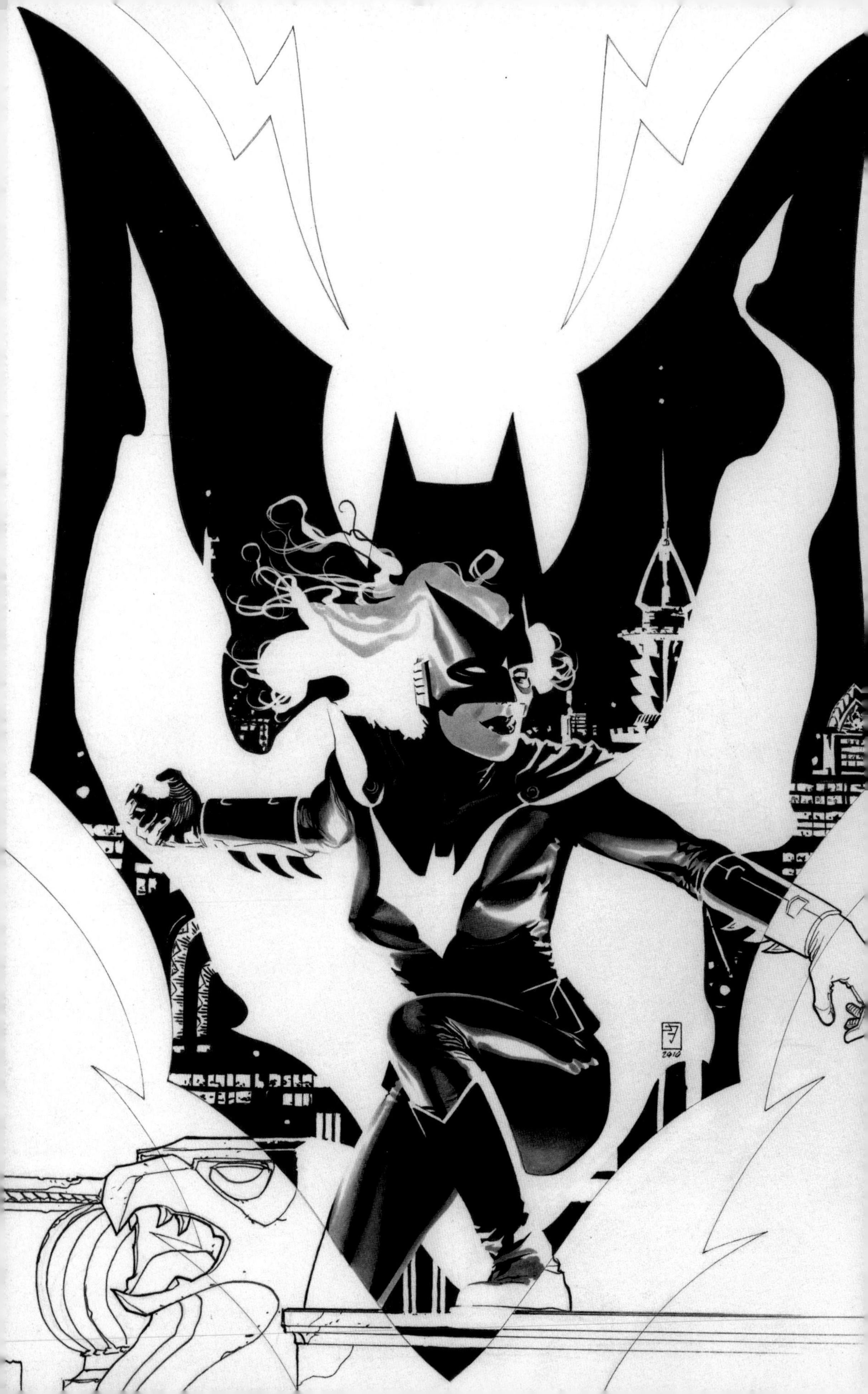

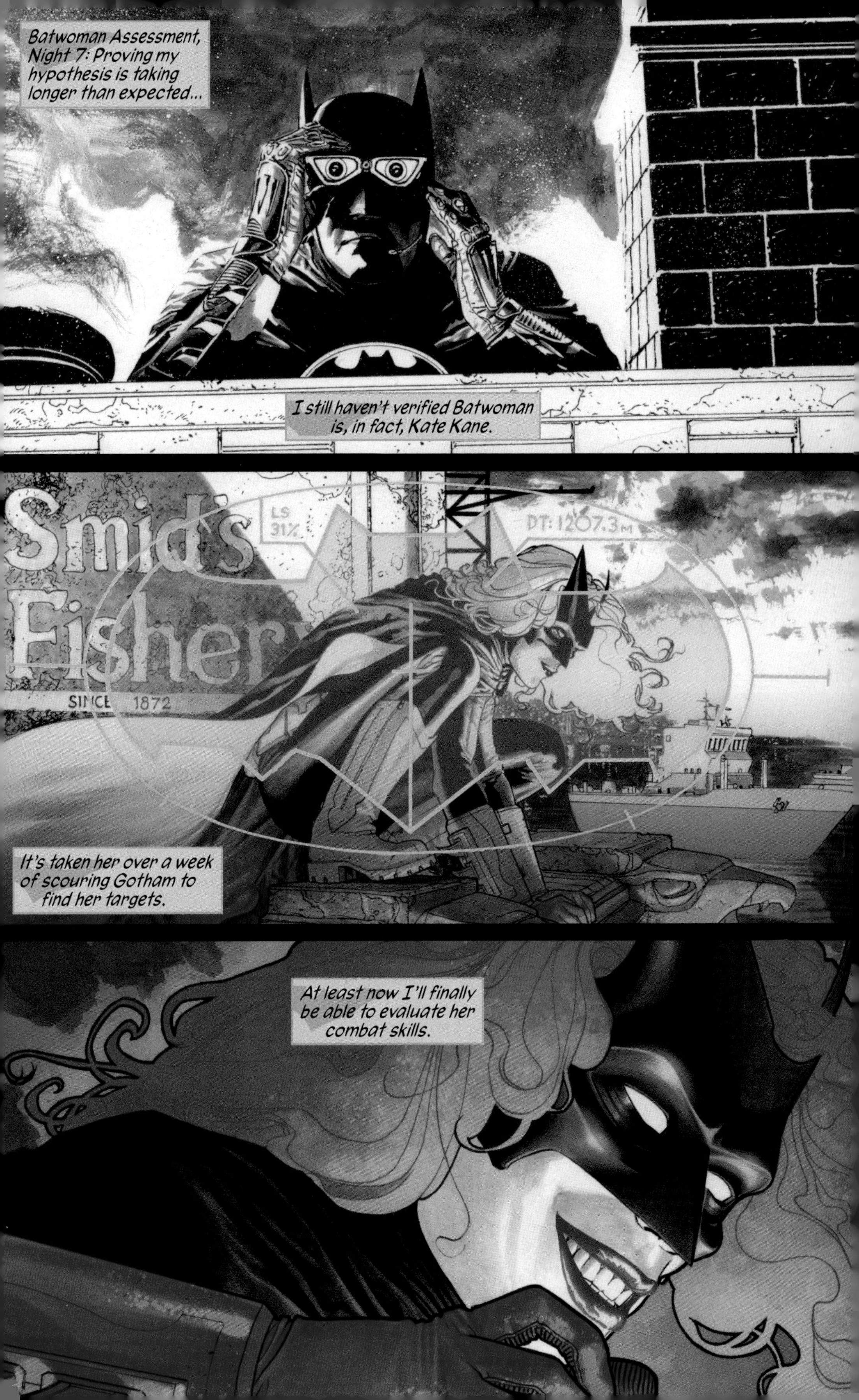
Batwoman Assessment, Night 7: Proving my hypothesis is taking longer than expected...
I still haven't verified Batwoman is, in fact, Kate Kane.
Smid's Fisher
SINCE 1872
LS 31%
DT: 1207.3M
It's taken her over a week of scouring Gotham to find her targets.
At least now I'll finally be able to evaluate her combat skills.

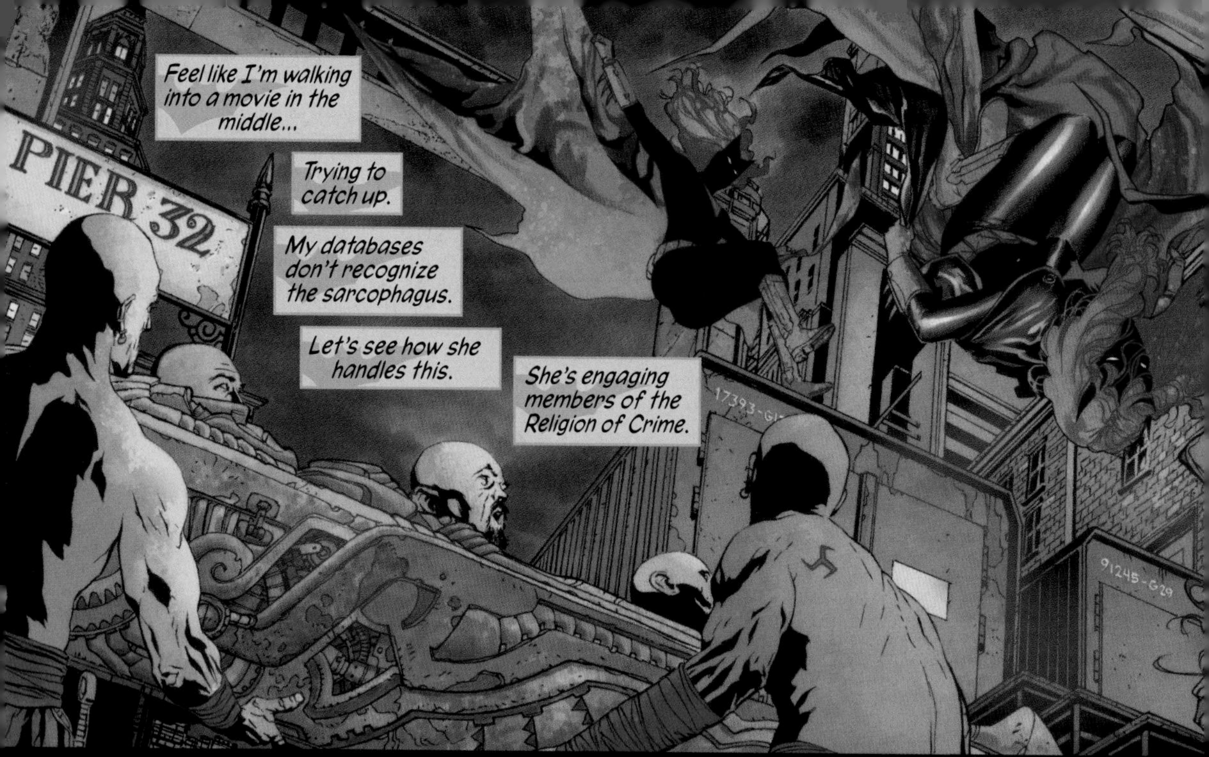
Feel like I'm walking into a movie in the middle...
Trying to catch up.
My databases don't recognize the sarcophagus.
Let's see how she handles this.
She's engaging members of the Religion of Crime.
PIER 32
17393-G1
91245-G29

BEYOND A

J.H. WILLIAMS III: writer - artist
W. HADEN BLACKMAN: co-writer
AMY REEDER: artist - Kate sequence
RICHARD FRIEND: inker - Kate sequence

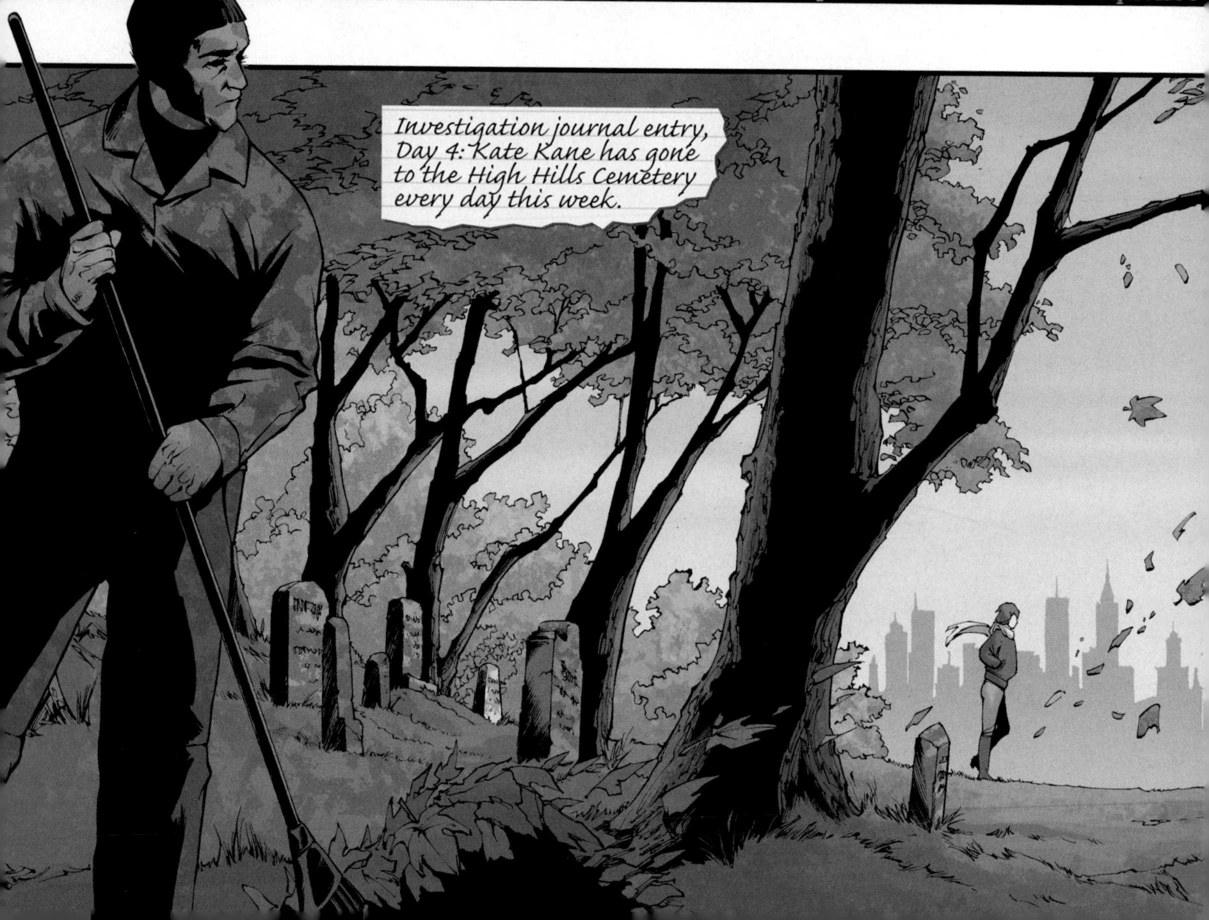
Investigation journal entry, Day 4: Kate Kane has gone to the High Hills Cemetery every day this week.

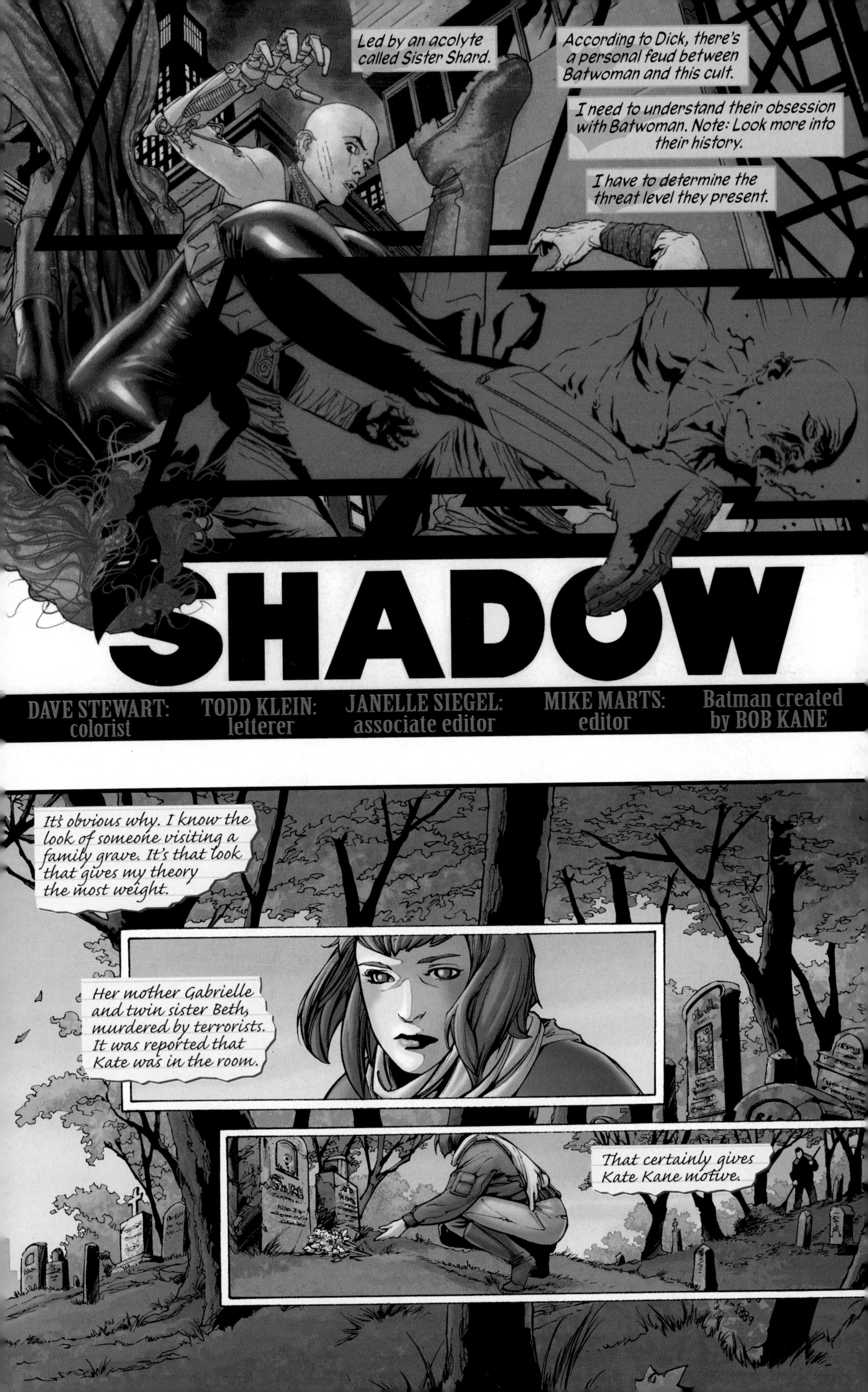
Led by an acolyte called Sister Shard.
According to Dick, there's a personal feud between Batwoman and this cult.
I need to understand their obsession with Batwoman. Note: Look more into their history.
I have to determine the threat level they present.
SHADOW
DAVE STEWART: colorist
TODD KLEIN: letterer
JANELLE SIEGEL: associate editor
MIKE MARTS: editor
Batman created by BOB KANE
It's obvious why. I know the look of someone visiting a family grave. It's that look that gives my theory the most weight.
Her mother Gabrielle and twin sister Beth, murdered by terrorists. It was reported that Kate was in the room.
That certainly gives Kate Kane motive.

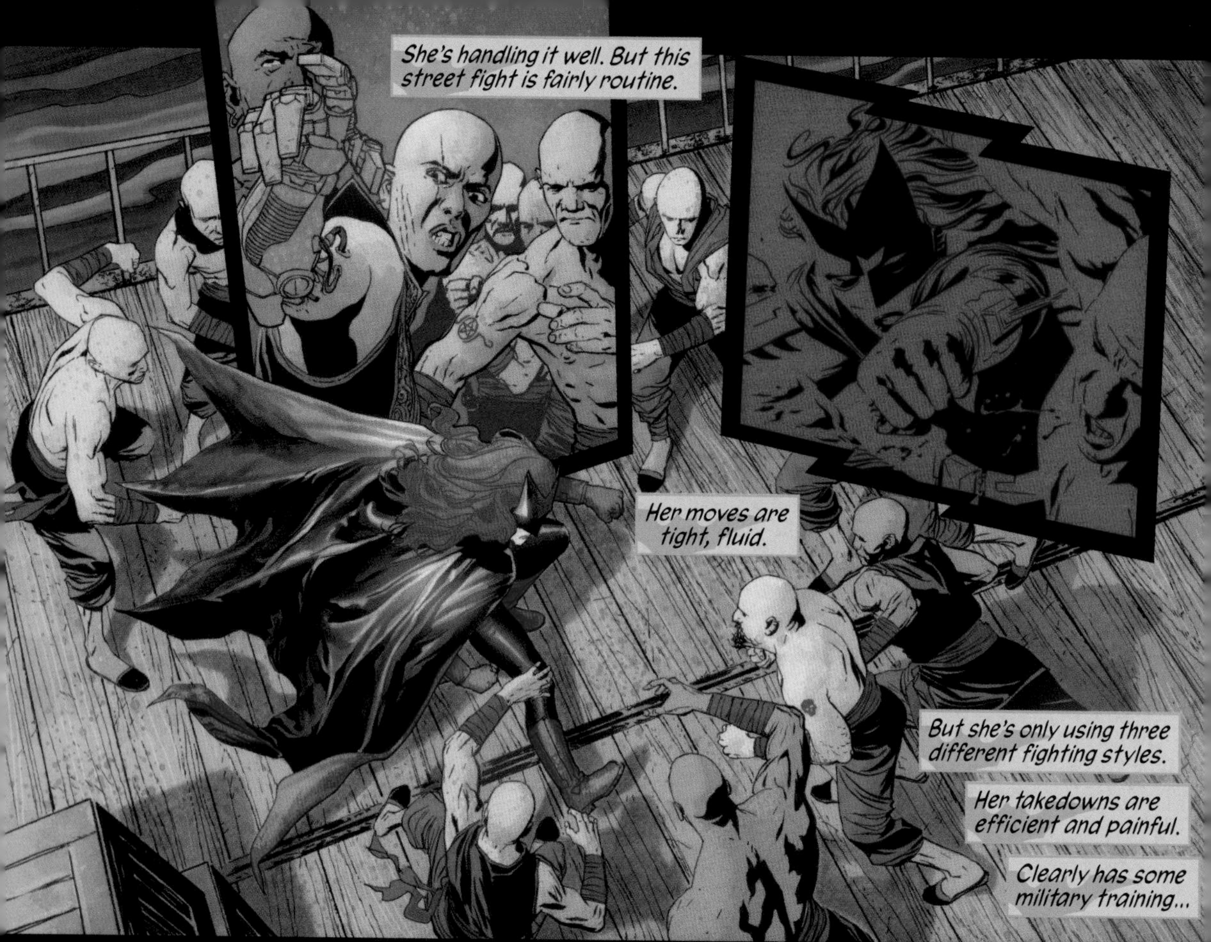
She's handling it well. But this street fight is fairly routine.
Her moves are tight, fluid.
But she's only using three different fighting styles.
Her takedowns are efficient and painful.
Clearly has some military training...

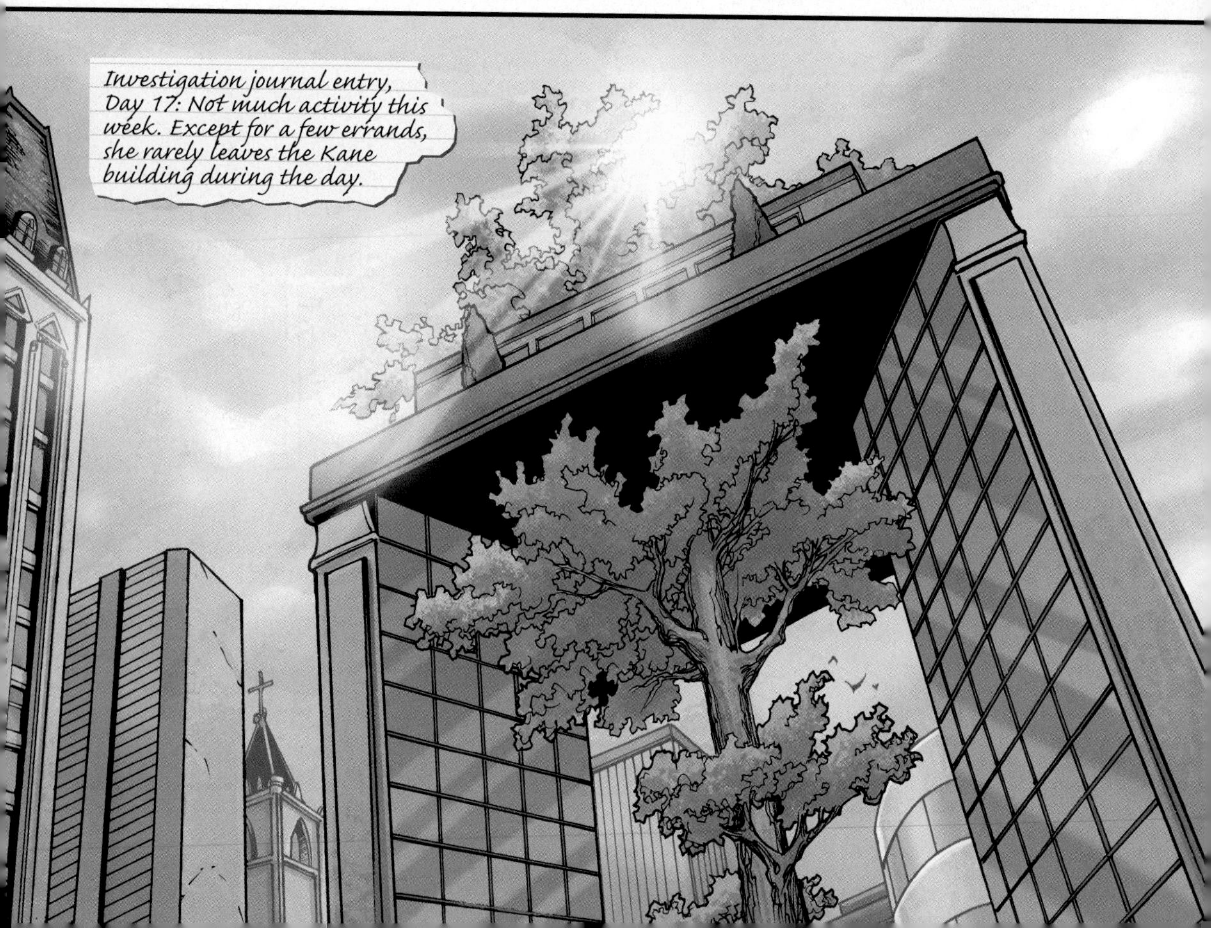
Investigation journal entry, Day 17: Not much activity this week. Except for a few errands, she rarely leaves the Kane building during the day.

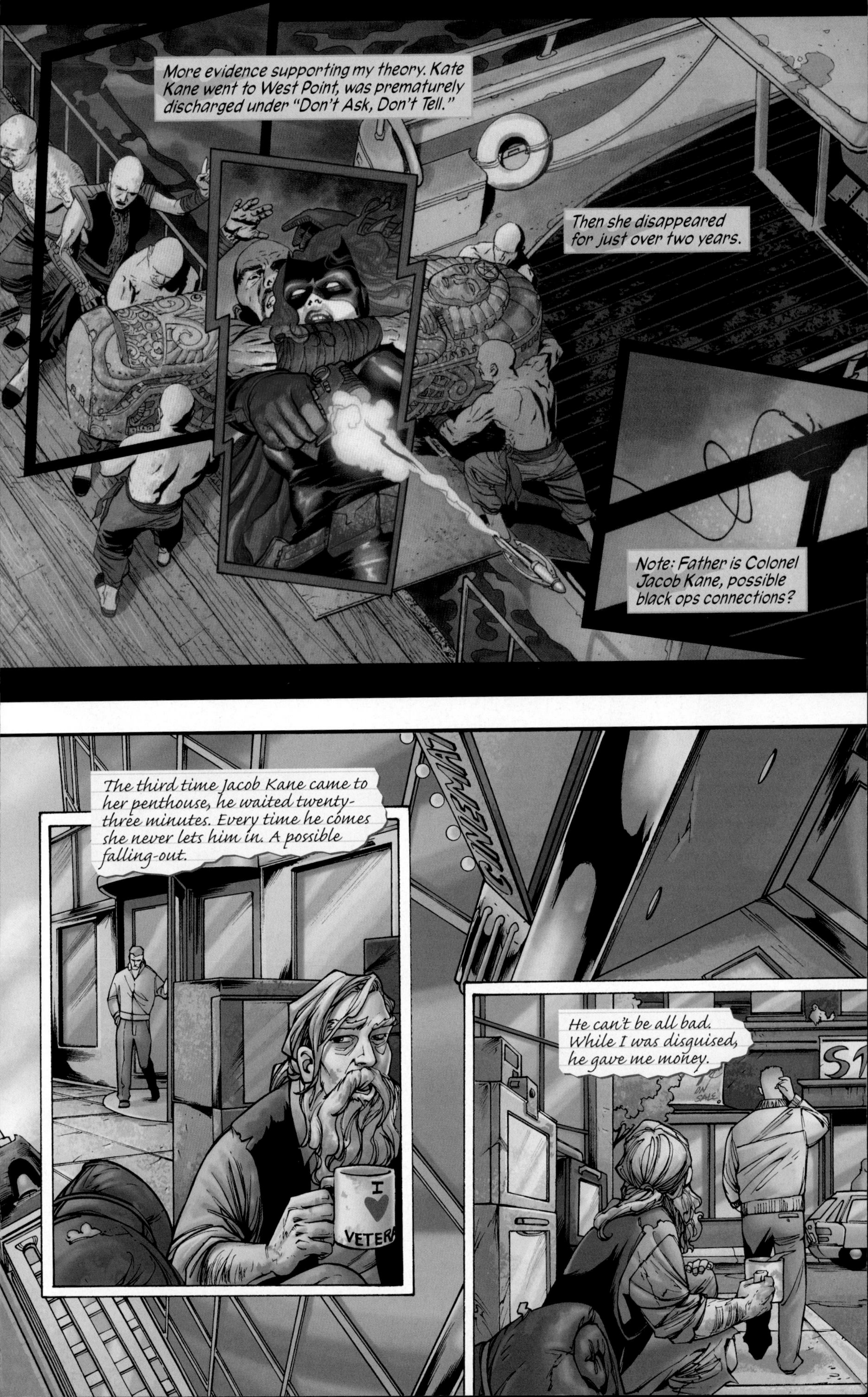
More evidence supporting my theory. Kate Kane went to West Point, was prematurely discharged under "Don't Ask, Don't Tell."
Then she disappeared for just over two years.
Note: Father is Colonel Jacob Kane, possible black ops connections?
The third time Jacob Kane came to her penthouse, he waited twenty-three minutes. Every time he comes she never lets him in. A possible falling-out.
He can't be all bad. While I was disguised, he gave me money.

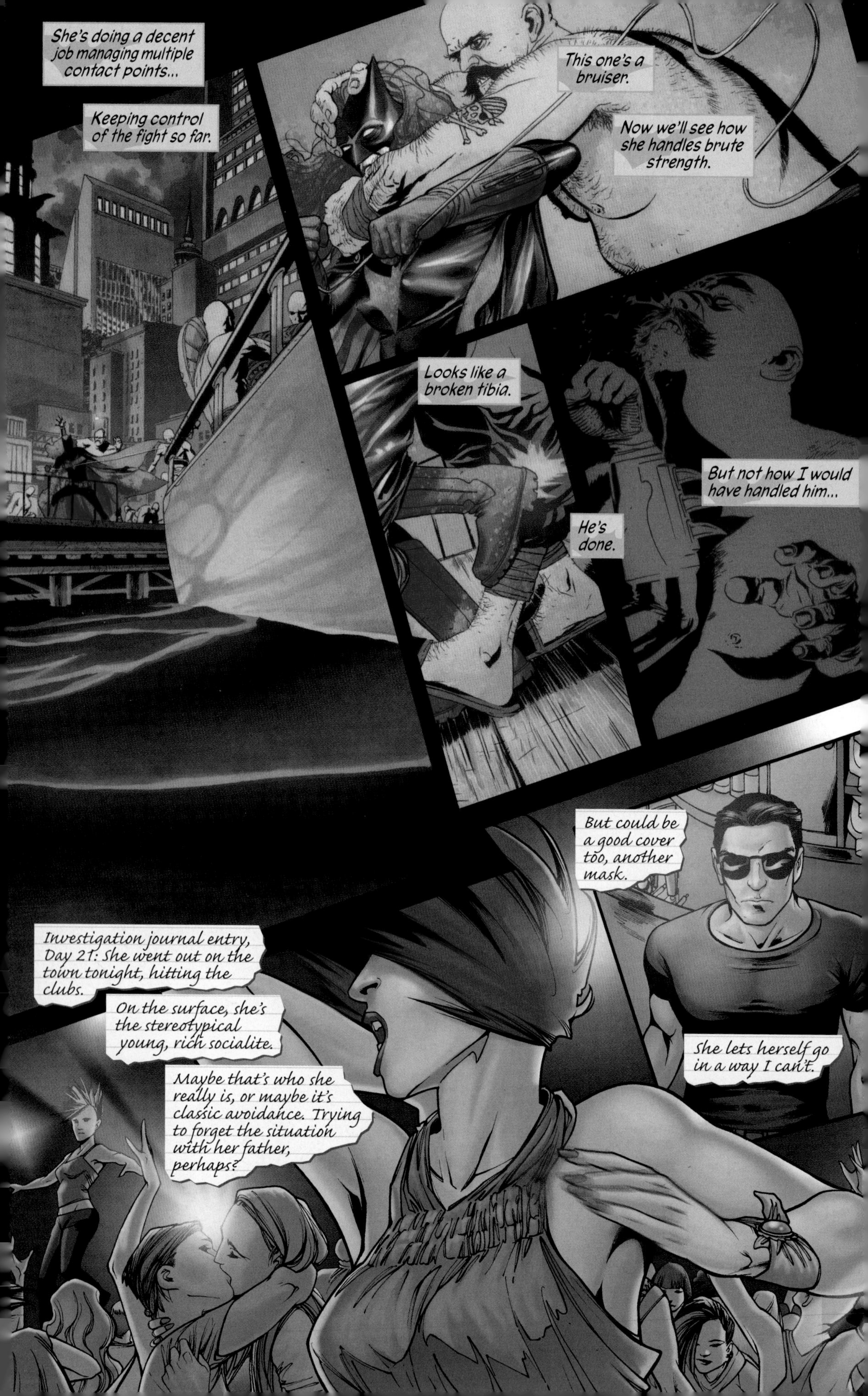
She's doing a decent job managing multiple contact points...
Keeping control of the fight so far.
This one's a bruiser.
Now we'll see how she handles brute strength.
Looks like a broken tibia.
He's done.
But not how I would have handled him...
But could be a good cover too, another mask.
Investigation journal entry, Day 21: She went out on the town tonight, hitting the clubs.
On the surface, she's the stereotypical young, rich socialite.
Maybe that's who she really is, or maybe it's classic avoidance. Trying to forget the situation with her father, perhaps?
She lets herself go in a way I can't.

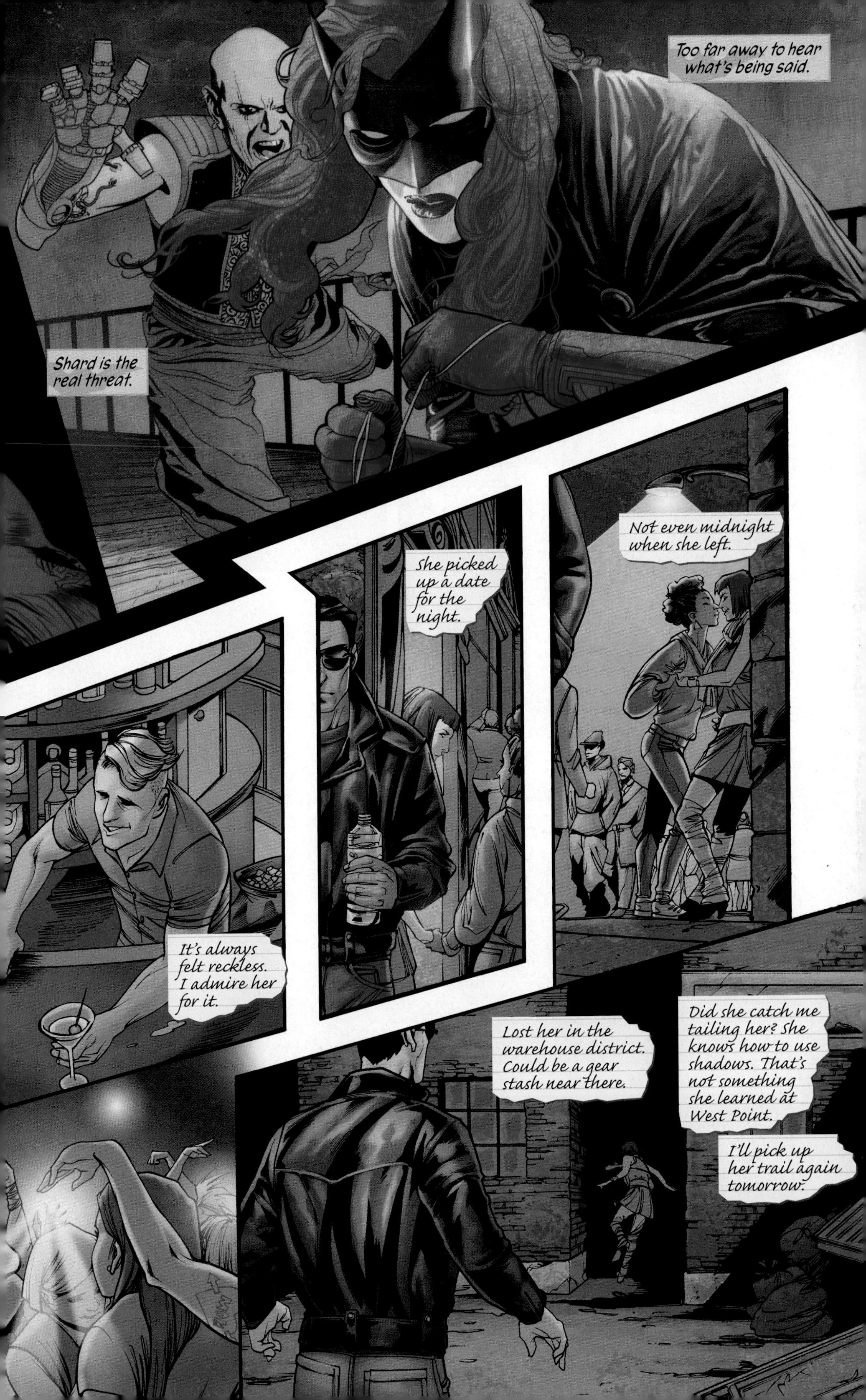
Too far away to hear what's being said.
Shard is the real threat.
It's always felt reckless. I admire her for it.
She picked up a date for the night.
Not even midnight when she left.
Lost her in the warehouse district. Could be a gear stash near there.
Did she catch me tailing her? She knows how to use shadows. That's not something she learned at West Point.
I'll pick up her trail again tomorrow.

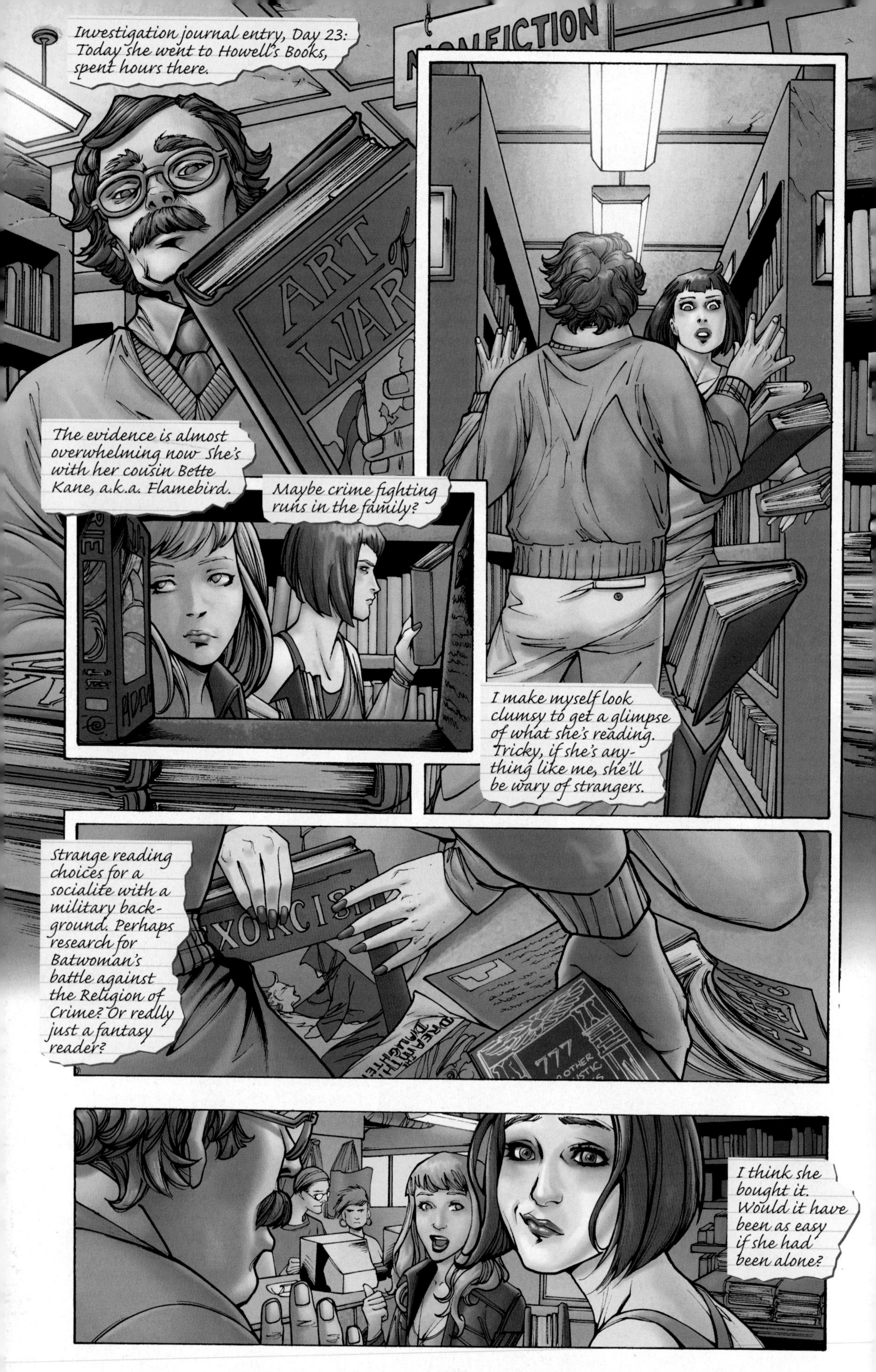
NONFICTION
Investigation journal entry, Day 23: Today she went to Howell's Books, spent hours there.
ART WAR
The evidence is almost overwhelming now. She's with her cousin Bette Kane, a.k.a. Flamebird.
Maybe crime fighting runs in the family?
I make myself look clumsy to get a glimpse of what she's reading. Tricky, if she's anything like me, she'll be wary of strangers.
Strange reading choices for a socialite with a military background. Perhaps research for Batwoman's battle against the Religion of Crime? Or really just a fantasy reader?
EXORCISM
777
I think she bought it. Would it have been as easy if she had been alone?

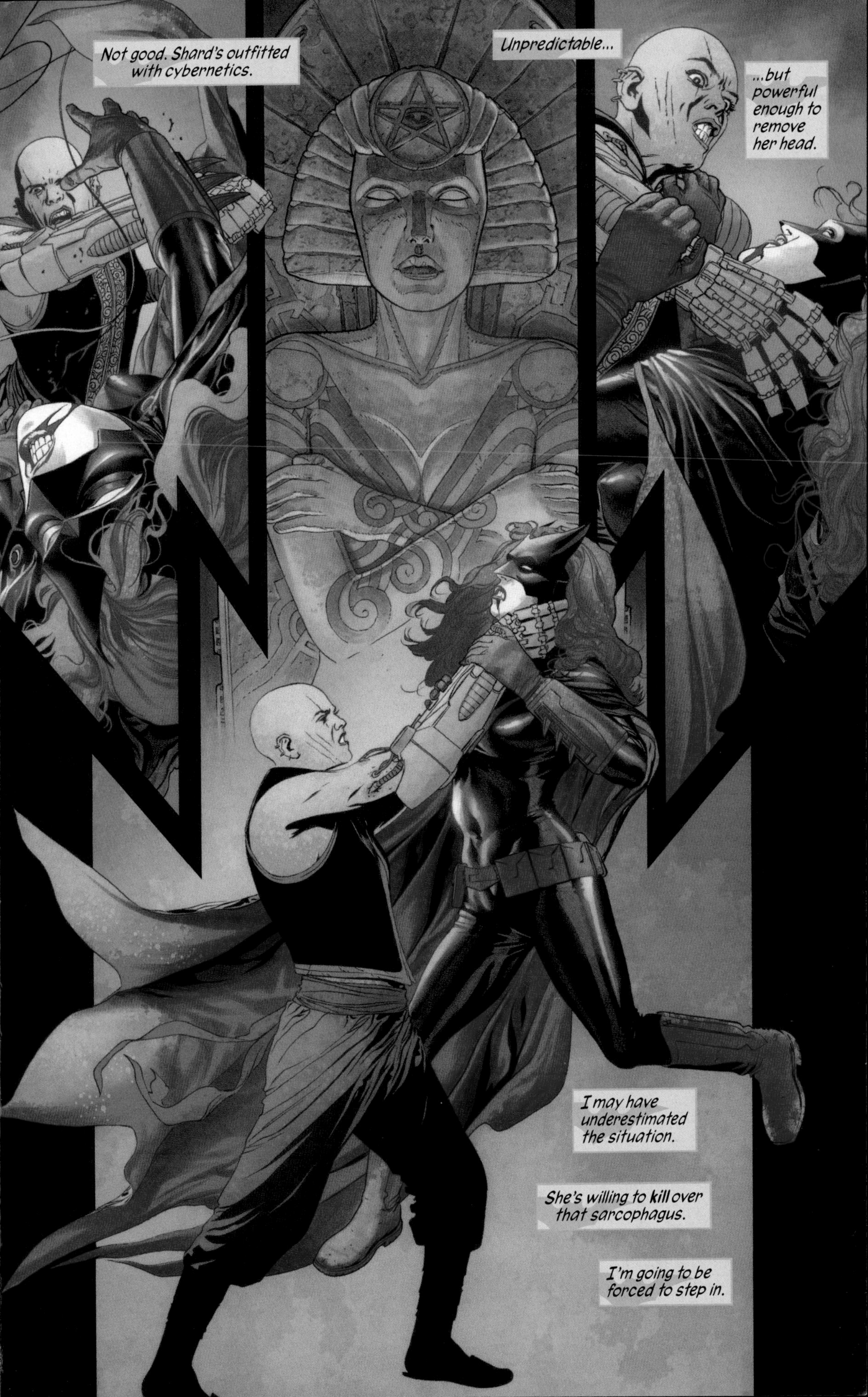
Not good. Shard's outfitted with cybernetics.
Unpredictable...
...but powerful enough to remove her head.
I may have underestimated the situation.
She's willing to kill over that sarcophagus.
I'm going to be forced to step in.

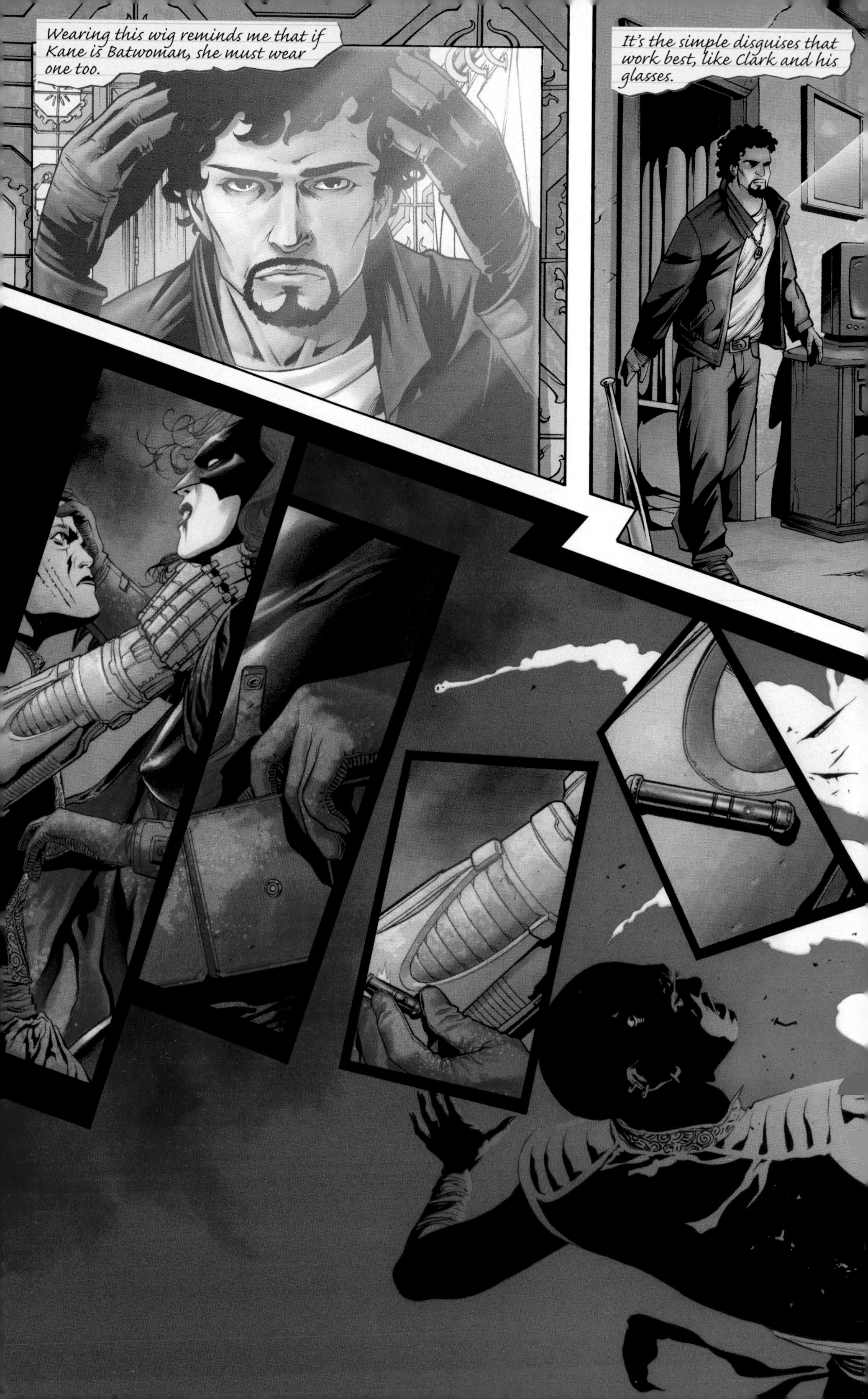
Wearing this wig reminds me that if Kane is Batwoman, she must wear one too.
It's the simple disguises that work best, like Clark and his glasses.

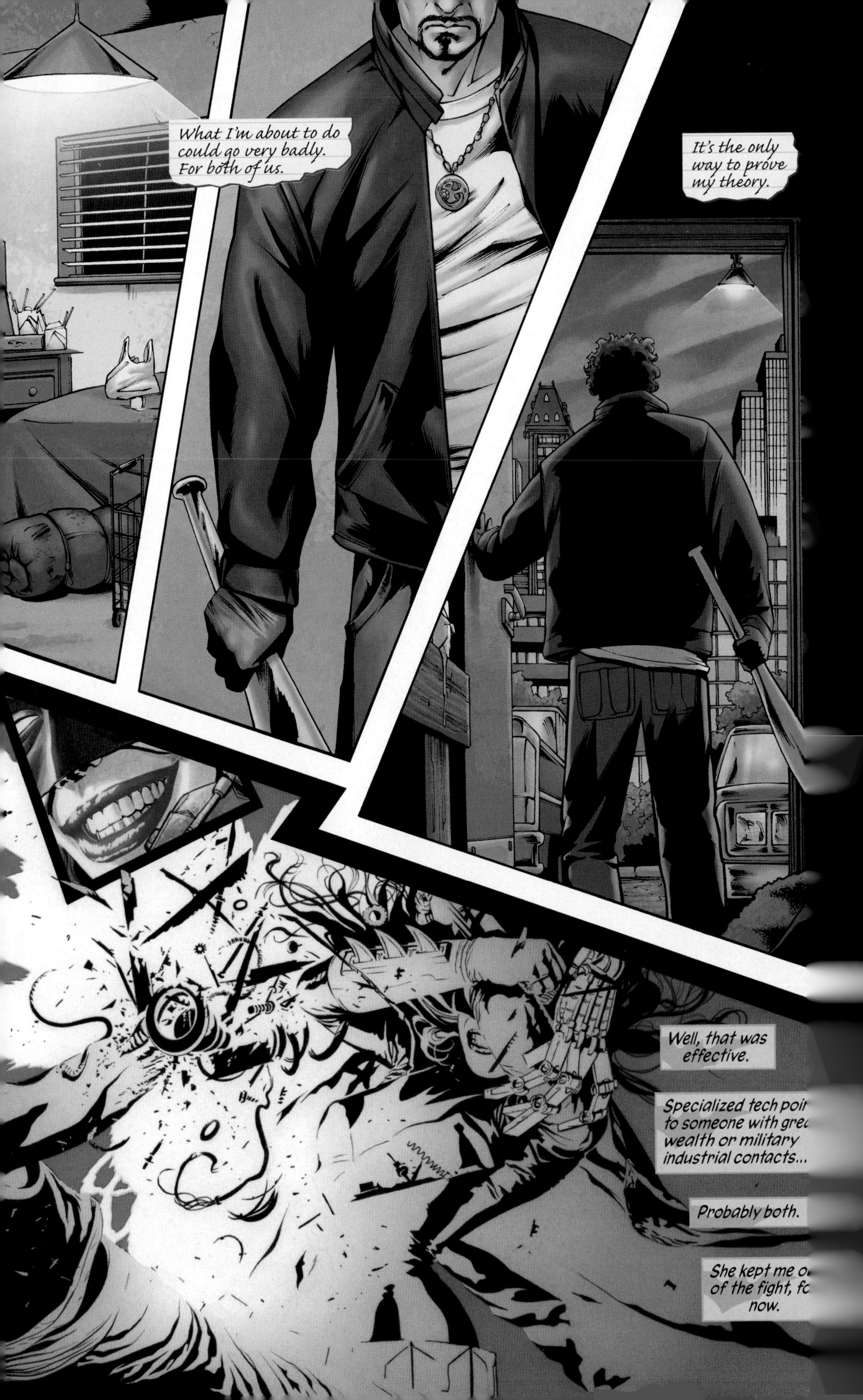

What I'm about to do could go very badly. For both of us.
It's the only way to prove my theory.
Well, that was effective.
Specialized tech poi
to someone with gre
wealth or military
industrial contacts...
Probably both.
She kept me o
of the fight, fo
now.

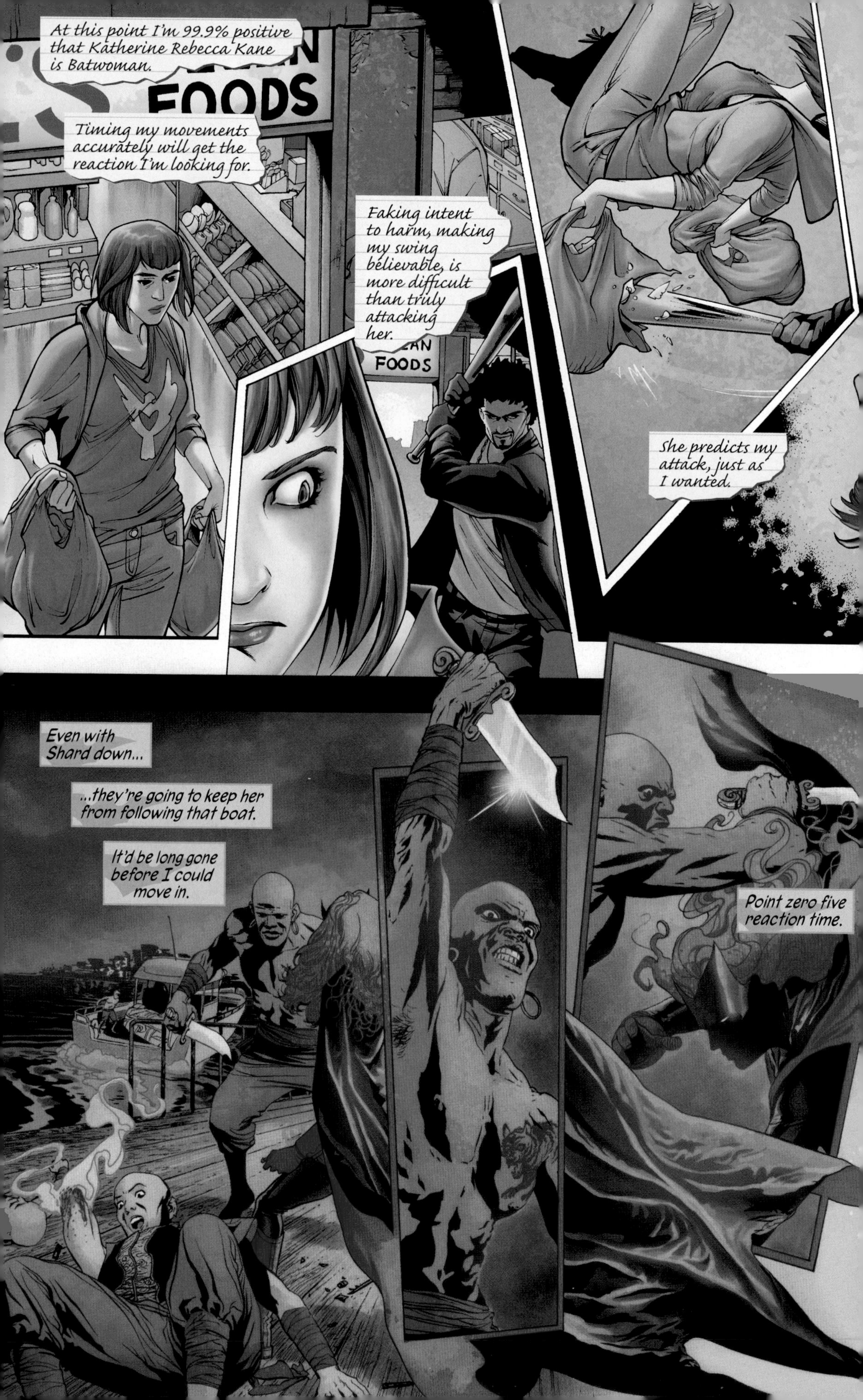
At this point I'm 99.9% positive that Katherine Rebecca Kane is Batwoman.
FOODS
Timing my movements accurately will get the reaction I'm looking for.
Faking intent to harm, making my swing believable, is more difficult than truly attacking her.
FOODS
She predicts my attack, just as I wanted.
Even with Shard down...
...they're going to keep her from following that boat.
It'd be long gone before I could move in.
Point zero five reaction time.

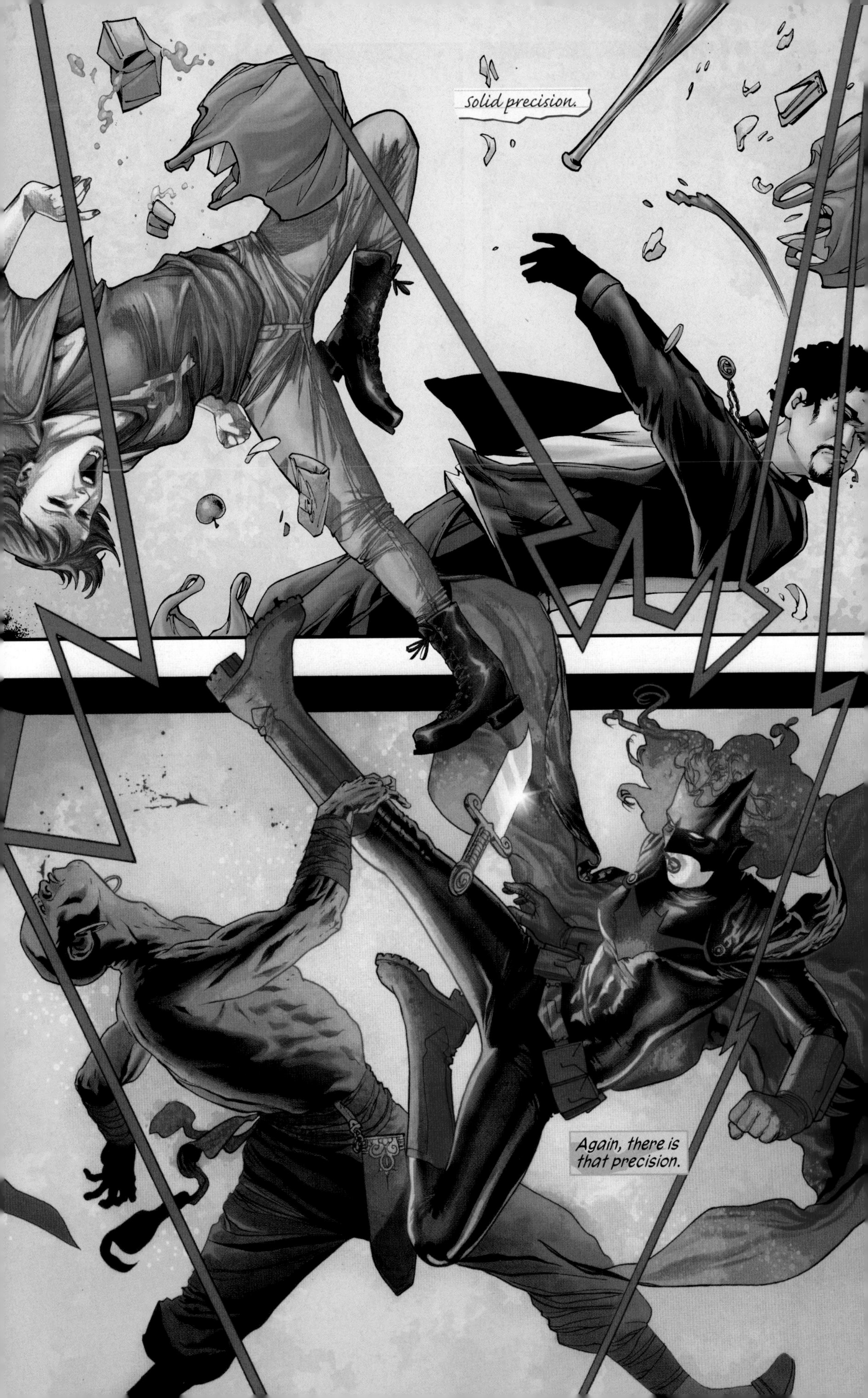
solid precision.
Again, there is that precision.

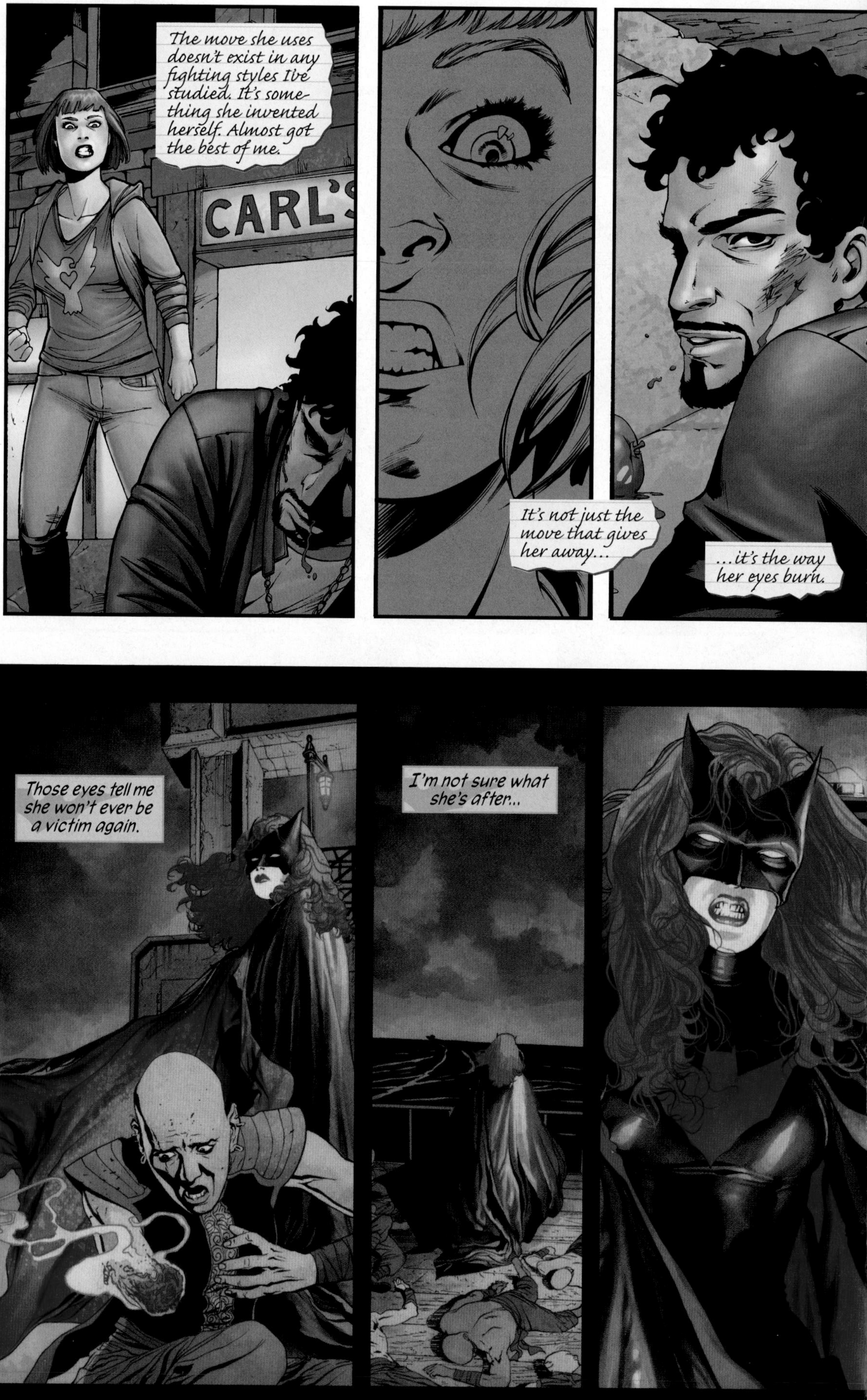
The move she uses doesn't exist in any fighting styles I've studied. It's something she invented herself. Almost got the best of me.
CARL'S
It's not just the move that gives her away...
...it's the way her eyes burn.
Those eyes tell me she won't ever be a victim again.
I'm not sure what she's after...

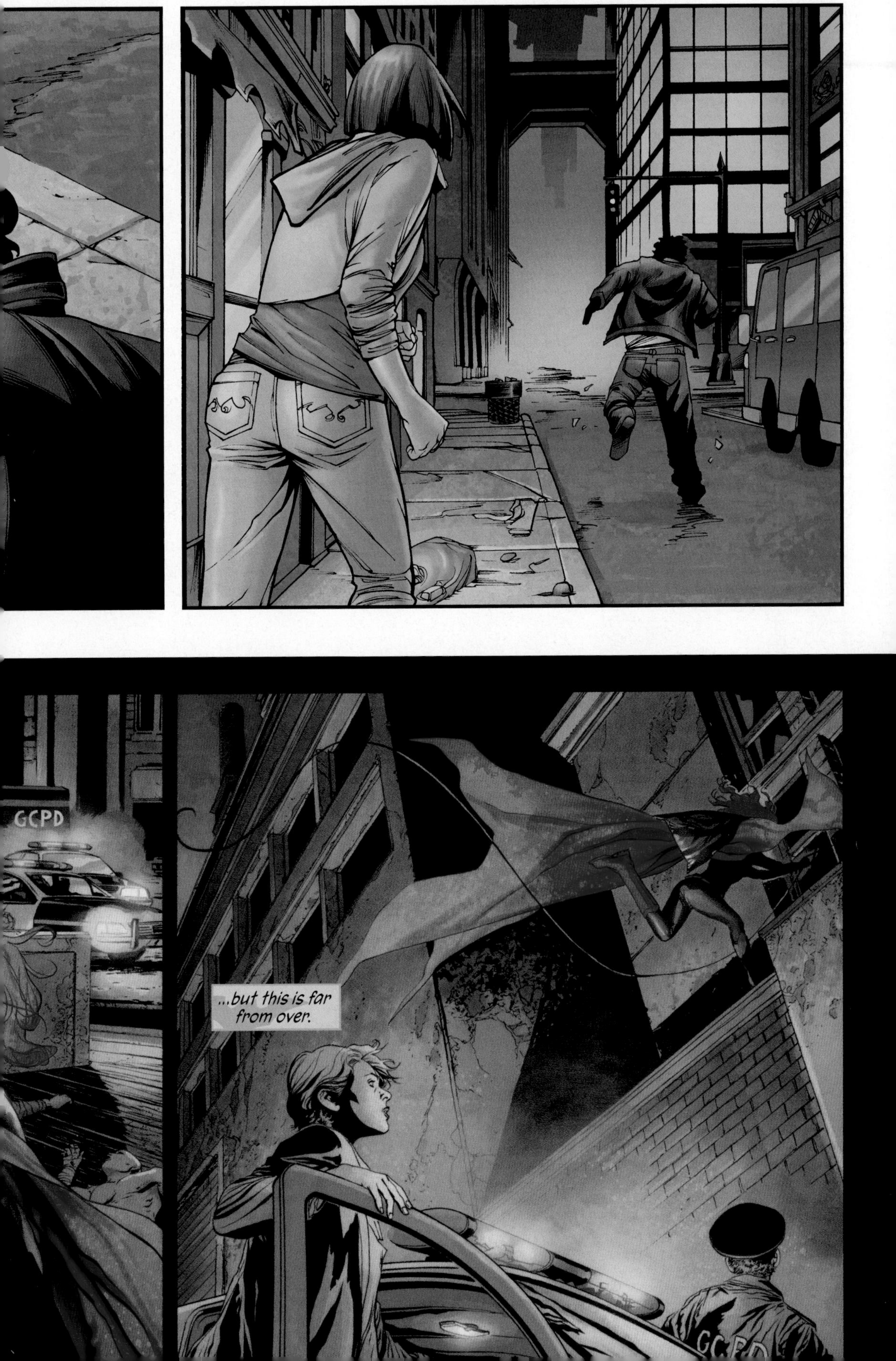
GCPD
...but this is far from over.
GCPD

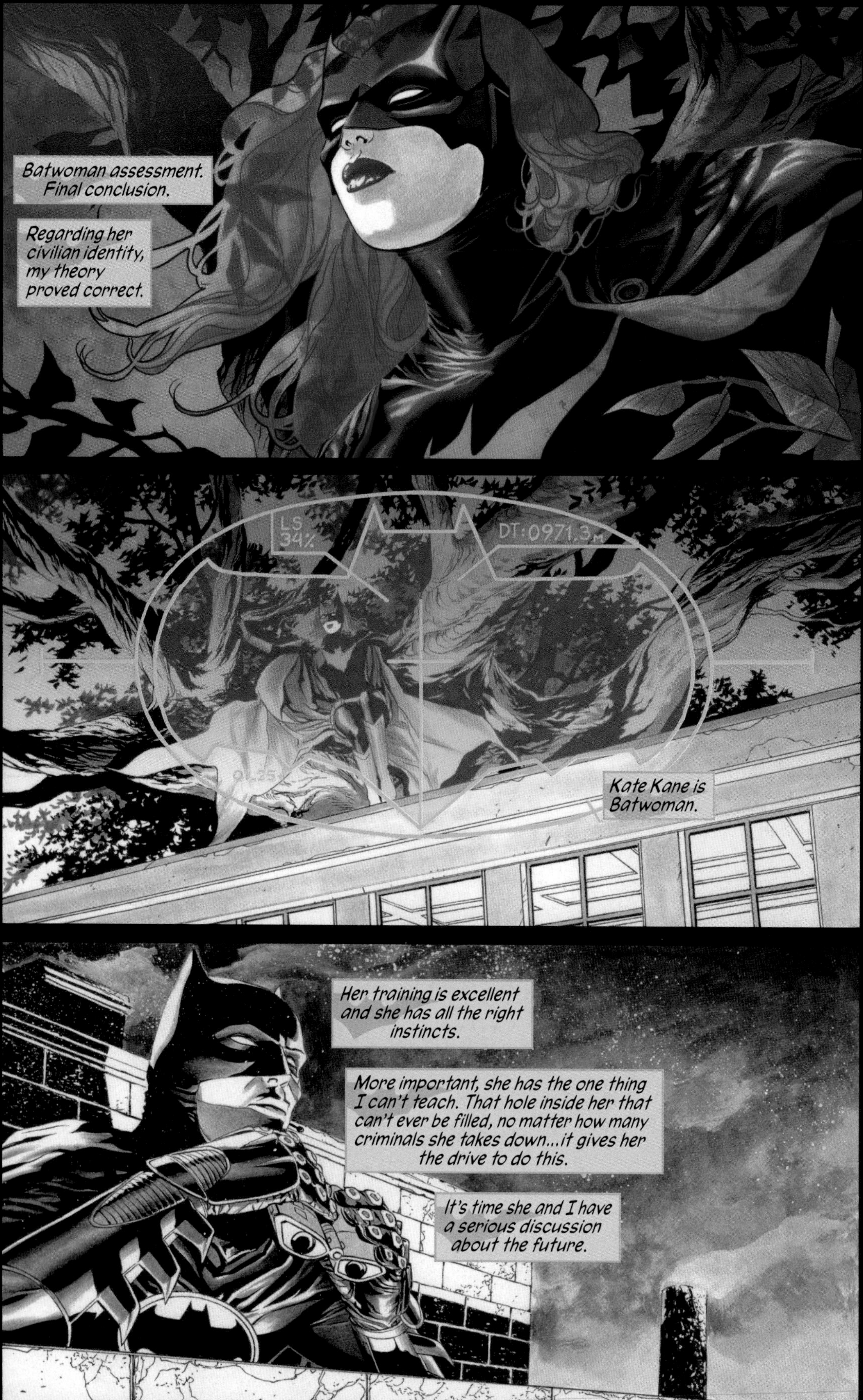
Batwoman assessment. Final conclusion.
Regarding her civilian identity, my theory proved correct.
LS 34%
DT:0971.3M
Kate Kane is Batwoman.
Her training is excellent and she has all the right instincts.
More important, she has the one thing I can't teach. That hole inside her that can't ever be filled, no matter how many criminals she takes down...it gives her the drive to do this.
It's time she and I have a serious discussion about the future.

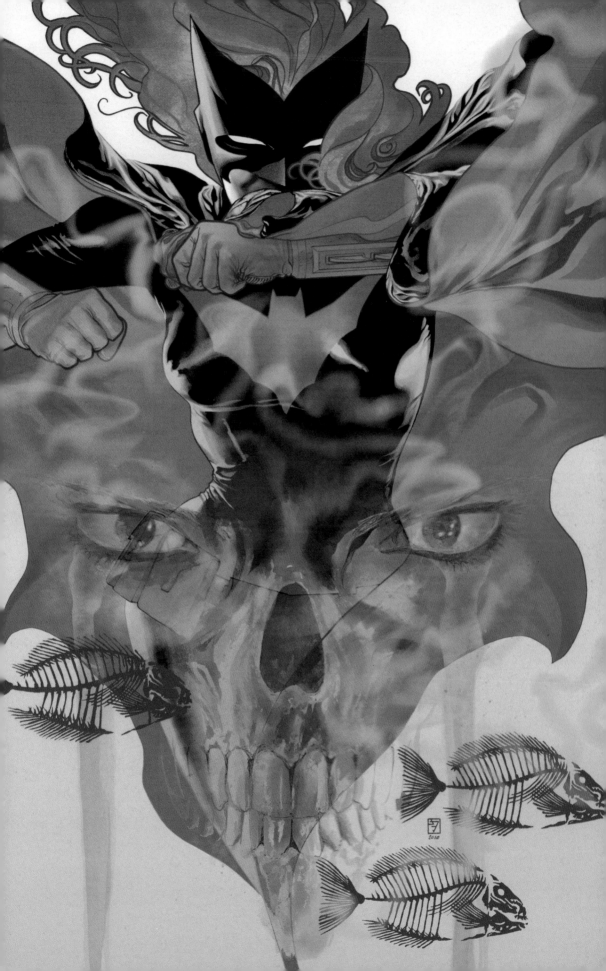

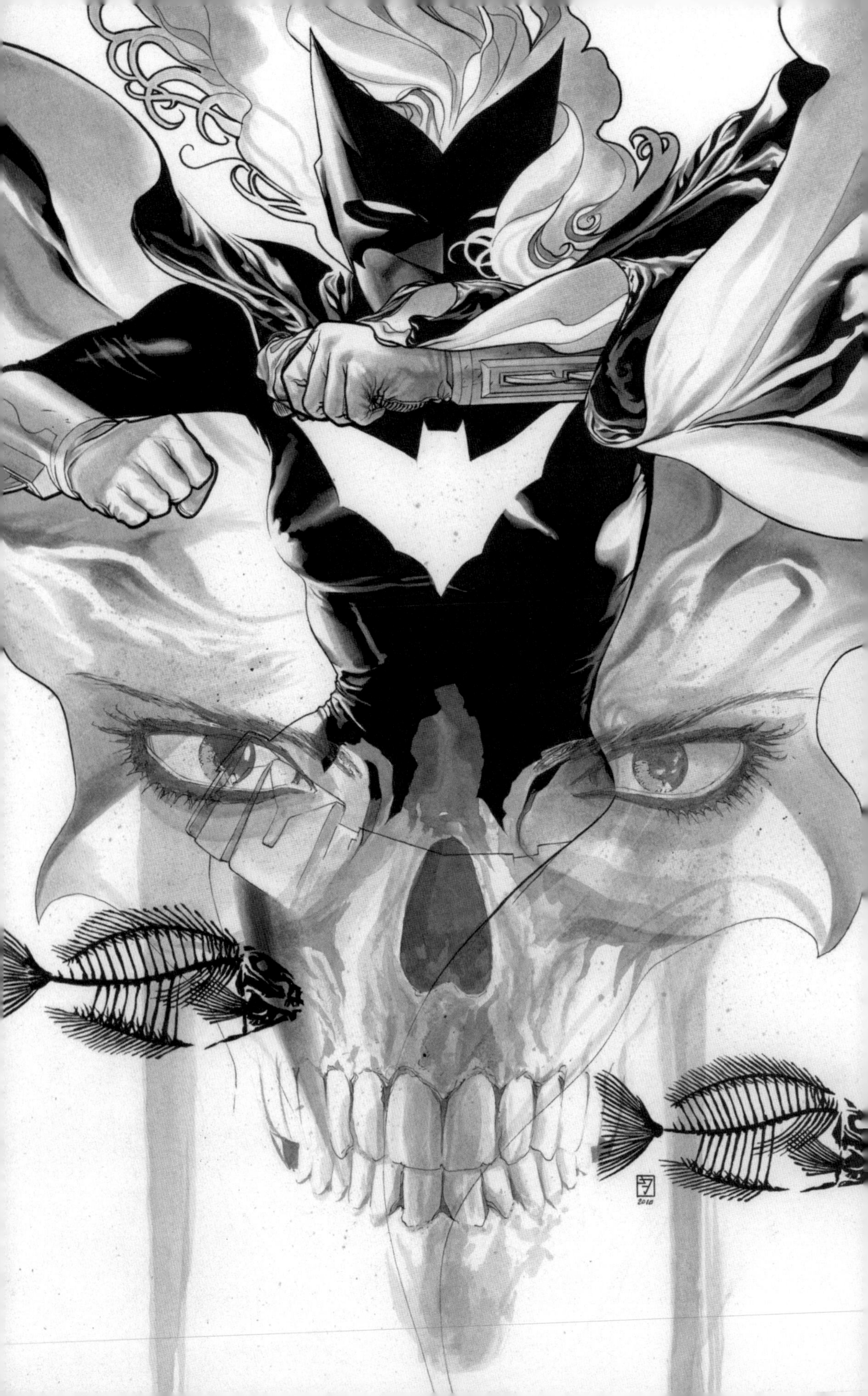

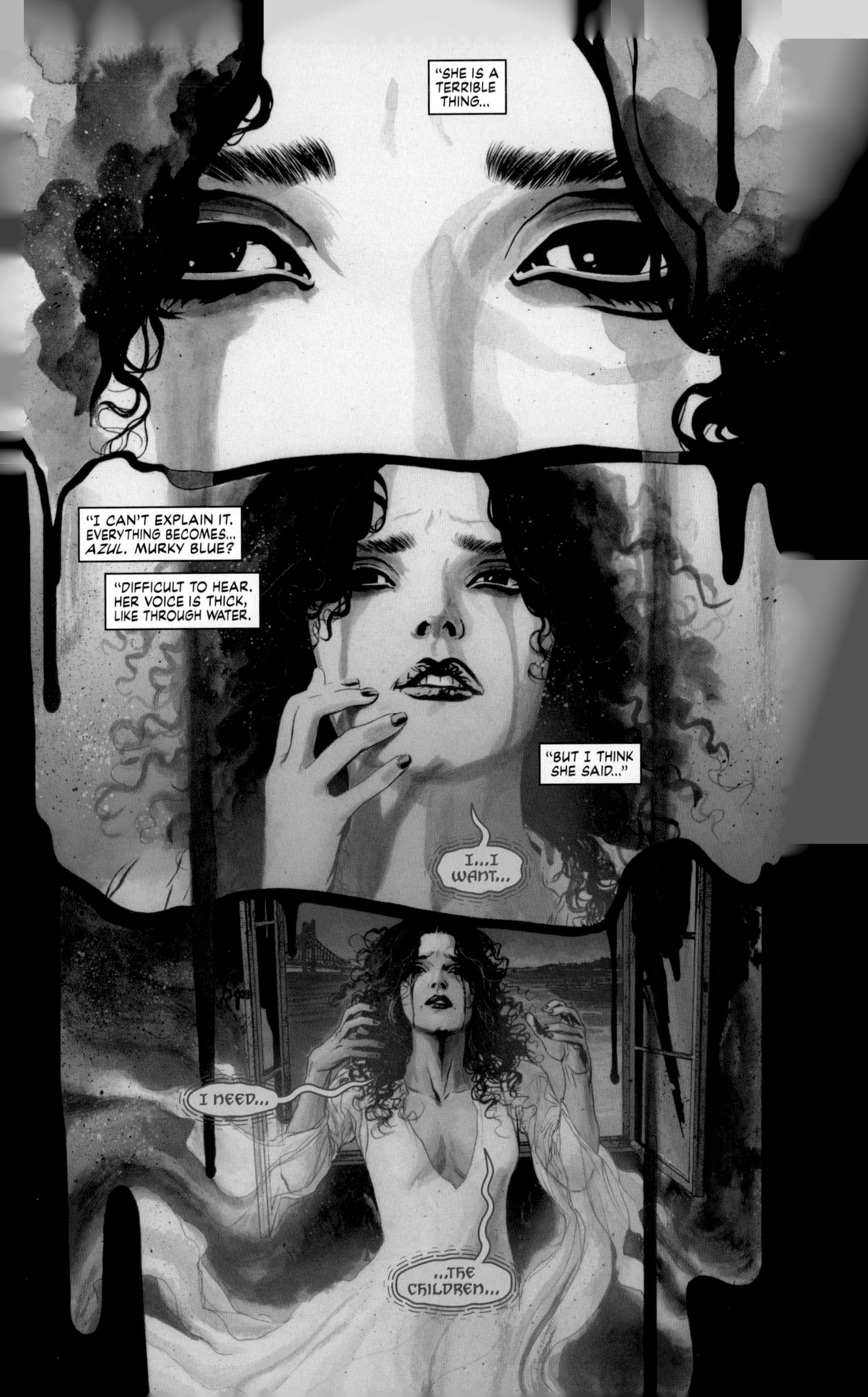
"SHE IS A TERRIBLE THING...
"I CAN'T EXPLAIN IT. EVERYTHING BECOMES... *AZUL*. MURKY BLUE?
"DIFFICULT TO HEAR. HER VOICE IS THICK, LIKE THROUGH WATER.
"BUT I THINK SHE SAID..."
I...I WANT...
I NEED...
...THE CHILDREN...

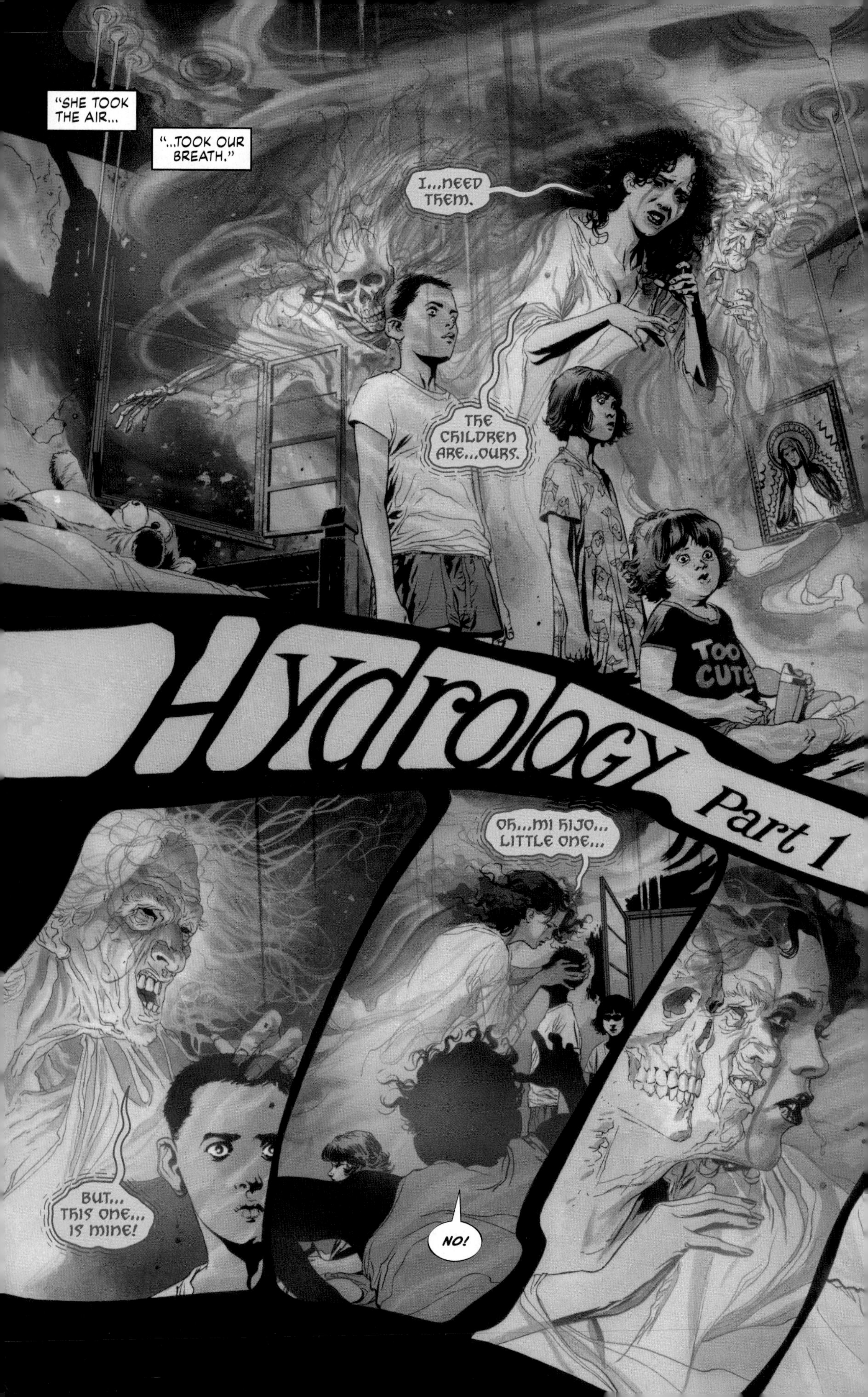
"SHE TOOK THE AIR...
"...TOOK OUR BREATH."
I...NEED THEM.
THE CHILDREN ARE...OURS.
TOO CUTE
Hydrology Part 1
BUT... THIS ONE... IS MINE!
OH...MI HIJO... LITTLE ONE...
NO!

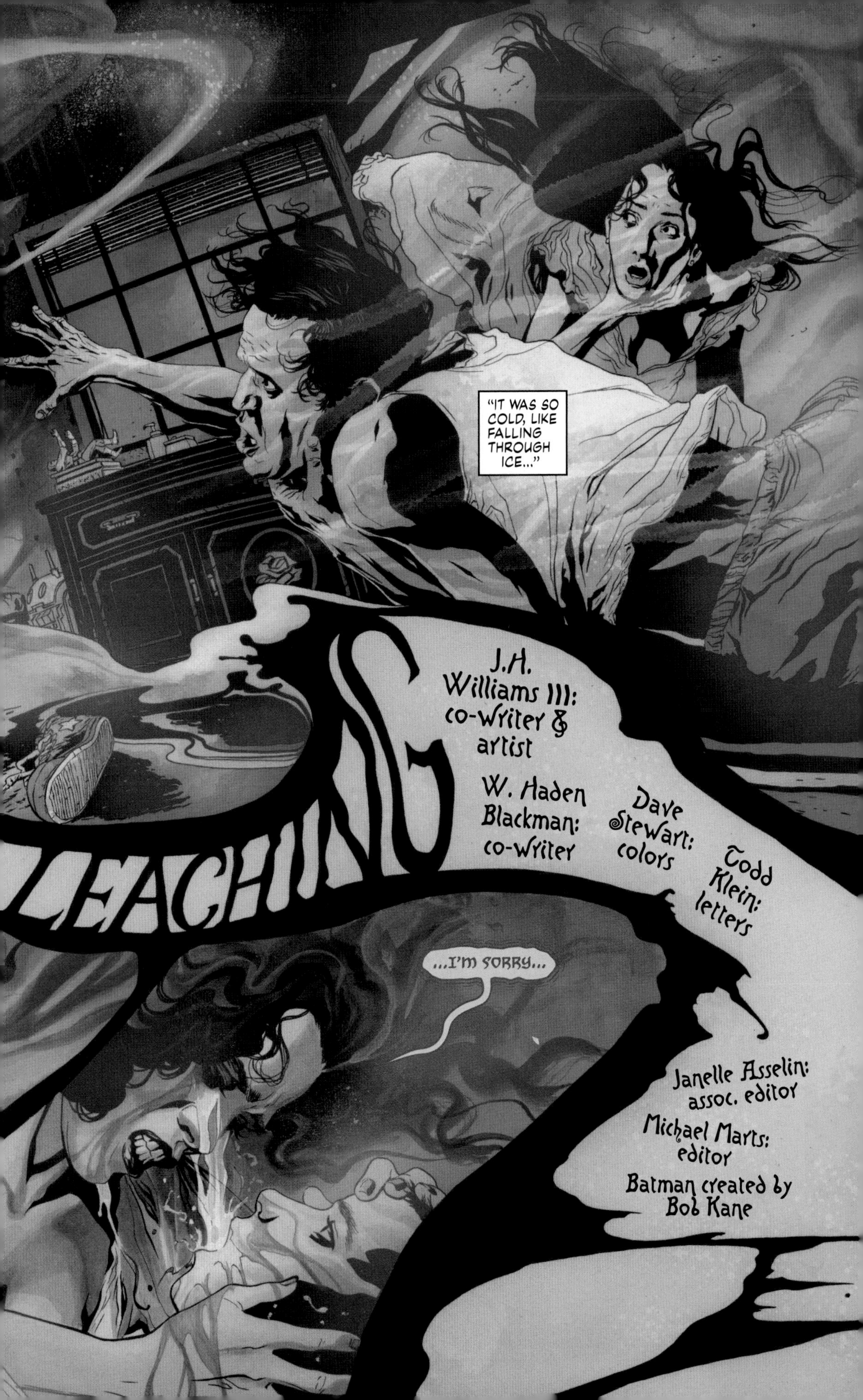
"IT WAS SO COLD, LIKE FALLING THROUGH ICE..."
LEACHING
J.H. Williams III: co-writer & artist
W. Haden Blackman: co-writer
Dave Stewart: colors
Todd Klein: letters
...I'M SORRY...
Janelle Asselin: assoc. editor
Michael Marts: editor
Batman created by Bob Kane

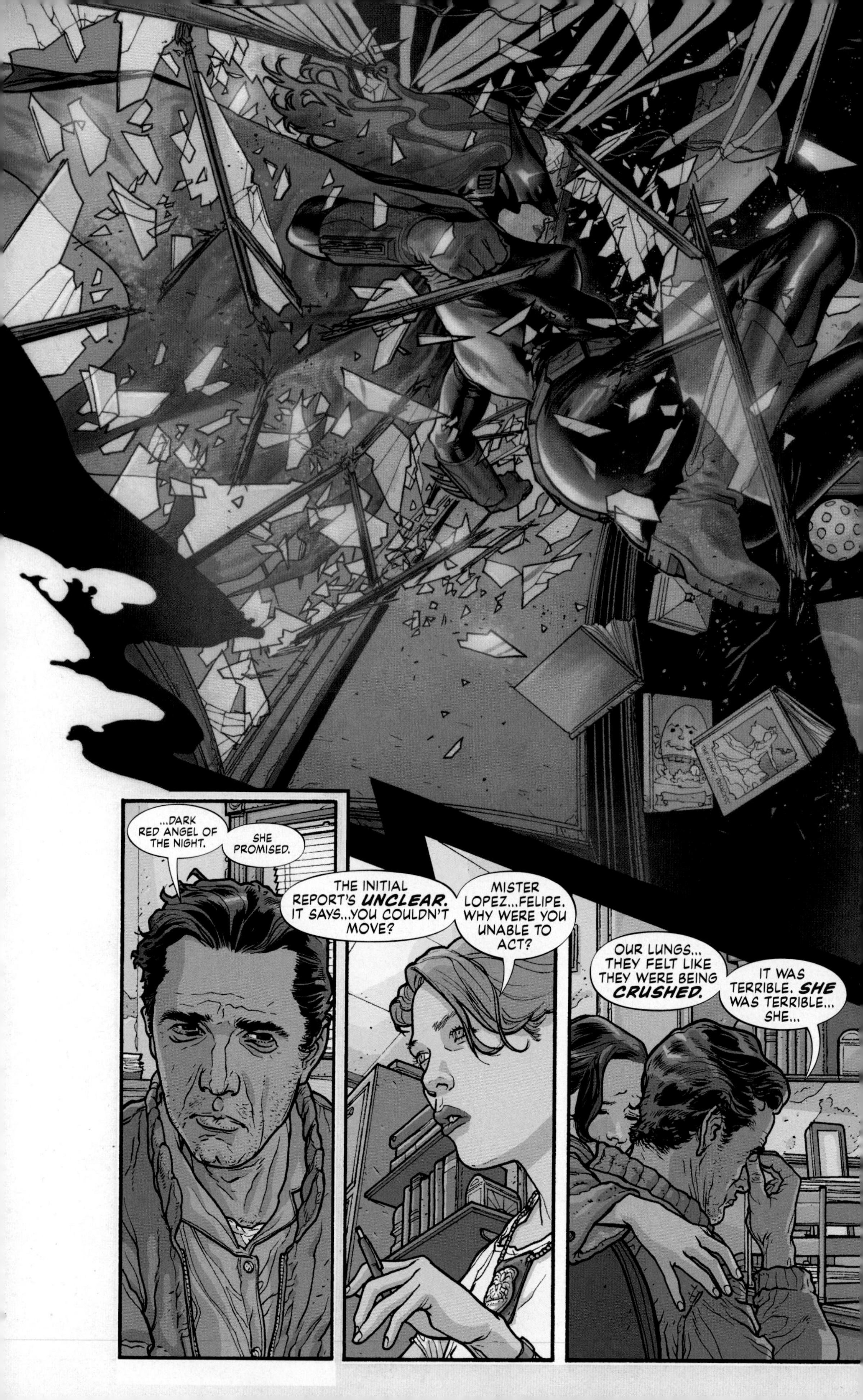
...DARK RED ANGEL OF THE NIGHT.
SHE PROMISED.
THE INITIAL REPORT'S UNCLEAR. IT SAYS...YOU COULDN'T MOVE?
MISTER LOPEZ...FELIPE. WHY WERE YOU UNABLE TO ACT?
OUR LUNGS... THEY FELT LIKE THEY WERE BEING CRUSHED.
IT WAS TERRIBLE. SHE WAS TERRIBLE... SHE...

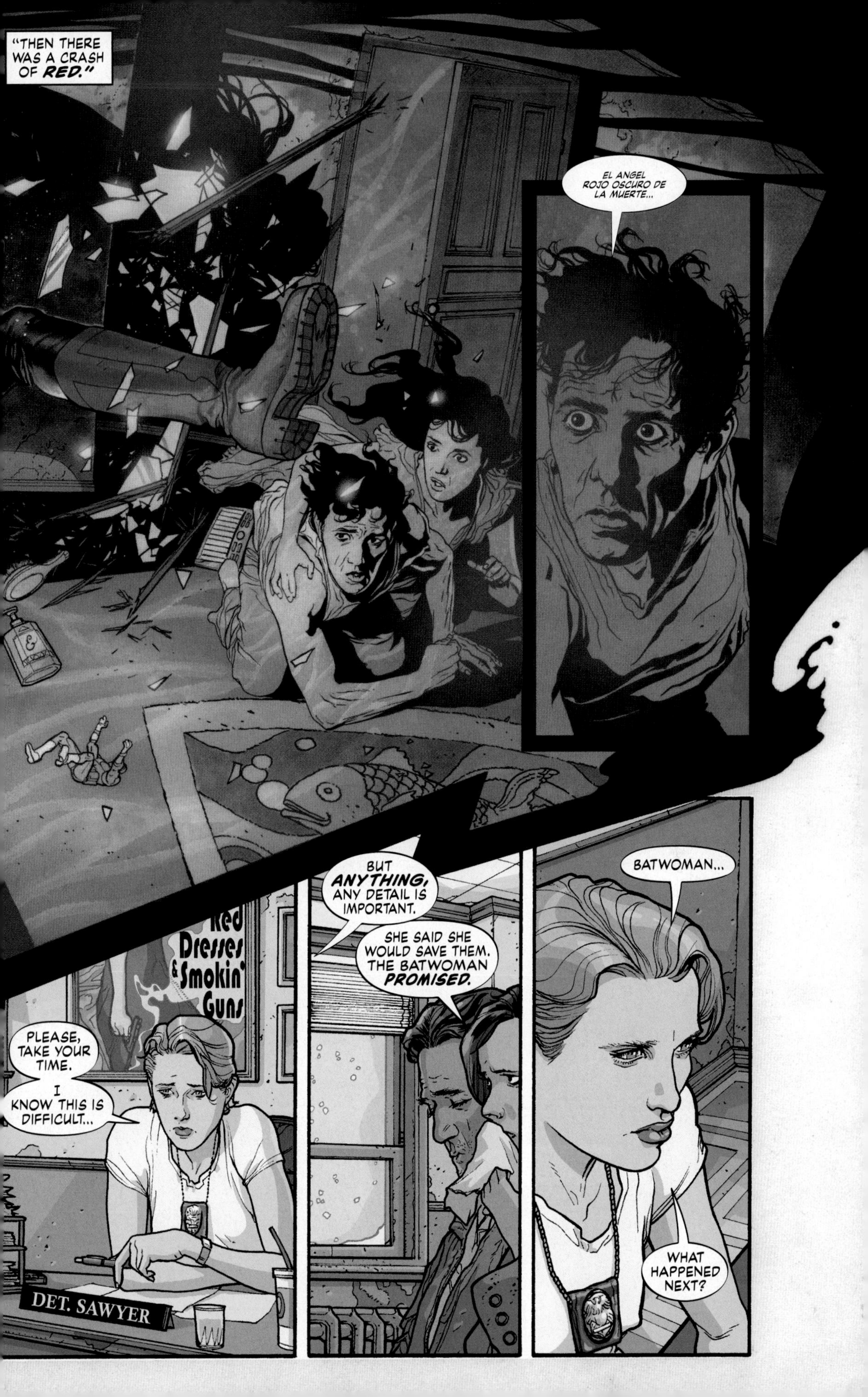
"THEN THERE WAS A CRASH OF RED."
EL ANGEL ROJO OSCURO DE LA MUERTE...
Red Dresses & Smokin' Guns
PLEASE, TAKE YOUR TIME.
I KNOW THIS IS DIFFICULT...
DET. SAWYER
BUT ANYTHING, ANY DETAIL IS IMPORTANT.
SHE SAID SHE WOULD SAVE THEM. THE BATWOMAN PROMISED.
BATWOMAN...
WHAT HAPPENED NEXT?

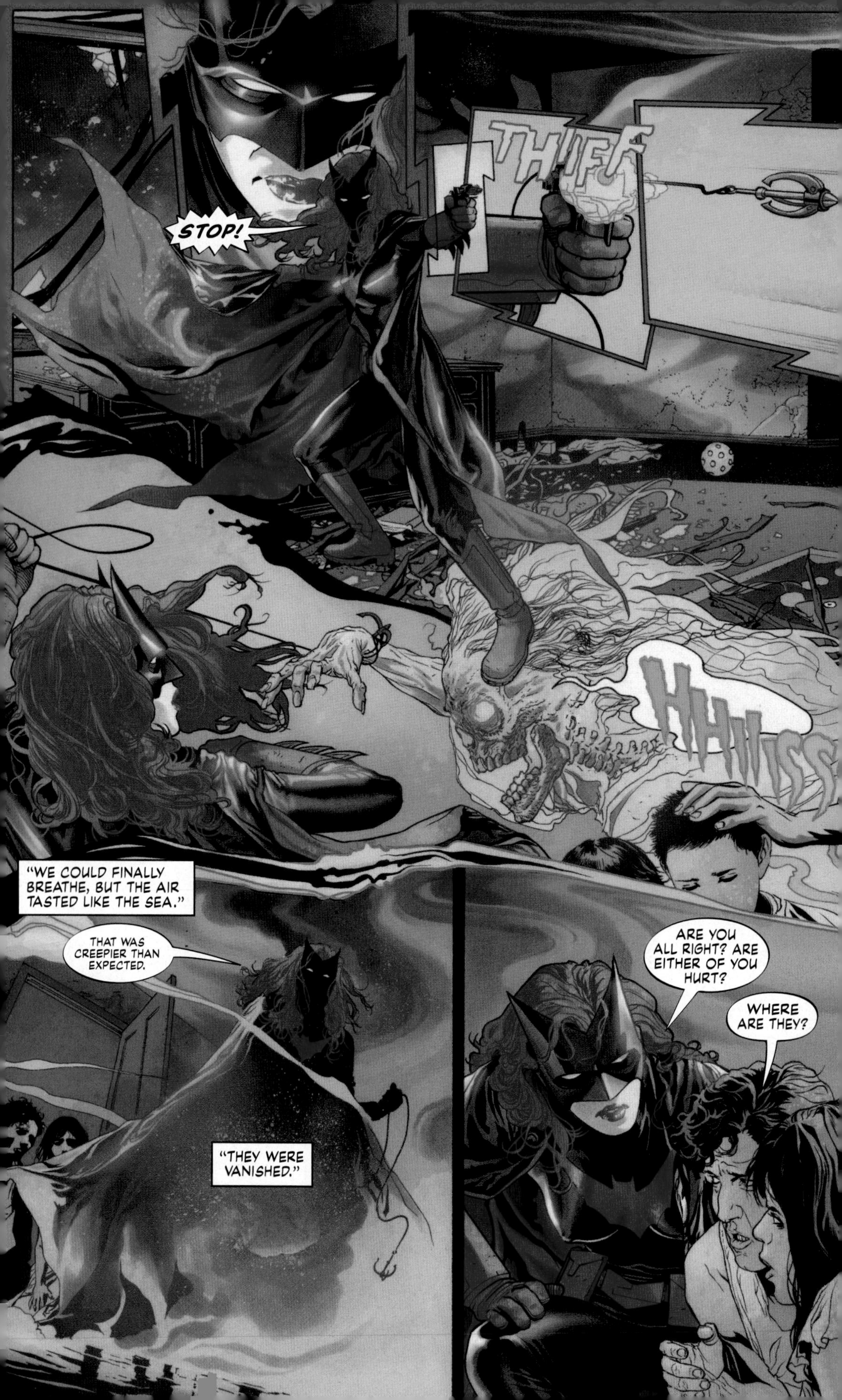
STOP!
THIEF
HHHISSS
"WE COULD FINALLY BREATHE, BUT THE AIR TASTED LIKE THE SEA."
THAT WAS CREEPIER THAN EXPECTED.
"THEY WERE VANISHED."
ARE YOU ALL RIGHT? ARE EITHER OF YOU HURT?
WHERE ARE THEY?

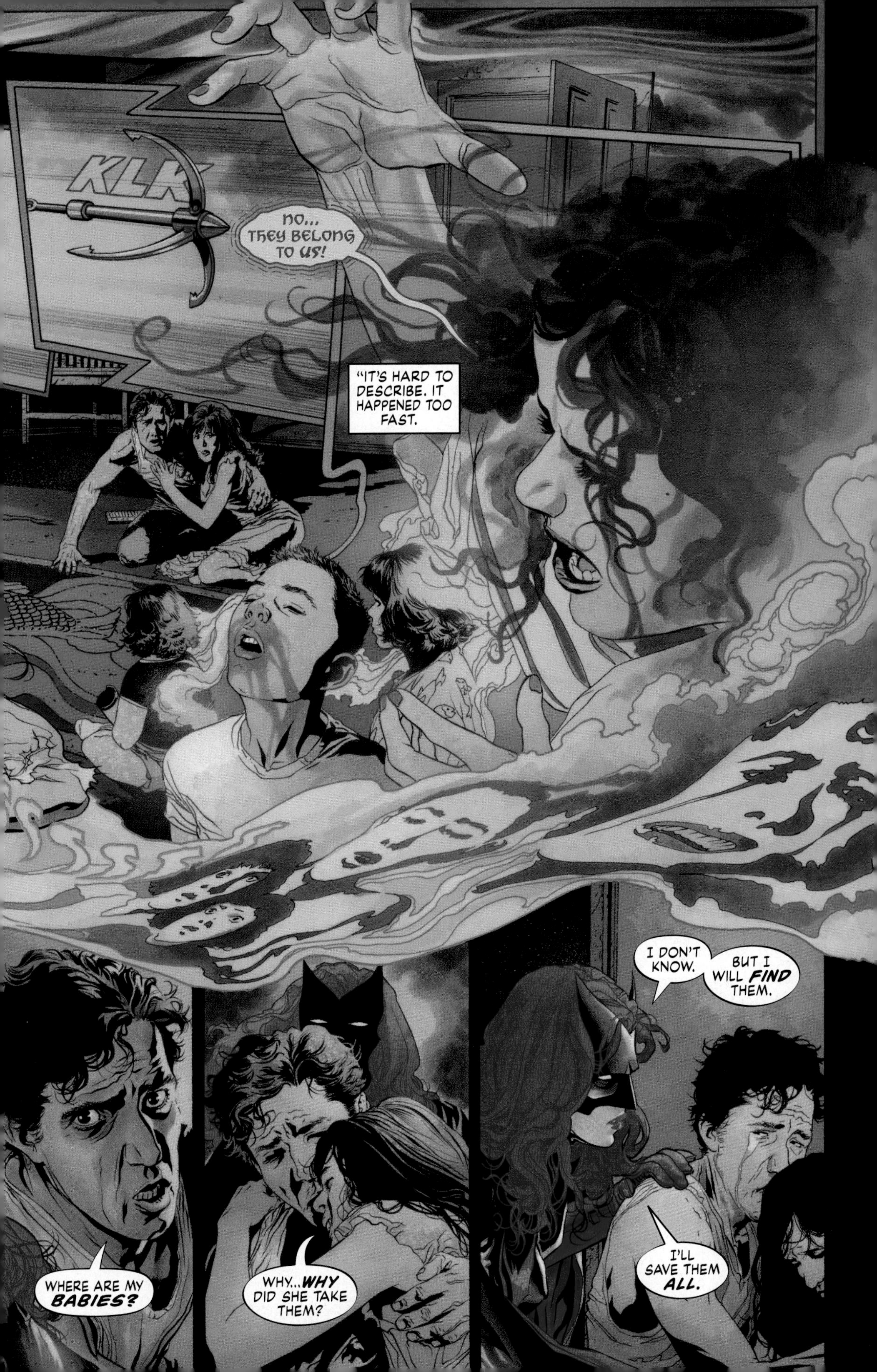
KLK
NO... THEY BELONG TO US!
"IT'S HARD TO DESCRIBE. IT HAPPENED TOO FAST.
WHERE ARE MY BABIES?
WHY...WHY DID SHE TAKE THEM?
I DON'T KNOW.
BUT I WILL FIND THEM.
I'LL SAVE THEM ALL.

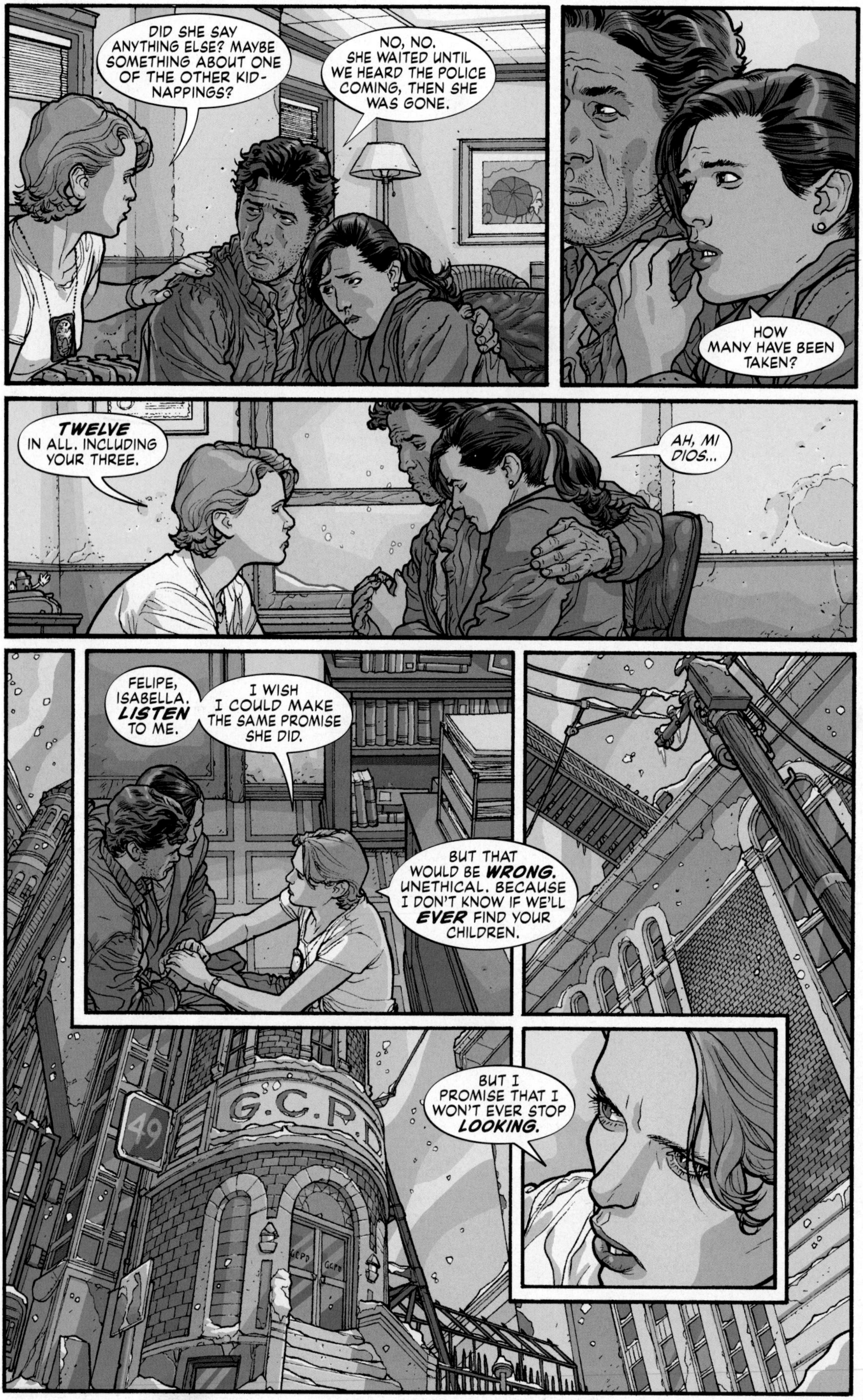
DID SHE SAY ANYTHING ELSE? MAYBE SOMETHING ABOUT ONE OF THE OTHER KID-NAPPINGS?
NO, NO. SHE WAITED UNTIL WE HEARD THE POLICE COMING, THEN SHE WAS GONE.
HOW MANY HAVE BEEN TAKEN?
TWELVE IN ALL. INCLUDING YOUR THREE.
AH, MI DIOS...
FELIPE, ISABELLA. LISTEN TO ME.
I WISH I COULD MAKE THE SAME PROMISE SHE DID.
BUT THAT WOULD BE WRONG. UNETHICAL. BECAUSE I DON'T KNOW IF WE'LL EVER FIND YOUR CHILDREN.
G.C.P.D
49
BUT I PROMISE THAT I WON'T EVER STOP LOOKING.

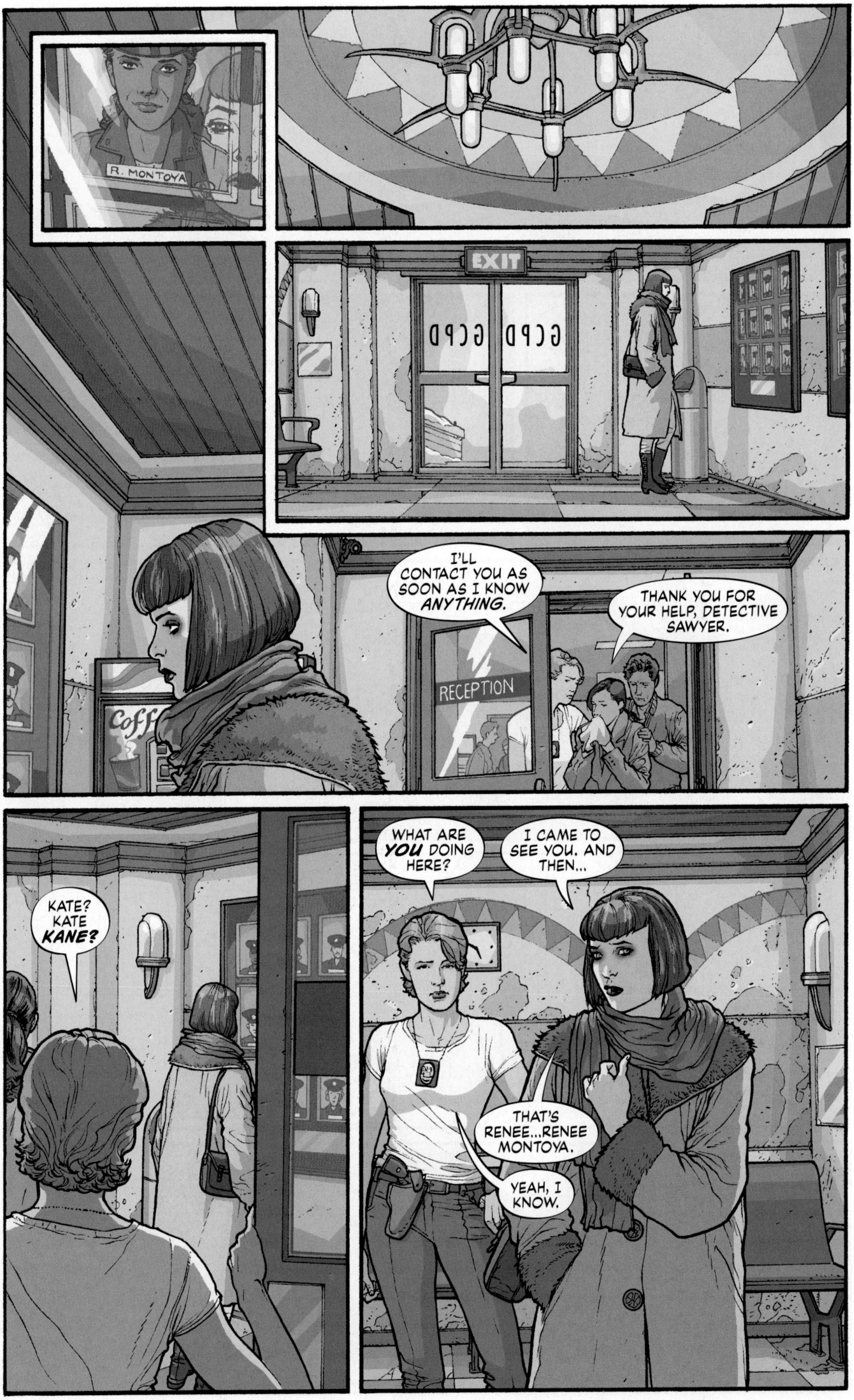
R. MONTOYA
EXIT
GCPD GCPD
I'LL CONTACT YOU AS SOON AS I KNOW *ANYTHING.*
THANK YOU FOR YOUR HELP, DETECTIVE SAWYER.
RECEPTION
KATE? KATE ***KANE?***
WHAT ARE ***YOU*** DOING HERE?
I CAME TO SEE YOU. AND THEN...
THAT'S RENEE...RENEE MONTOYA.
YEAH, I KNOW.

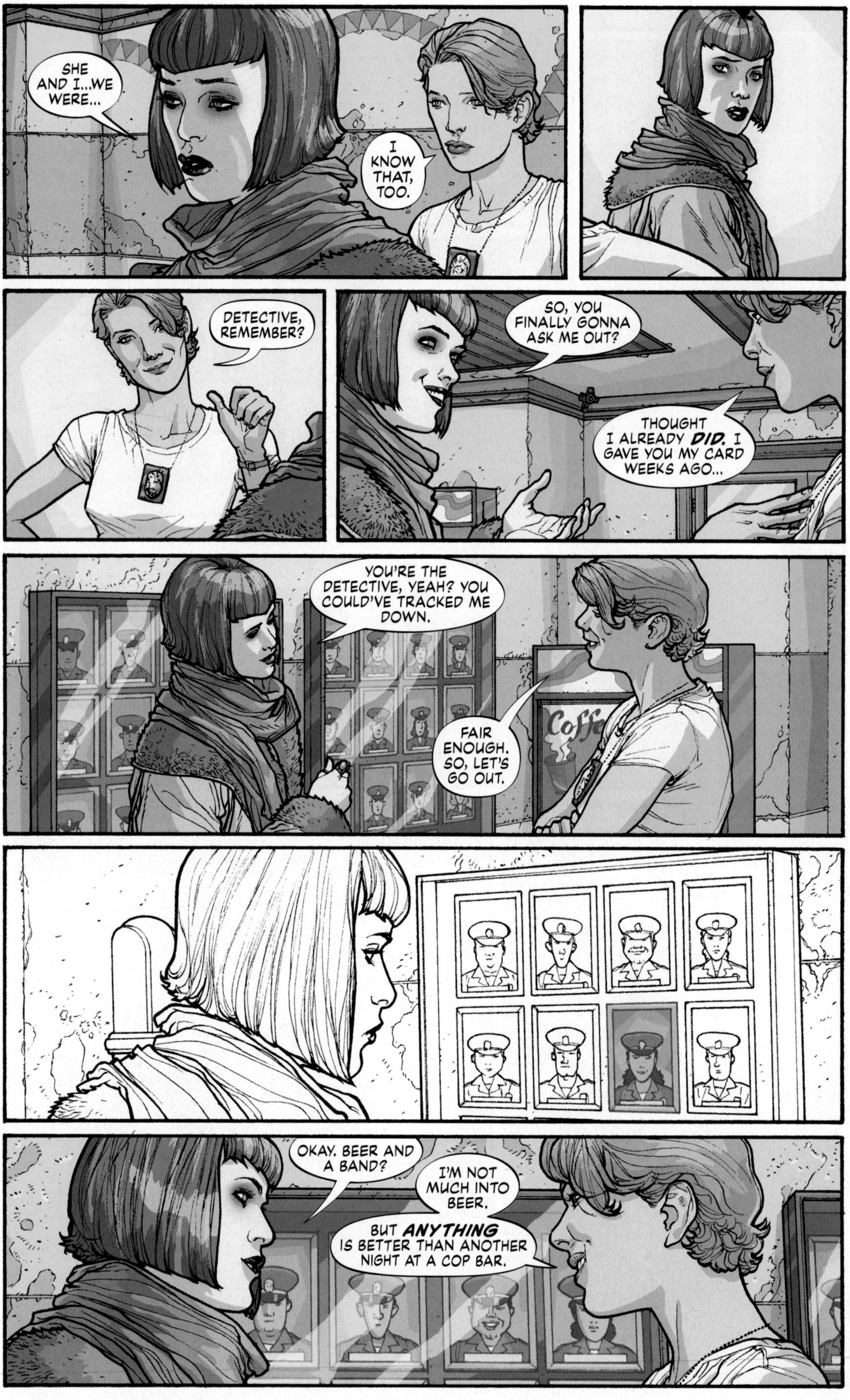
SHE AND I...WE WERE...
I KNOW THAT, TOO.
DETECTIVE, REMEMBER?
SO, YOU FINALLY GONNA ASK ME OUT?
THOUGHT I ALREADY DID. I GAVE YOU MY CARD WEEKS AGO...
YOU'RE THE DETECTIVE, YEAH? YOU COULD'VE TRACKED ME DOWN.
FAIR ENOUGH. SO, LET'S GO OUT.
OKAY. BEER AND A BAND?
I'M NOT MUCH INTO BEER.
BUT ANYTHING IS BETTER THAN ANOTHER NIGHT AT A COP BAR.

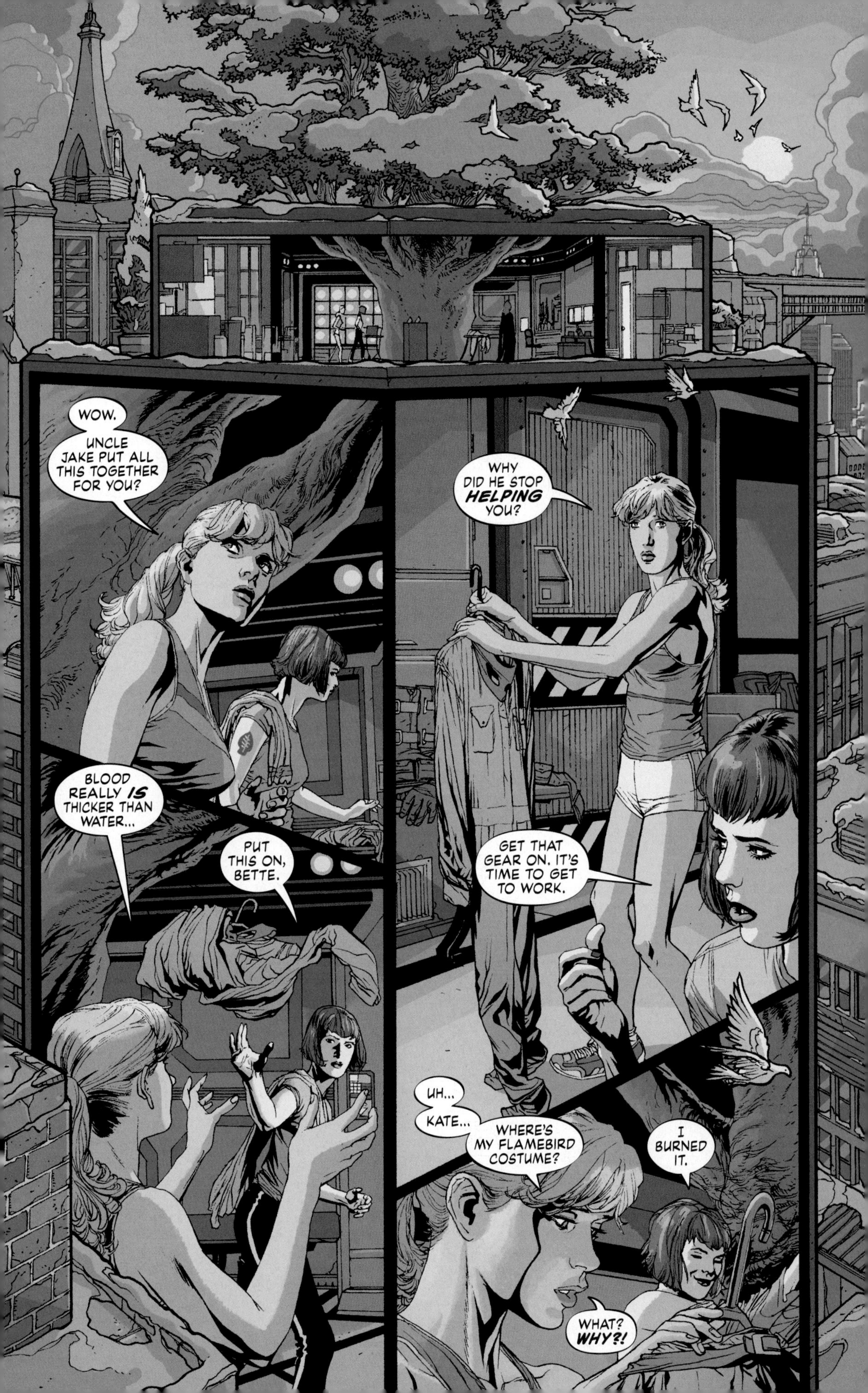
WOW.
UNCLE JAKE PUT ALL THIS TOGETHER FOR YOU?
WHY DID HE STOP HELPING YOU?
BLOOD REALLY IS THICKER THAN WATER...
PUT THIS ON, BETTE.
GET THAT GEAR ON. IT'S TIME TO GET TO WORK.
UH...
KATE...
WHERE'S MY FLAMEBIRD COSTUME?
I BURNED IT.
WHAT? WHY?!

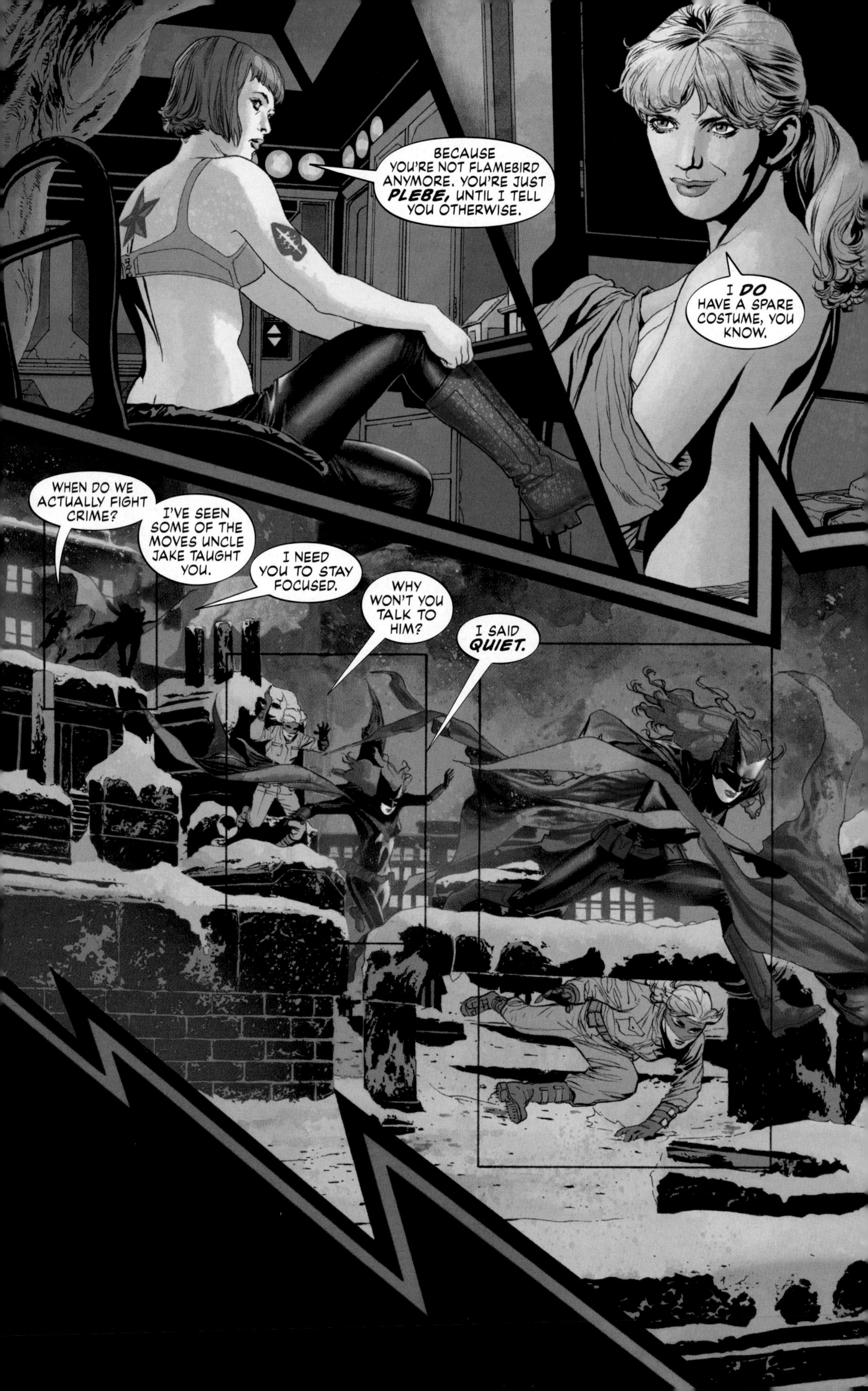

BECAUSE YOU'RE NOT FLAMEBIRD ANYMORE. YOU'RE JUST *PLEBE,* UNTIL I TELL YOU OTHERWISE.
I *DO* HAVE A SPARE COSTUME, YOU KNOW.
WHEN DO WE ACTUALLY FIGHT CRIME?
I'VE SEEN SOME OF THE MOVES UNCLE JAKE TAUGHT YOU.
I NEED YOU TO STAY FOCUSED.
WHY WON'T YOU TALK TO HIM?
I SAID *QUIET.*

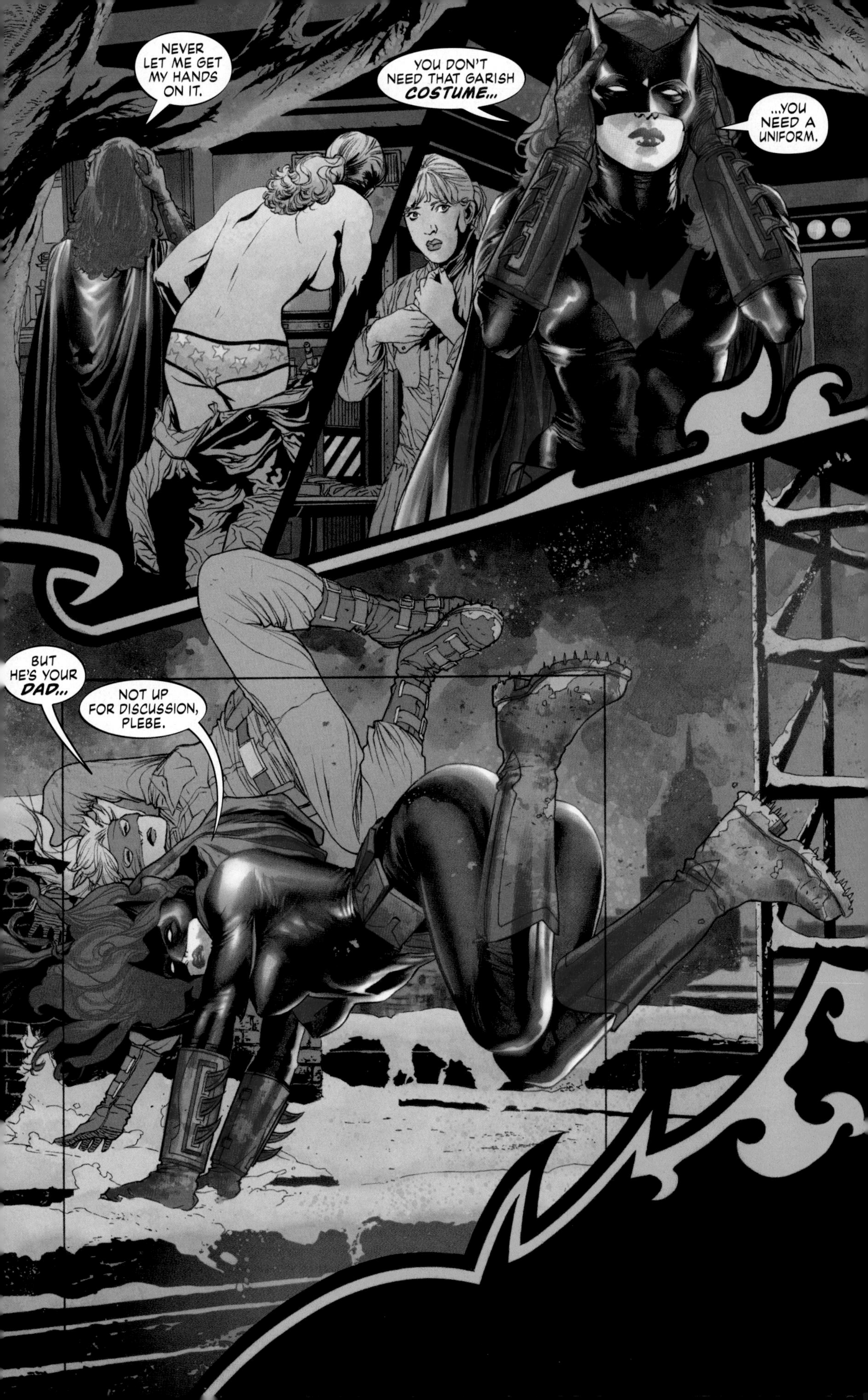
NEVER LET ME GET MY HANDS ON IT.
YOU DON'T NEED THAT GARISH COSTUME...
...YOU NEED A UNIFORM.
BUT HE'S YOUR DAD...
NOT UP FOR DISCUSSION, PLEBE.

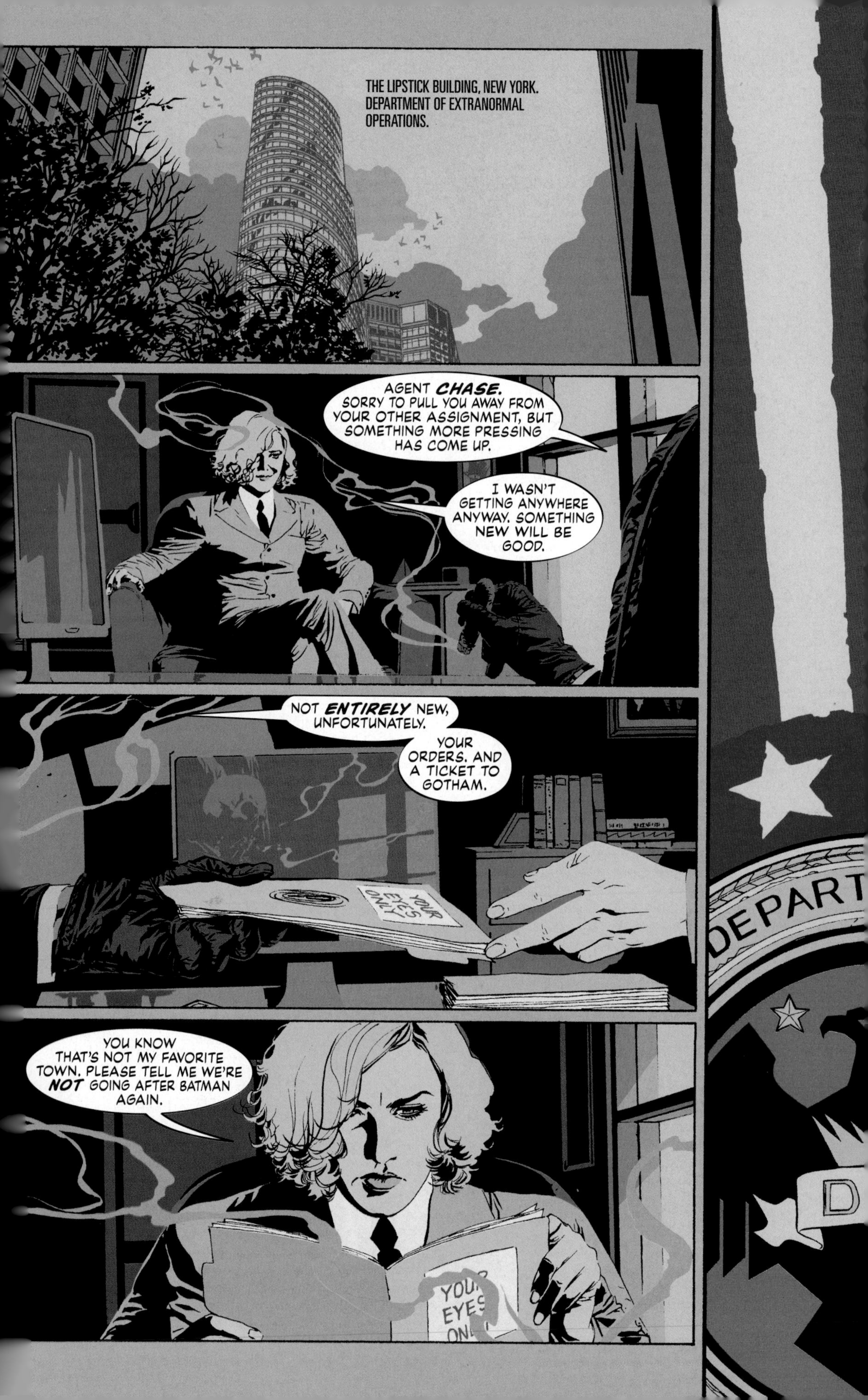
THE LIPSTICK BUILDING, NEW YORK. DEPARTMENT OF EXTRANORMAL OPERATIONS.
AGENT CHASE. SORRY TO PULL YOU AWAY FROM YOUR OTHER ASSIGNMENT, BUT SOMETHING MORE PRESSING HAS COME UP.
I WASN'T GETTING ANYWHERE ANYWAY. SOMETHING NEW WILL BE GOOD.
NOT ENTIRELY NEW, UNFORTUNATELY.
YOUR ORDERS. AND A TICKET TO GOTHAM.
YOUR EYES ONLY
YOU KNOW THAT'S NOT MY FAVORITE TOWN. PLEASE TELL ME WE'RE NOT GOING AFTER BATMAN AGAIN.
DEPART

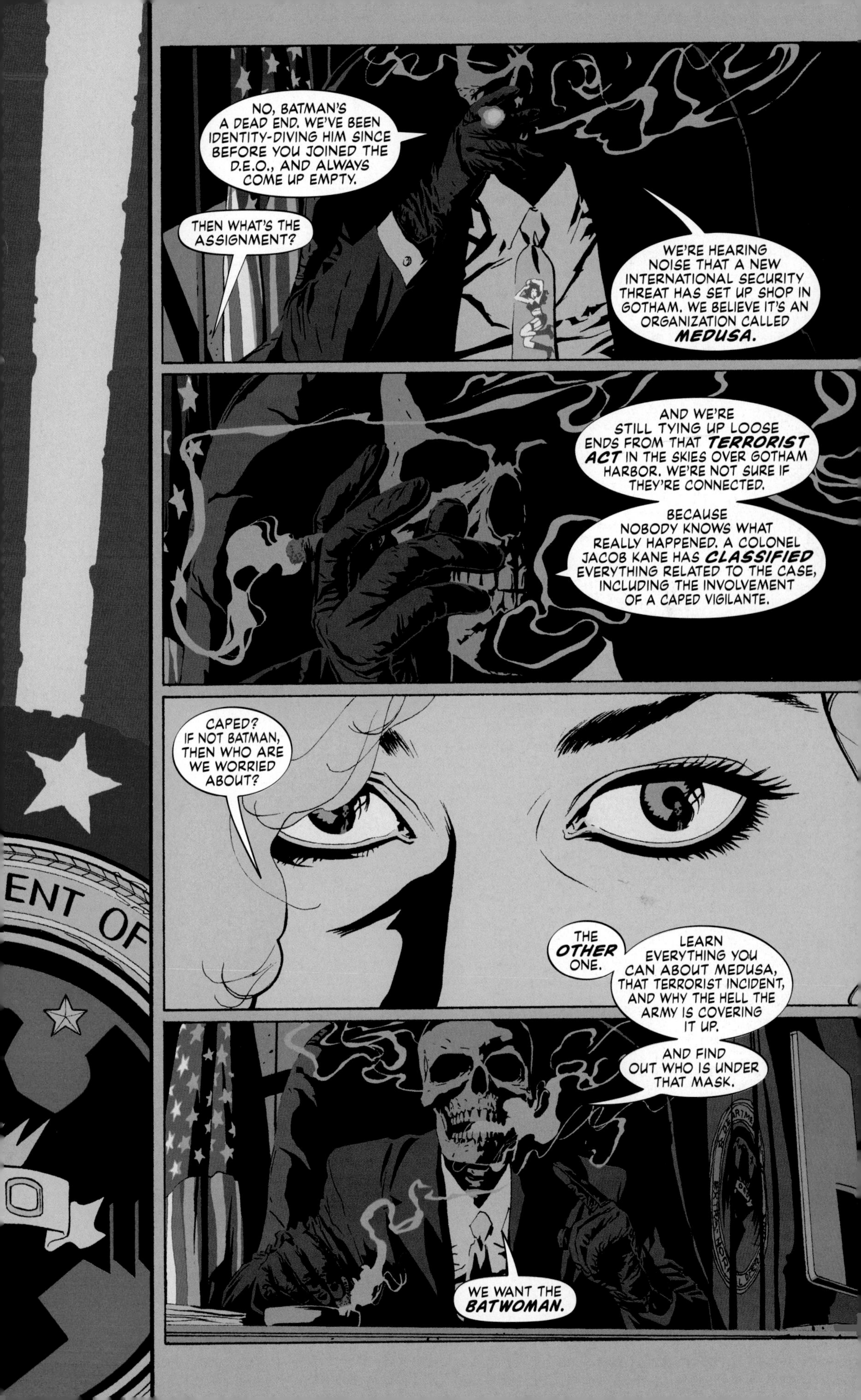
NO, BATMAN'S A DEAD END. WE'VE BEEN IDENTITY-DIVING HIM SINCE BEFORE YOU JOINED THE D.E.O., AND ALWAYS COME UP EMPTY.
THEN WHAT'S THE ASSIGNMENT?
WE'RE HEARING NOISE THAT A NEW INTERNATIONAL SECURITY THREAT HAS SET UP SHOP IN GOTHAM. WE BELIEVE IT'S AN ORGANIZATION CALLED MEDUSA.
AND WE'RE STILL TYING UP LOOSE ENDS FROM THAT TERRORIST ACT IN THE SKIES OVER GOTHAM HARBOR. WE'RE NOT SURE IF THEY'RE CONNECTED.
BECAUSE NOBODY KNOWS WHAT REALLY HAPPENED. A COLONEL JACOB KANE HAS CLASSIFIED EVERYTHING RELATED TO THE CASE, INCLUDING THE INVOLVEMENT OF A CAPED VIGILANTE.
CAPED? IF NOT BATMAN, THEN WHO ARE WE WORRIED ABOUT?
THE OTHER ONE.
LEARN EVERYTHING YOU CAN ABOUT MEDUSA, THAT TERRORIST INCIDENT, AND WHY THE HELL THE ARMY IS COVERING IT UP.
AND FIND OUT WHO IS UNDER THAT MASK.
WE WANT THE BATWOMAN.
ENT OF

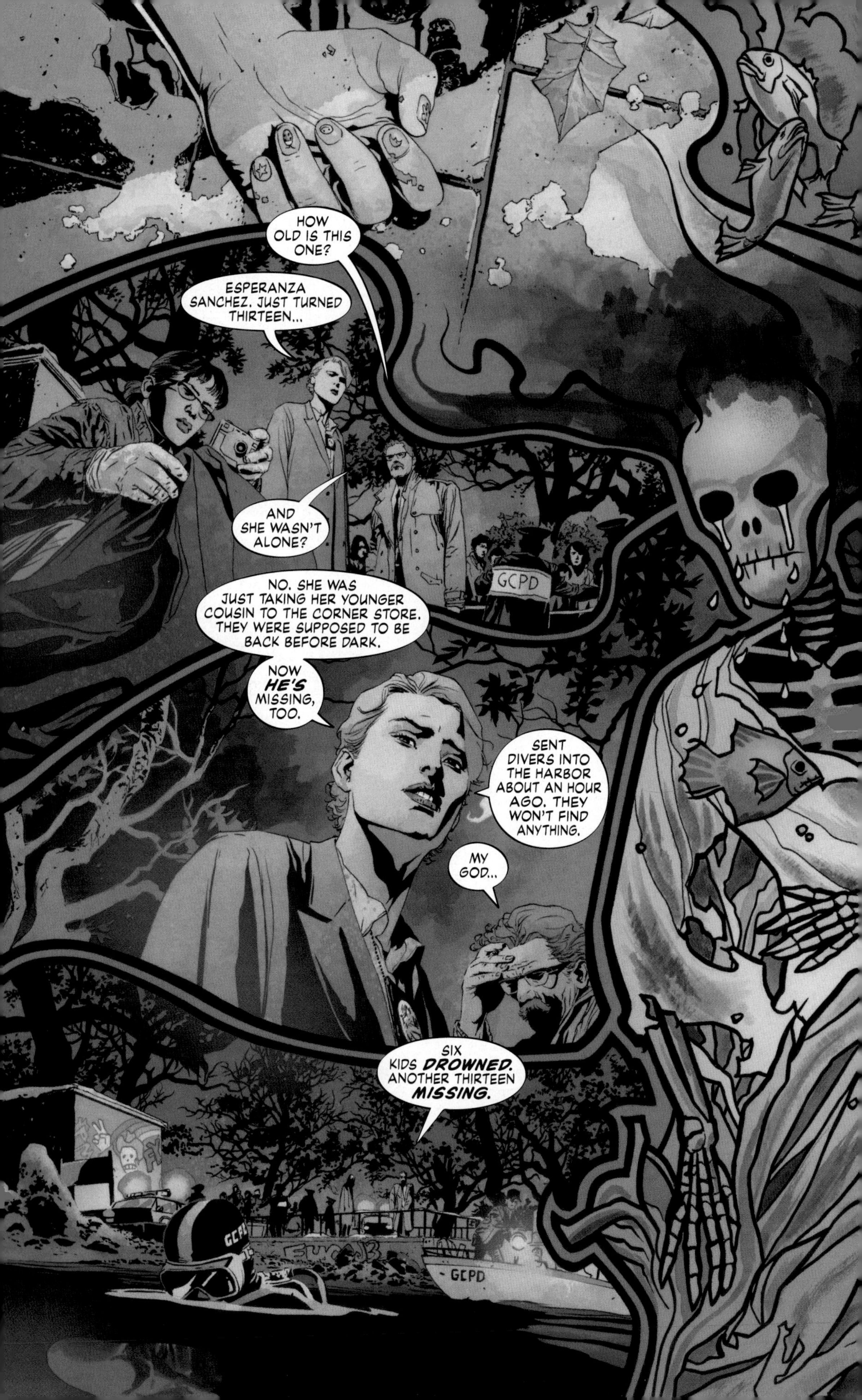
HOW OLD IS THIS ONE?
ESPERANZA SANCHEZ. JUST TURNED THIRTEEN...
AND SHE WASN'T ALONE?
GCPD
NO. SHE WAS JUST TAKING HER YOUNGER COUSIN TO THE CORNER STORE. THEY WERE SUPPOSED TO BE BACK BEFORE DARK.
NOW ***HE'S*** MISSING, TOO.
SENT DIVERS INTO THE HARBOR ABOUT AN HOUR AGO. THEY WON'T FIND ANYTHING.
MY GOD...
SIX KIDS ***DROWNED.*** ANOTHER THIRTEEN ***MISSING.***
GCPD
GCPD

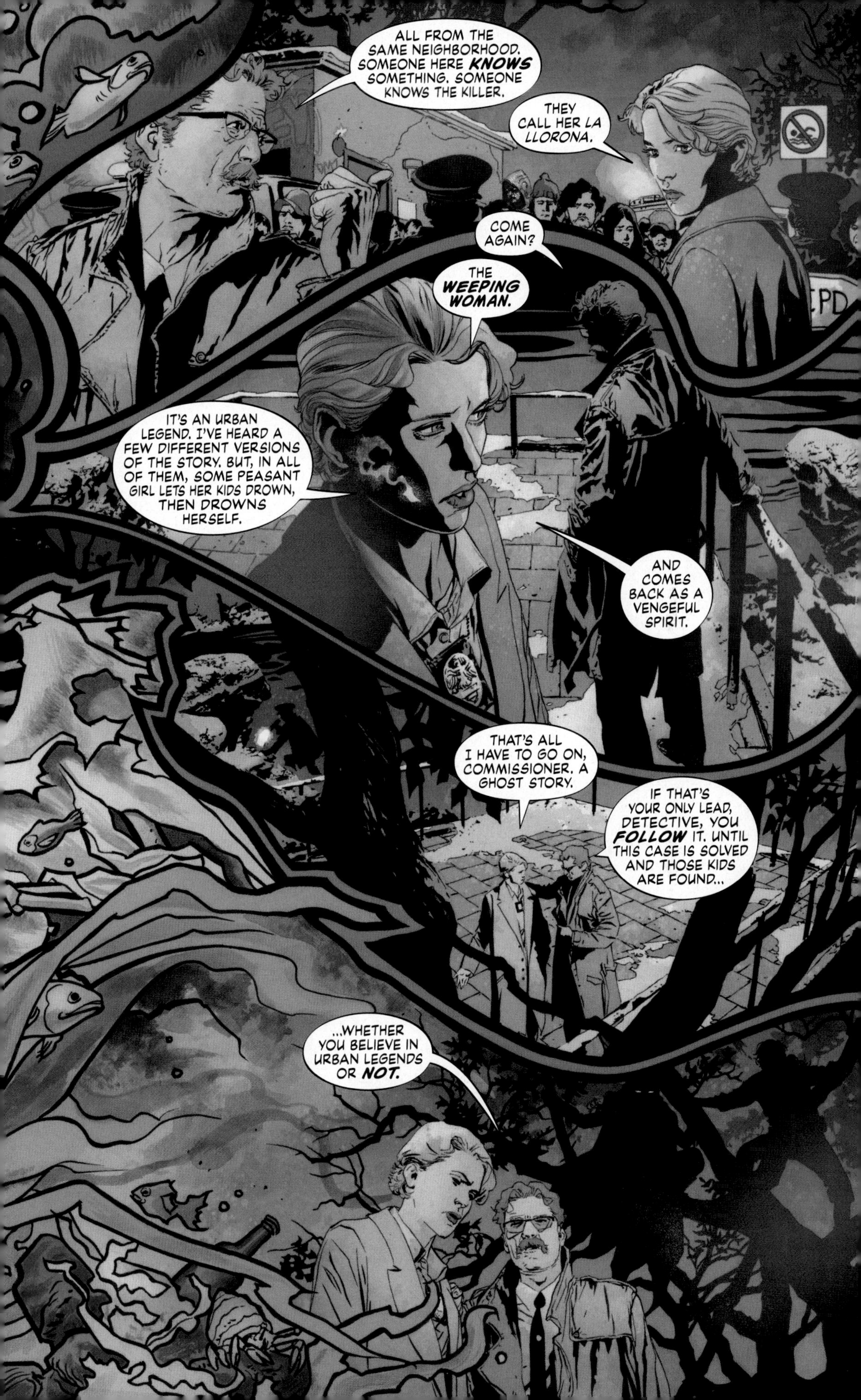
ALL FROM THE SAME NEIGHBORHOOD. SOMEONE HERE **KNOWS** SOMETHING. SOMEONE KNOWS THE KILLER.
THEY CALL HER *LA LLORONA*.
COME AGAIN?
THE ***WEEPING WOMAN.***
IT'S AN URBAN LEGEND. I'VE HEARD A FEW DIFFERENT VERSIONS OF THE STORY. BUT, IN ALL OF THEM, SOME PEASANT GIRL LETS HER KIDS DROWN, THEN DROWNS HERSELF.
AND COMES BACK AS A VENGEFUL SPIRIT.
THAT'S ALL I HAVE TO GO ON, COMMISSIONER. A GHOST STORY.
IF THAT'S YOUR ONLY LEAD, DETECTIVE, YOU ***FOLLOW*** IT. UNTIL THIS CASE IS SOLVED AND THOSE KIDS ARE FOUND...
...WHETHER YOU BELIEVE IN URBAN LEGENDS OR ***NOT.***

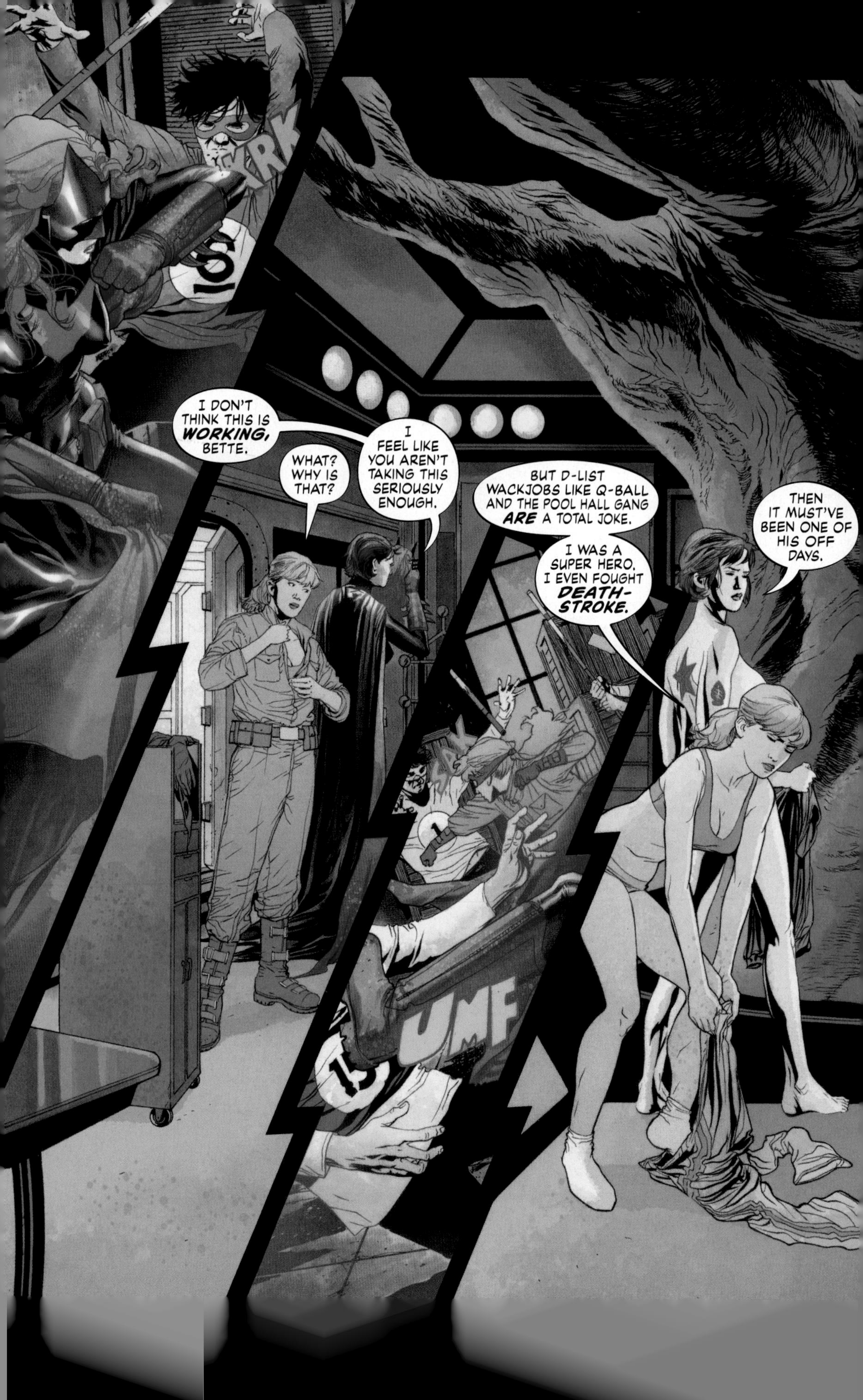

KRRK
I DON'T THINK THIS IS WORKING, BETTE.
WHAT? WHY IS THAT?
I FEEL LIKE YOU AREN'T TAKING THIS SERIOUSLY ENOUGH.
BUT D-LIST WACKJOBS LIKE Q-BALL AND THE POOL HALL GANG ARE A TOTAL JOKE.
I WAS A SUPER HERO. I EVEN FOUGHT DEATH-STROKE.
THEN IT MUST'VE BEEN ONE OF HIS OFF DAYS.
UMF

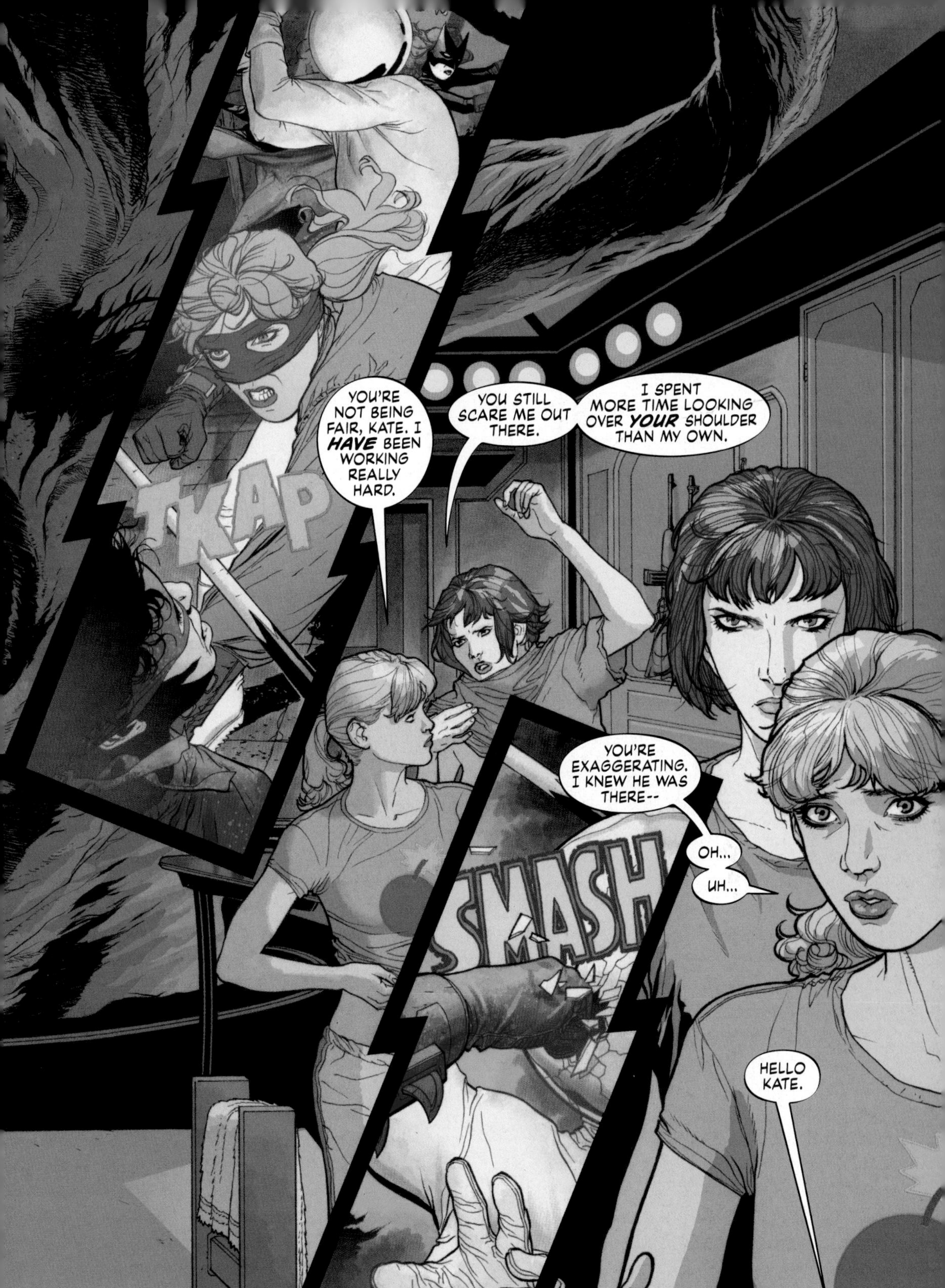
TKAP
YOU'RE NOT BEING FAIR, KATE. I *HAVE* BEEN WORKING REALLY HARD.
YOU STILL SCARE ME OUT THERE.
I SPENT MORE TIME LOOKING OVER *YOUR* SHOULDER THAN MY OWN.
YOU'RE EXAGGERATING. I KNEW HE WAS THERE--
SMASH
OH...
UH...
HELLO KATE.

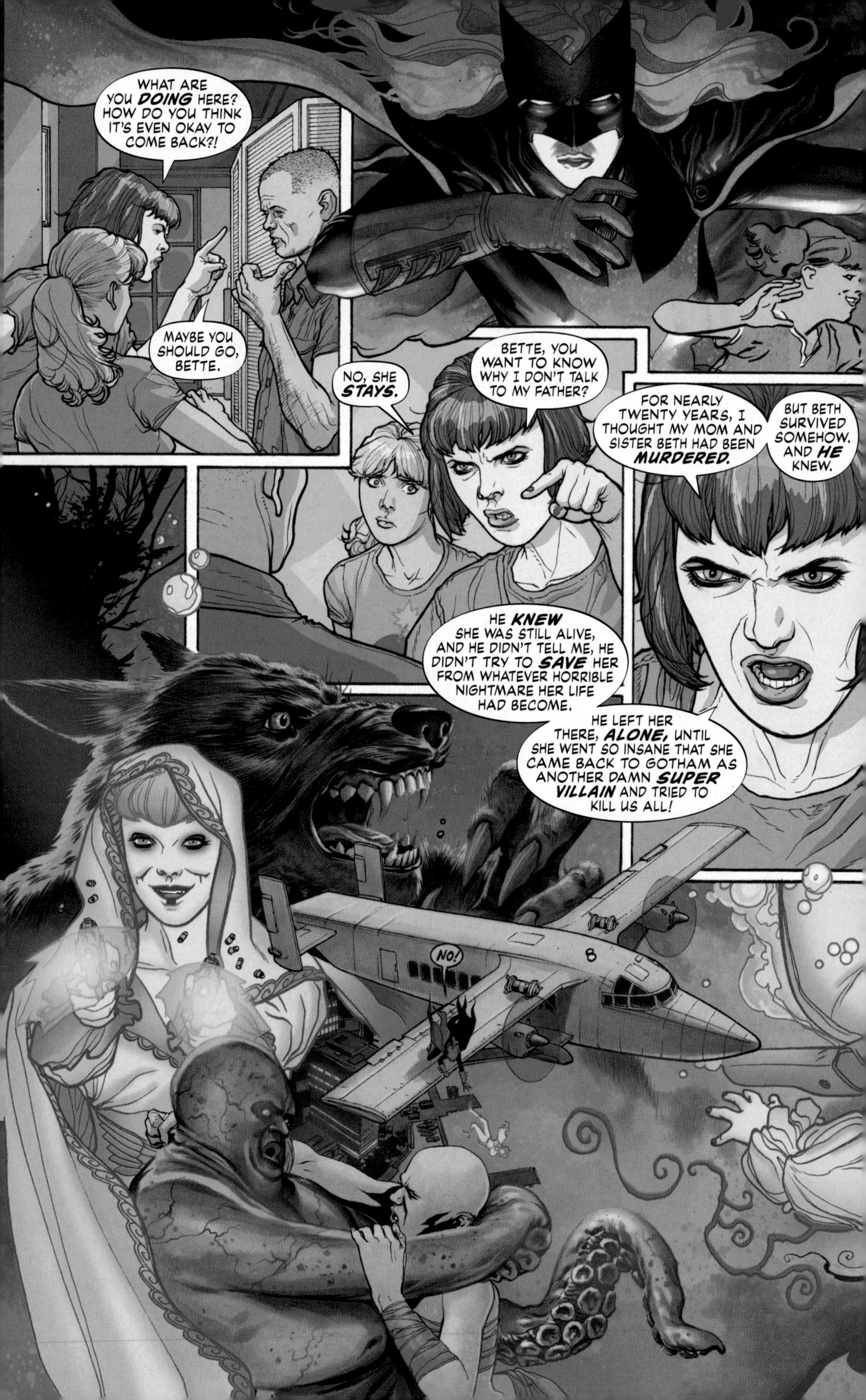
WHAT ARE YOU DOING HERE? HOW DO YOU THINK IT'S EVEN OKAY TO COME BACK?!
MAYBE YOU SHOULD GO, BETTE.
NO, SHE STAYS.
BETTE, YOU WANT TO KNOW WHY I DON'T TALK TO MY FATHER?
FOR NEARLY TWENTY YEARS, I THOUGHT MY MOM AND SISTER BETH HAD BEEN MURDERED.
BUT BETH SURVIVED SOMEHOW. AND HE KNEW.
HE KNEW SHE WAS STILL ALIVE, AND HE DIDN'T TELL ME, HE DIDN'T TRY TO SAVE HER FROM WHATEVER HORRIBLE NIGHTMARE HER LIFE HAD BECOME.
HE LEFT HER THERE, ALONE, UNTIL SHE WENT SO INSANE THAT SHE CAME BACK TO GOTHAM AS ANOTHER DAMN SUPER VILLAIN AND TRIED TO KILL US ALL!
NO!

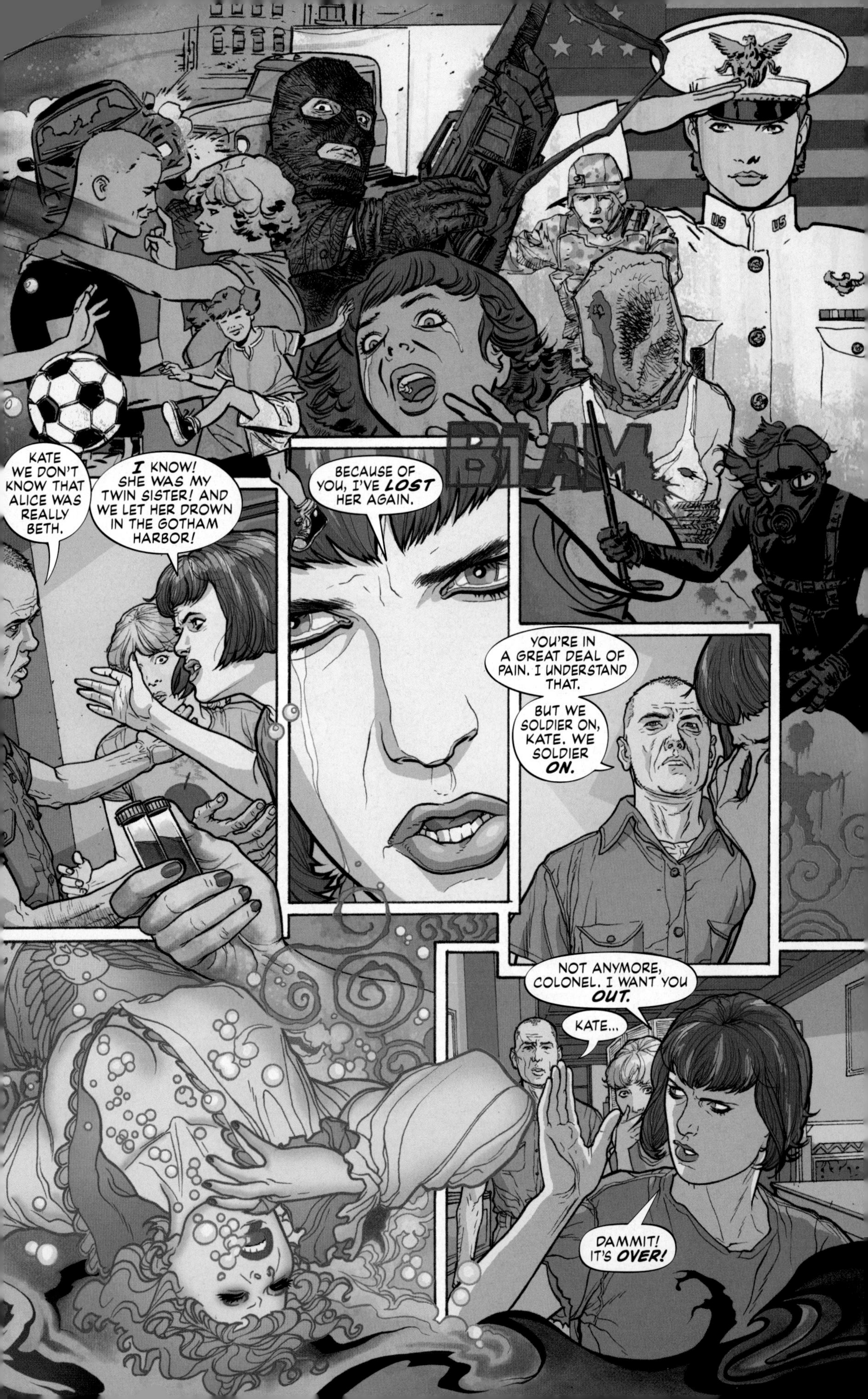
BLAM
KATE WE DON'T KNOW THAT ALICE WAS REALLY BETH.
I KNOW! SHE WAS MY TWIN SISTER! AND WE LET HER DROWN IN THE GOTHAM HARBOR!
BECAUSE OF YOU, I'VE LOST HER AGAIN.
YOU'RE IN A GREAT DEAL OF PAIN. I UNDERSTAND THAT.
BUT WE SOLDIER ON, KATE. WE SOLDIER ON.
NOT ANYMORE, COLONEL. I WANT YOU OUT.
KATE...
DAMMIT! IT'S OVER!

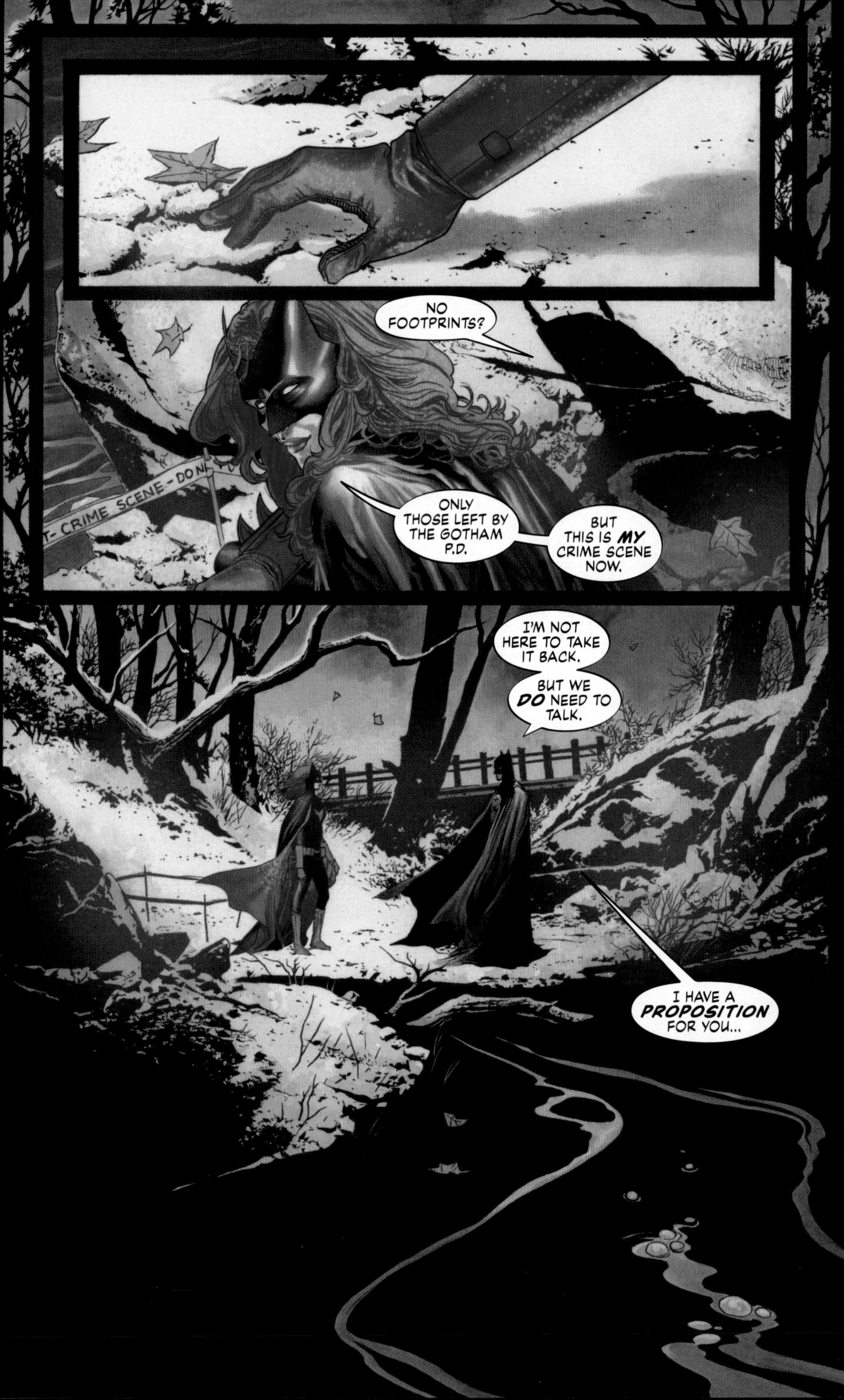
NO FOOTPRINTS?
CRIME SCENE-DO N
ONLY THOSE LEFT BY THE GOTHAM P.D.
BUT THIS IS MY CRIME SCENE NOW.
I'M NOT HERE TO TAKE IT BACK.
BUT WE DO NEED TO TALK.
I HAVE A PROPOSITION FOR YOU...

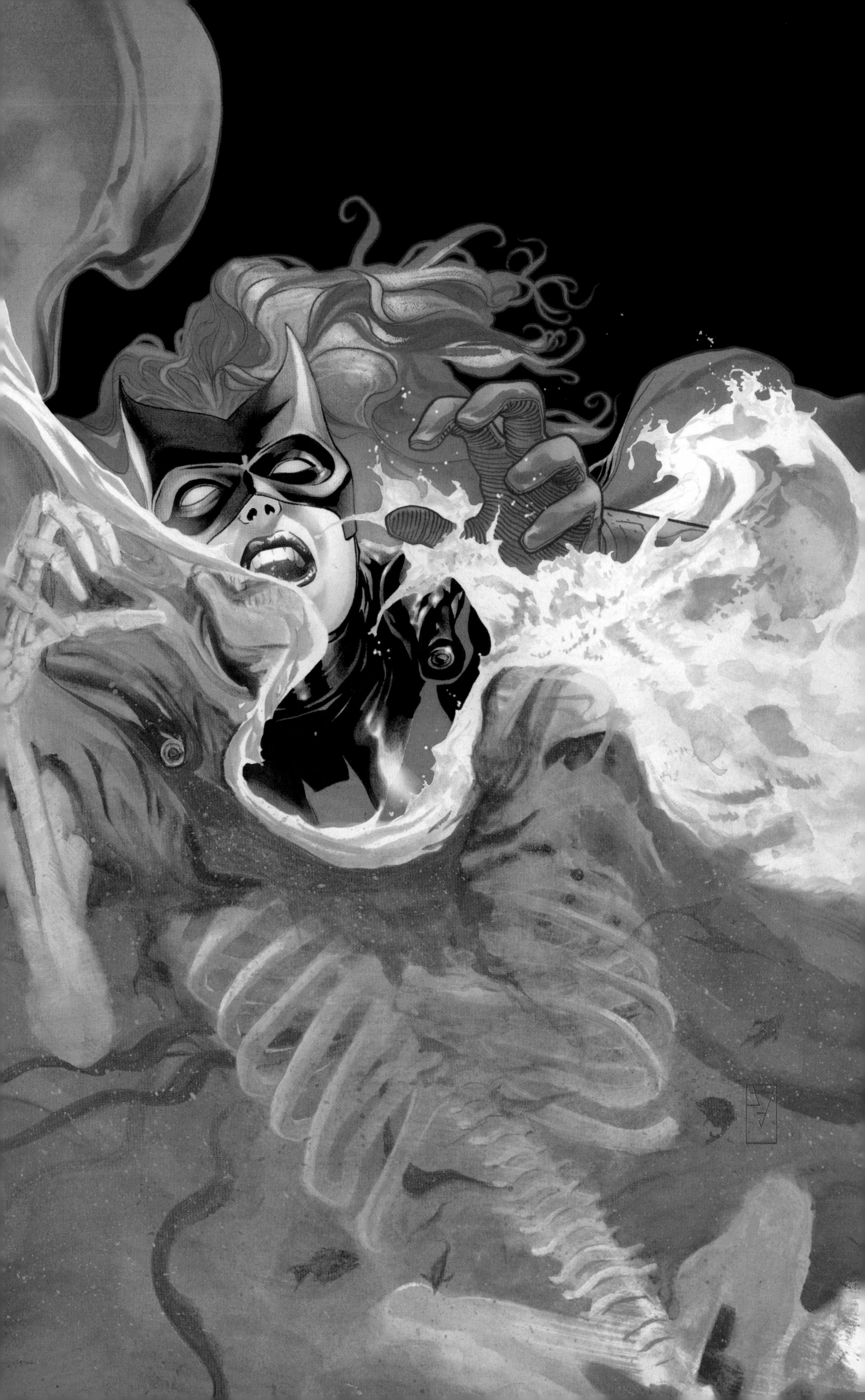

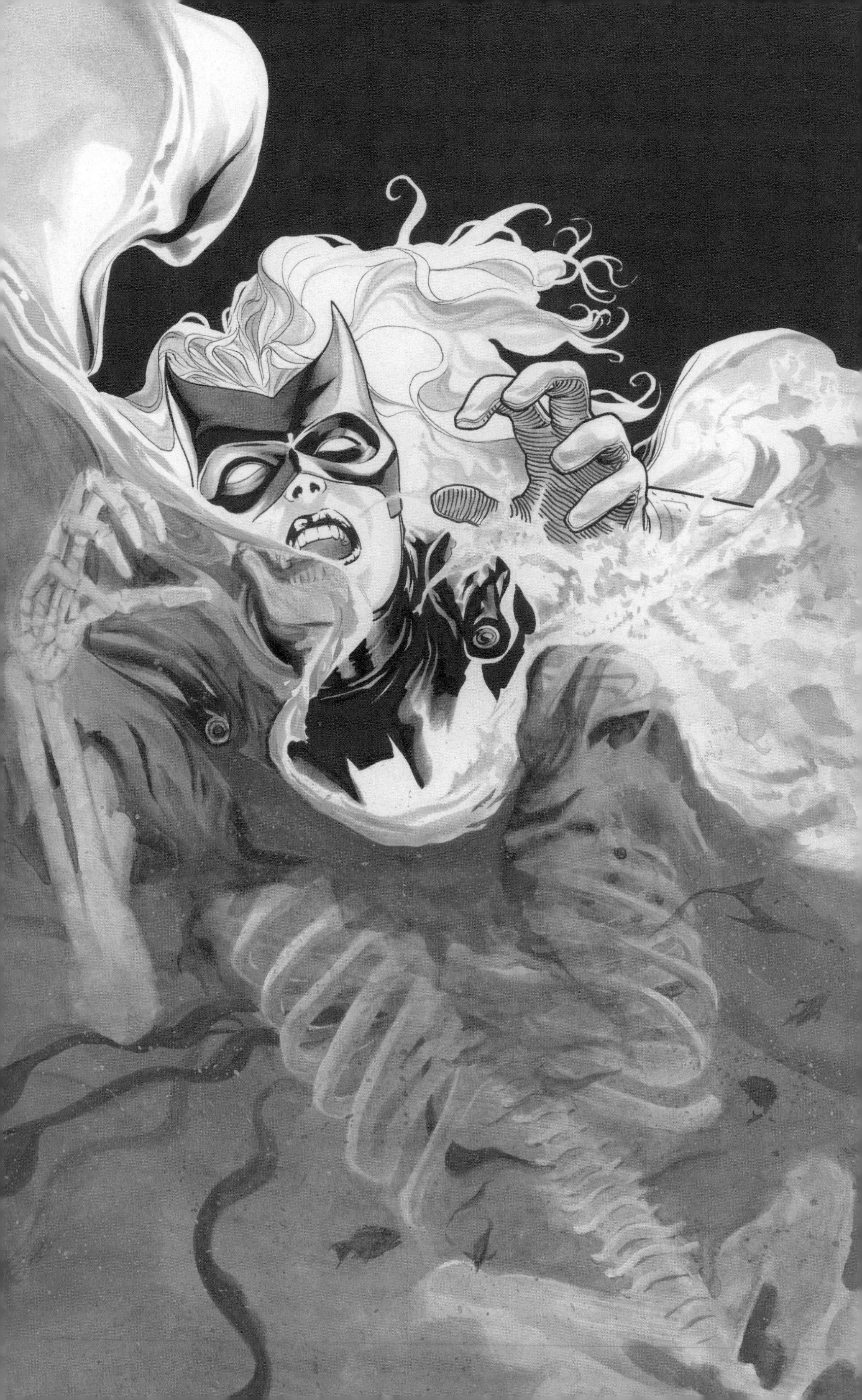

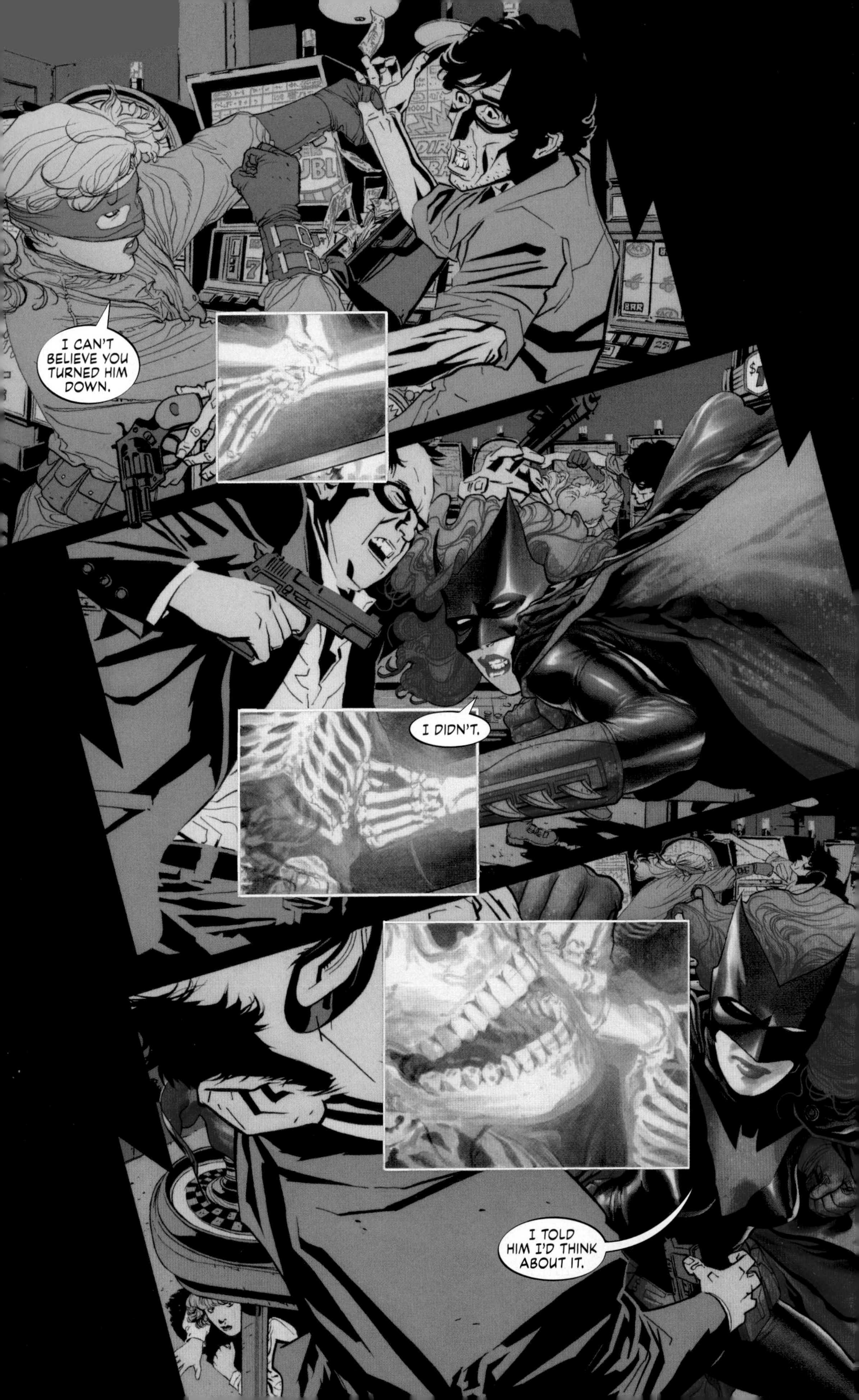
I CAN'T BELIEVE YOU TURNED HIM DOWN.
I DIDN'T.
I TOLD HIM I'D THINK ABOUT IT.

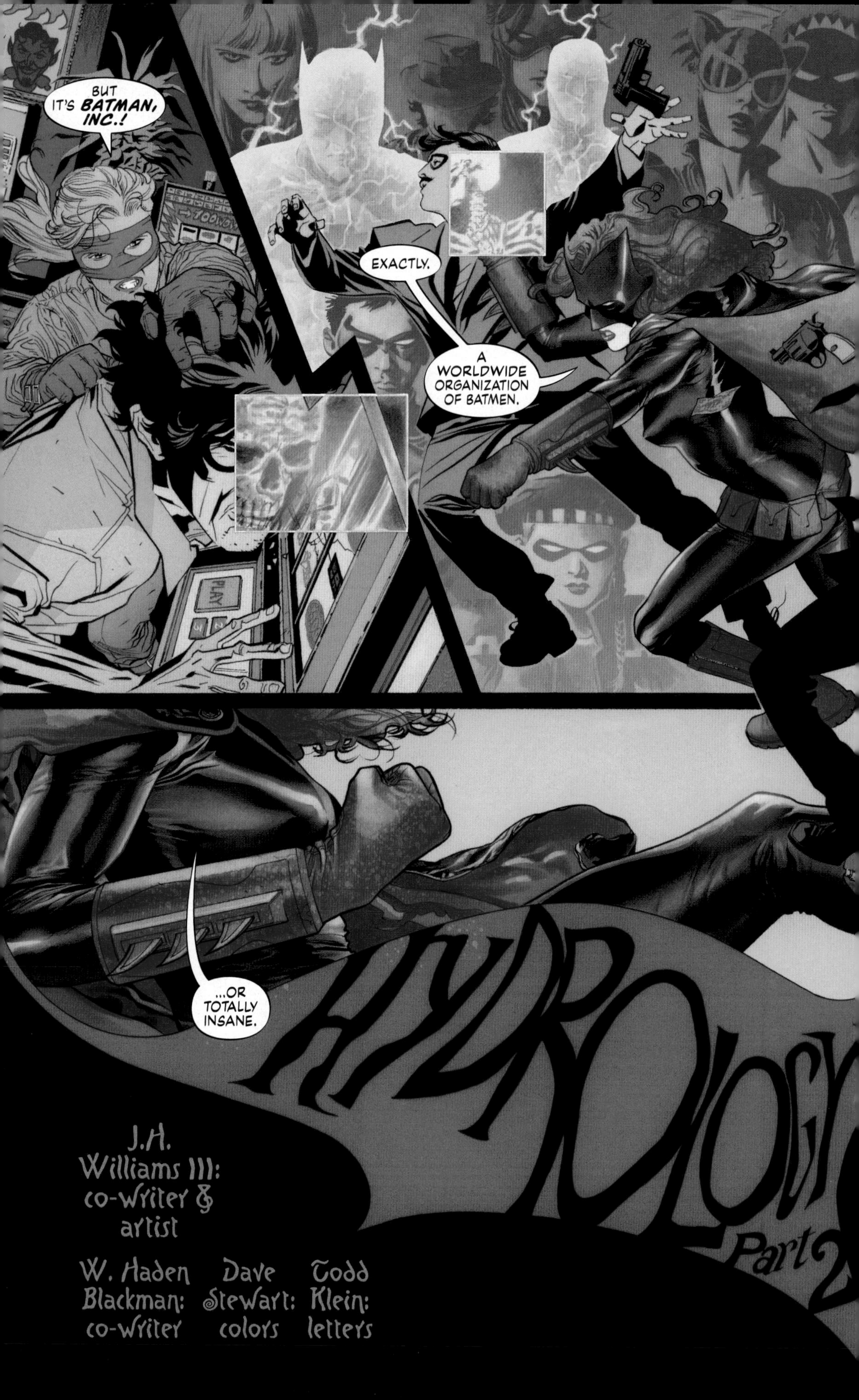

BUT IT'S BATMAN, INC.!
EXACTLY.
A WORLDWIDE ORGANIZATION OF BATMEN.
...OR TOTALLY INSANE.
HYDROLOGY
Part 2
J.H. Williams III: co-writer & artist
W. Haden Blackman: co-writer
Dave Stewart: colors
Todd Klein: letters

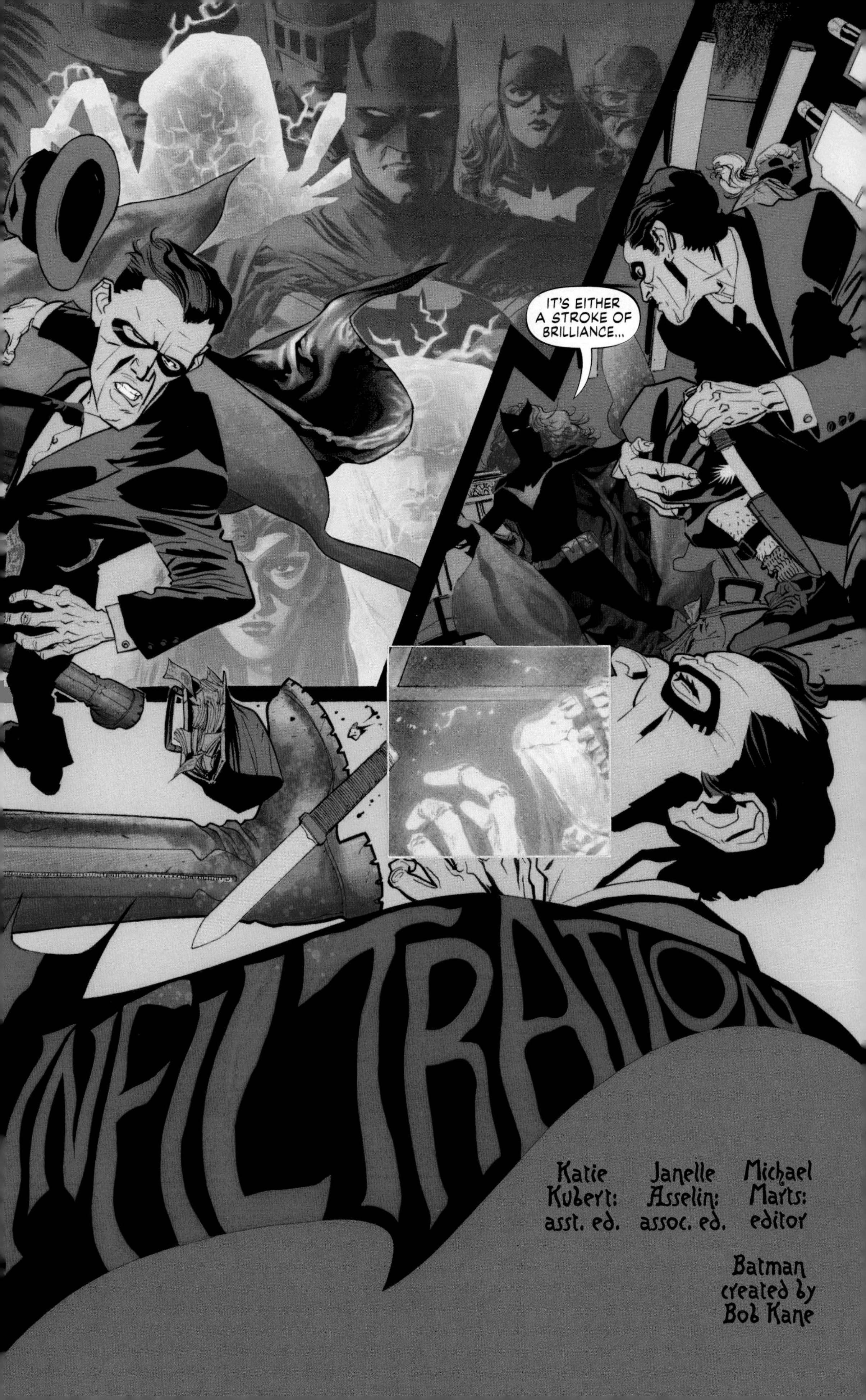
IT'S EITHER A STROKE OF BRILLIANCE...
INFILTRATION
Katie Kubert: asst. ed.
Janelle Asselin: assoc. ed.
Michael Marts: editor
Batman created by Bob Kane

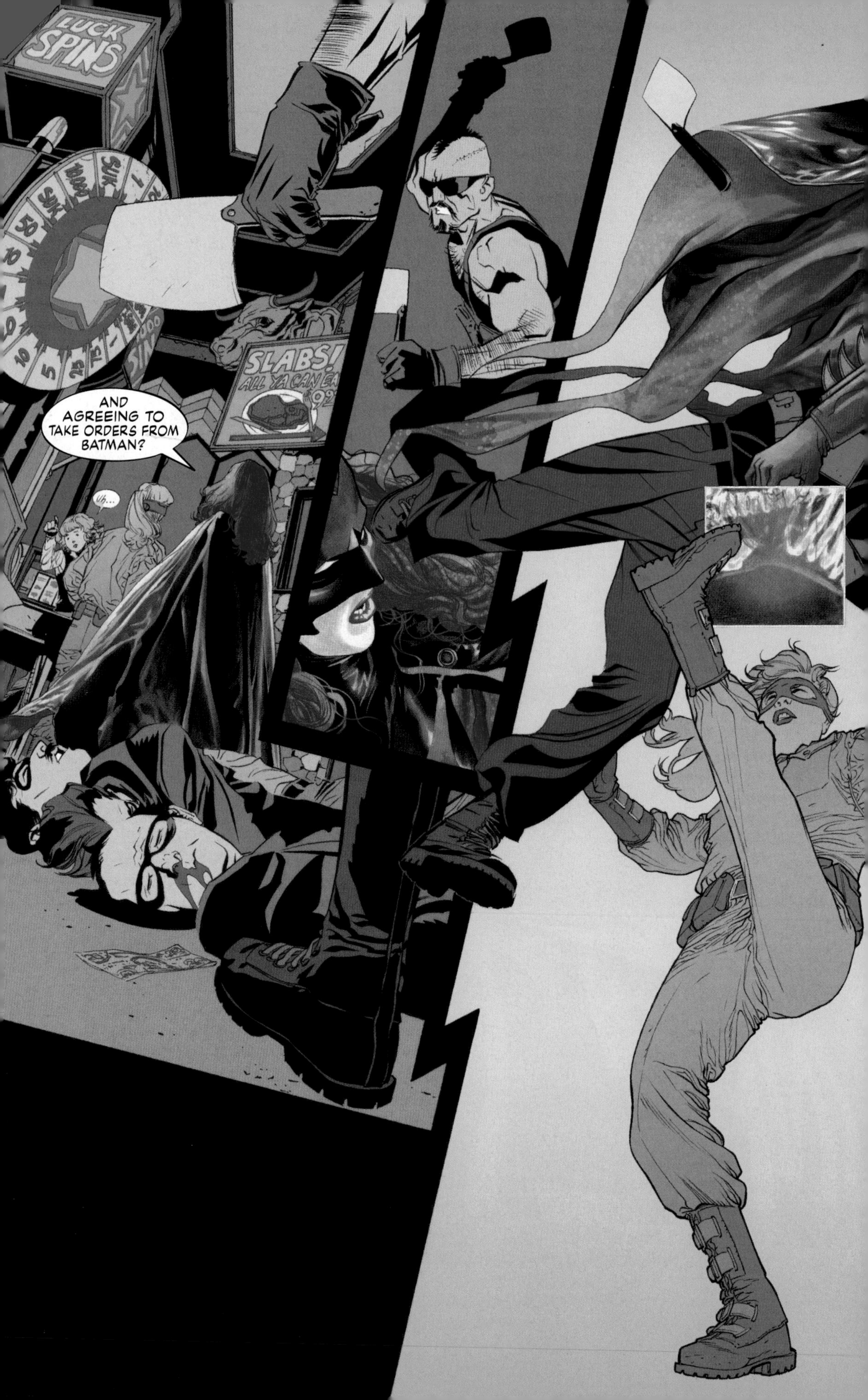
LUCK SPINS
SLABS! ALL YA CAN EAT
AND AGREEING TO TAKE ORDERS FROM BATMAN?
Uh...

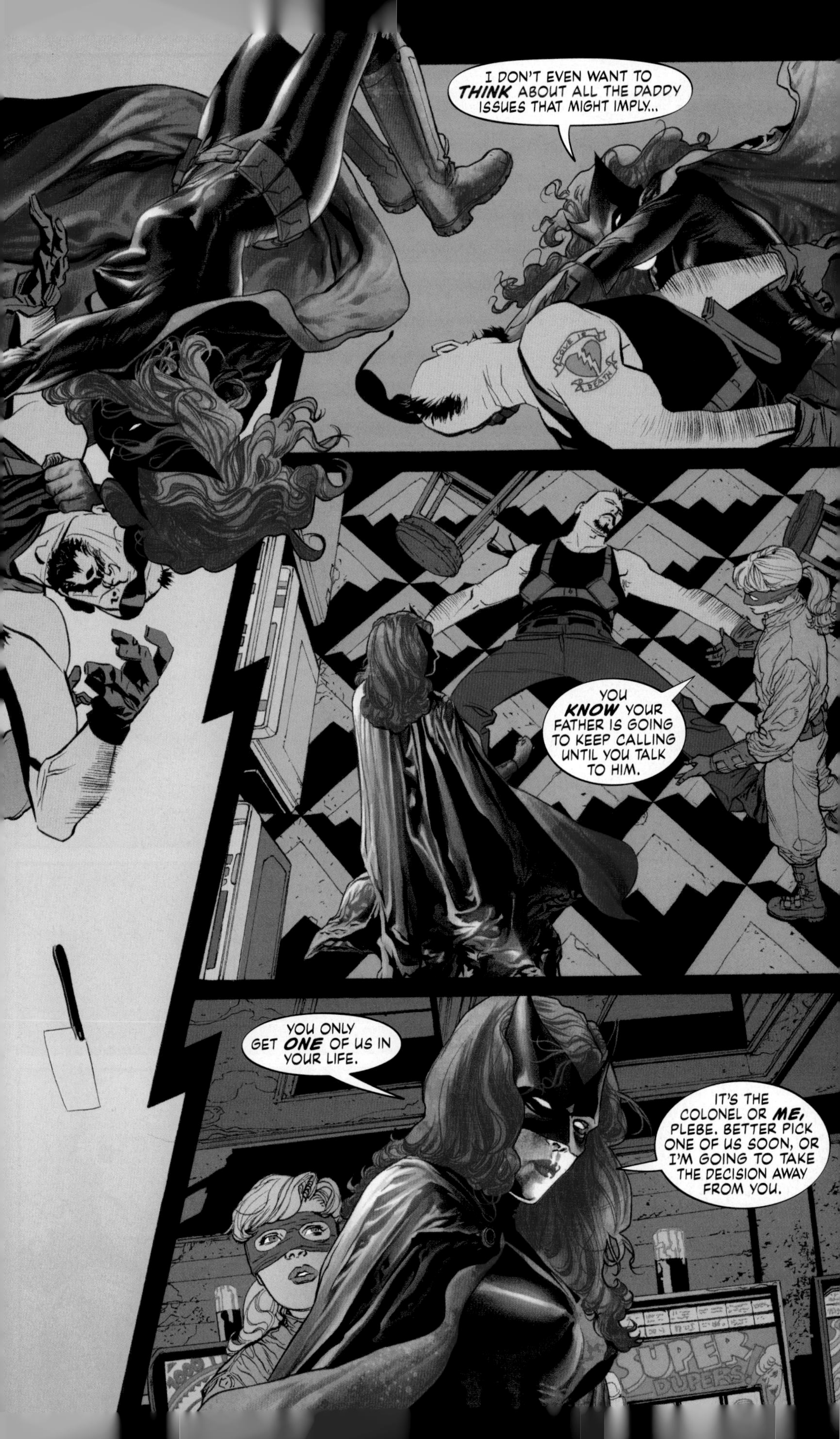
I DON'T EVEN WANT TO THINK ABOUT ALL THE DADDY ISSUES THAT MIGHT IMPLY...
YOU KNOW YOUR FATHER IS GOING TO KEEP CALLING UNTIL YOU TALK TO HIM.
YOU ONLY GET ONE OF US IN YOUR LIFE.
IT'S THE COLONEL OR ME, PLEBE. BETTER PICK ONE OF US SOON, OR I'M GOING TO TAKE THE DECISION AWAY FROM YOU.
SUPER DUPERS!

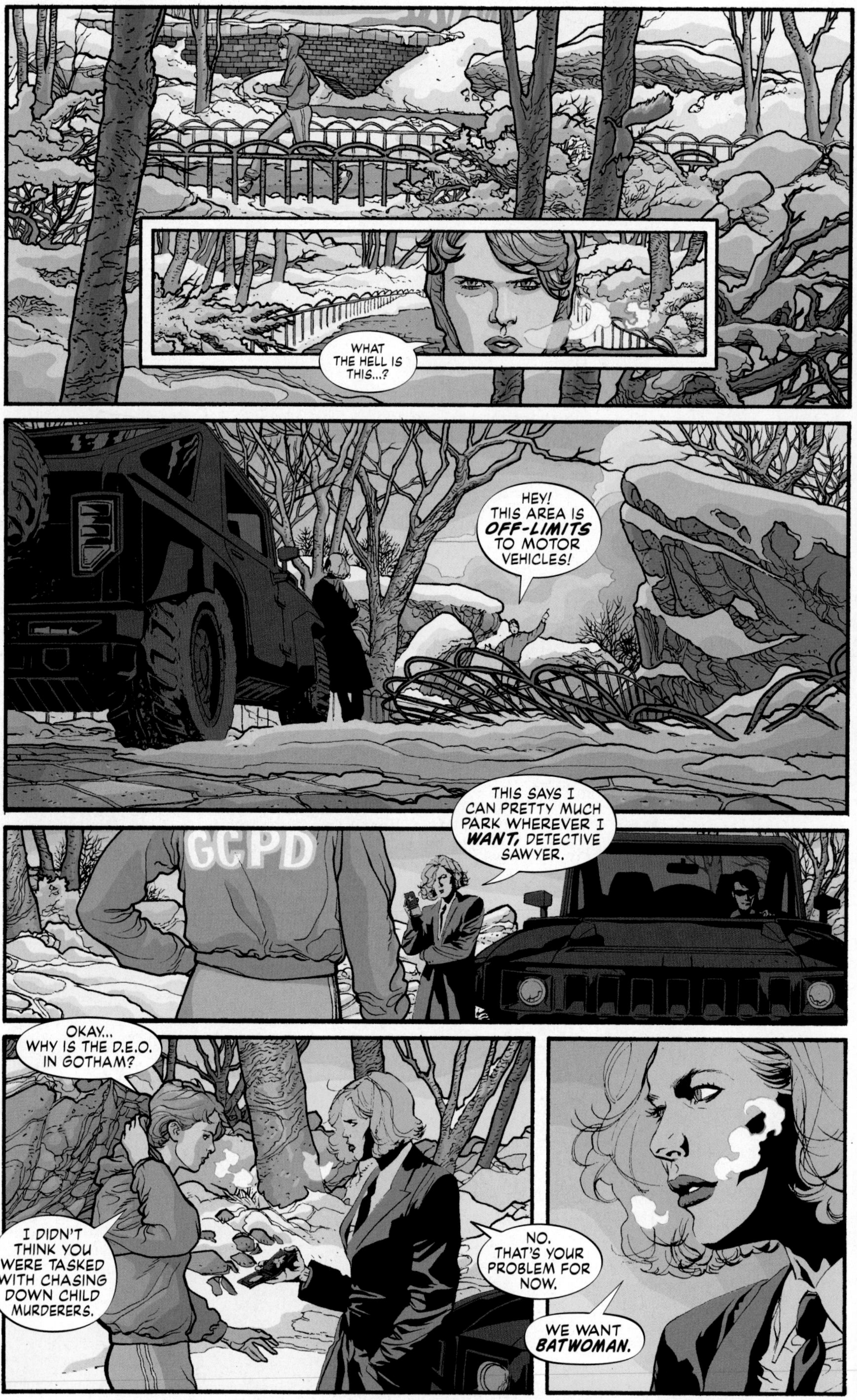

WHAT THE HELL IS THIS...?
HEY! THIS AREA IS OFF-LIMITS TO MOTOR VEHICLES!
THIS SAYS I CAN PRETTY MUCH PARK WHEREVER I WANT, DETECTIVE SAWYER.
GCPD
OKAY... WHY IS THE D.E.O. IN GOTHAM?
I DIDN'T THINK YOU WERE TASKED WITH CHASING DOWN CHILD MURDERERS.
NO. THAT'S YOUR PROBLEM FOR NOW.
WE WANT BATWOMAN.

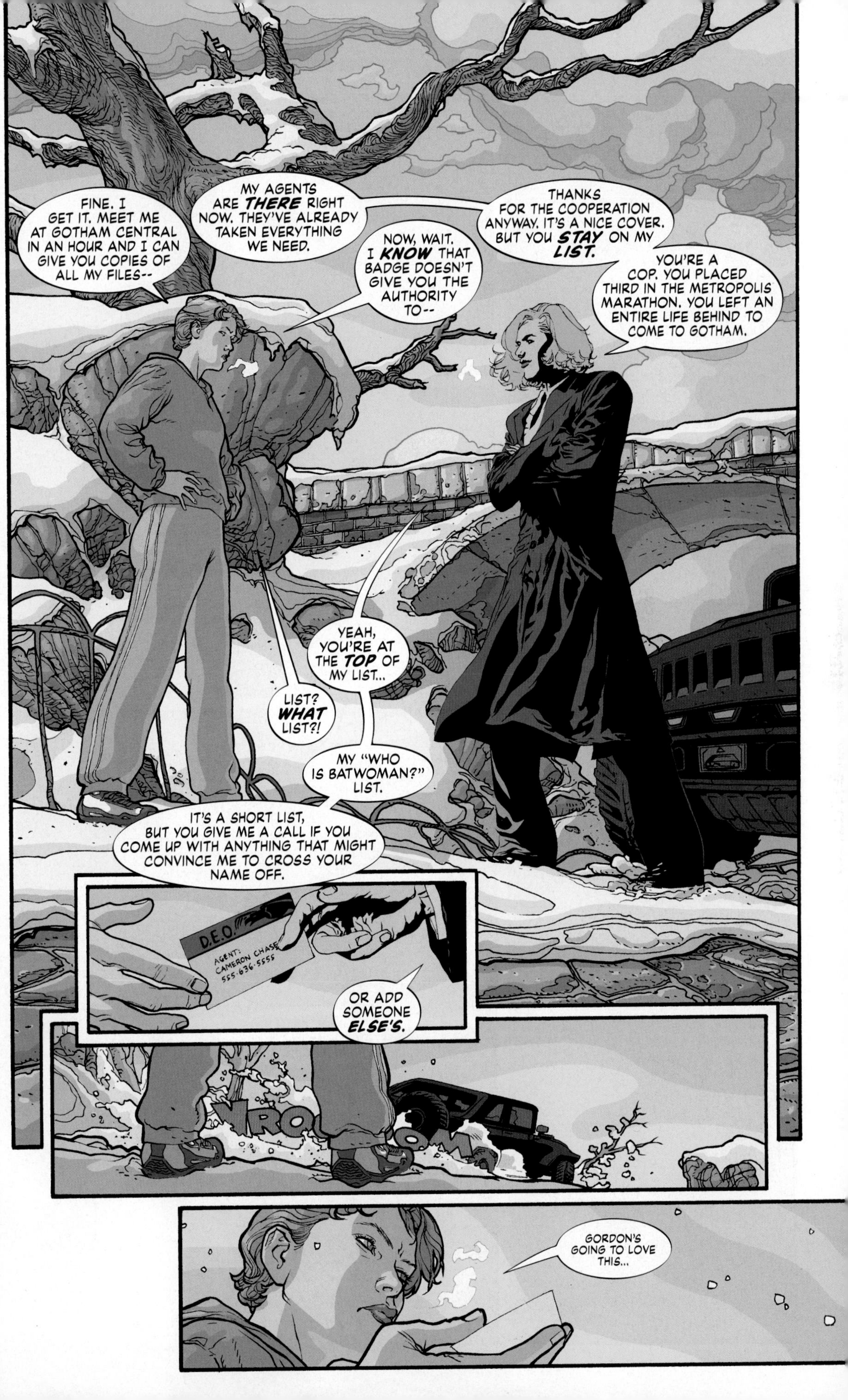
FINE. I GET IT. MEET ME AT GOTHAM CENTRAL IN AN HOUR AND I CAN GIVE YOU COPIES OF ALL MY FILES--
MY AGENTS ARE THERE RIGHT NOW. THEY'VE ALREADY TAKEN EVERYTHING WE NEED.
THANKS FOR THE COOPERATION ANYWAY. IT'S A NICE COVER. BUT YOU STAY ON MY LIST.
NOW, WAIT. I KNOW THAT BADGE DOESN'T GIVE YOU THE AUTHORITY TO--
YOU'RE A COP. YOU PLACED THIRD IN THE METROPOLIS MARATHON. YOU LEFT AN ENTIRE LIFE BEHIND TO COME TO GOTHAM.
YEAH, YOU'RE AT THE TOP OF MY LIST...
LIST? WHAT LIST?!
MY "WHO IS BATWOMAN?" LIST.
IT'S A SHORT LIST, BUT YOU GIVE ME A CALL IF YOU COME UP WITH ANYTHING THAT MIGHT CONVINCE ME TO CROSS YOUR NAME OFF.
D.E.O.
AGENT: CAMERON CHASE
555-636-5555
OR ADD SOMEONE ELSE'S.
VROOOOM
GORDON'S GOING TO LOVE THIS...

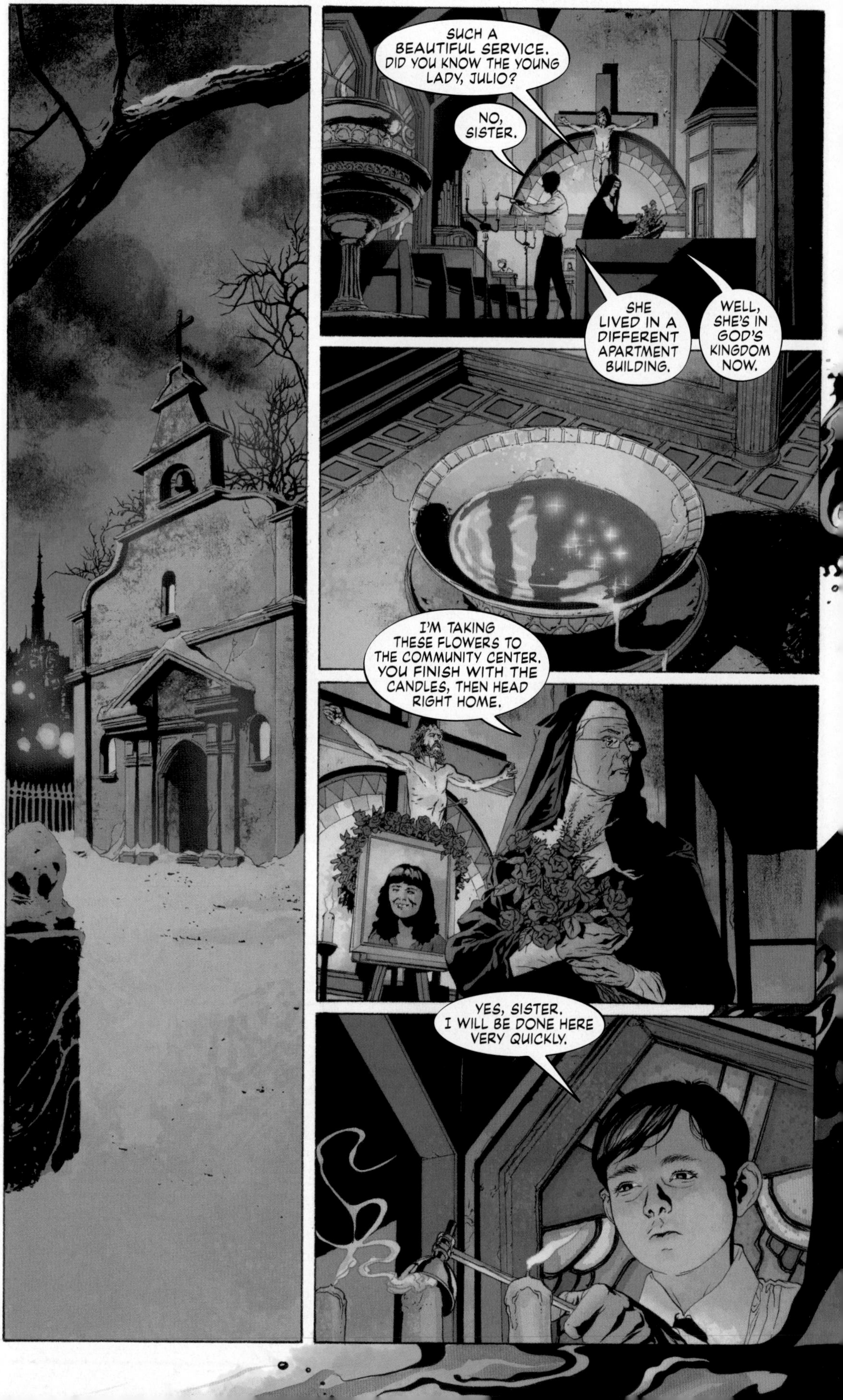
SUCH A BEAUTIFUL SERVICE. DID YOU KNOW THE YOUNG LADY, JULIO?
NO, SISTER.
SHE LIVED IN A DIFFERENT APARTMENT BUILDING.
WELL, SHE'S IN GOD'S KINGDOM NOW.
I'M TAKING THESE FLOWERS TO THE COMMUNITY CENTER. YOU FINISH WITH THE CANDLES, THEN HEAD RIGHT HOME.
YES, SISTER. I WILL BE DONE HERE VERY QUICKLY.

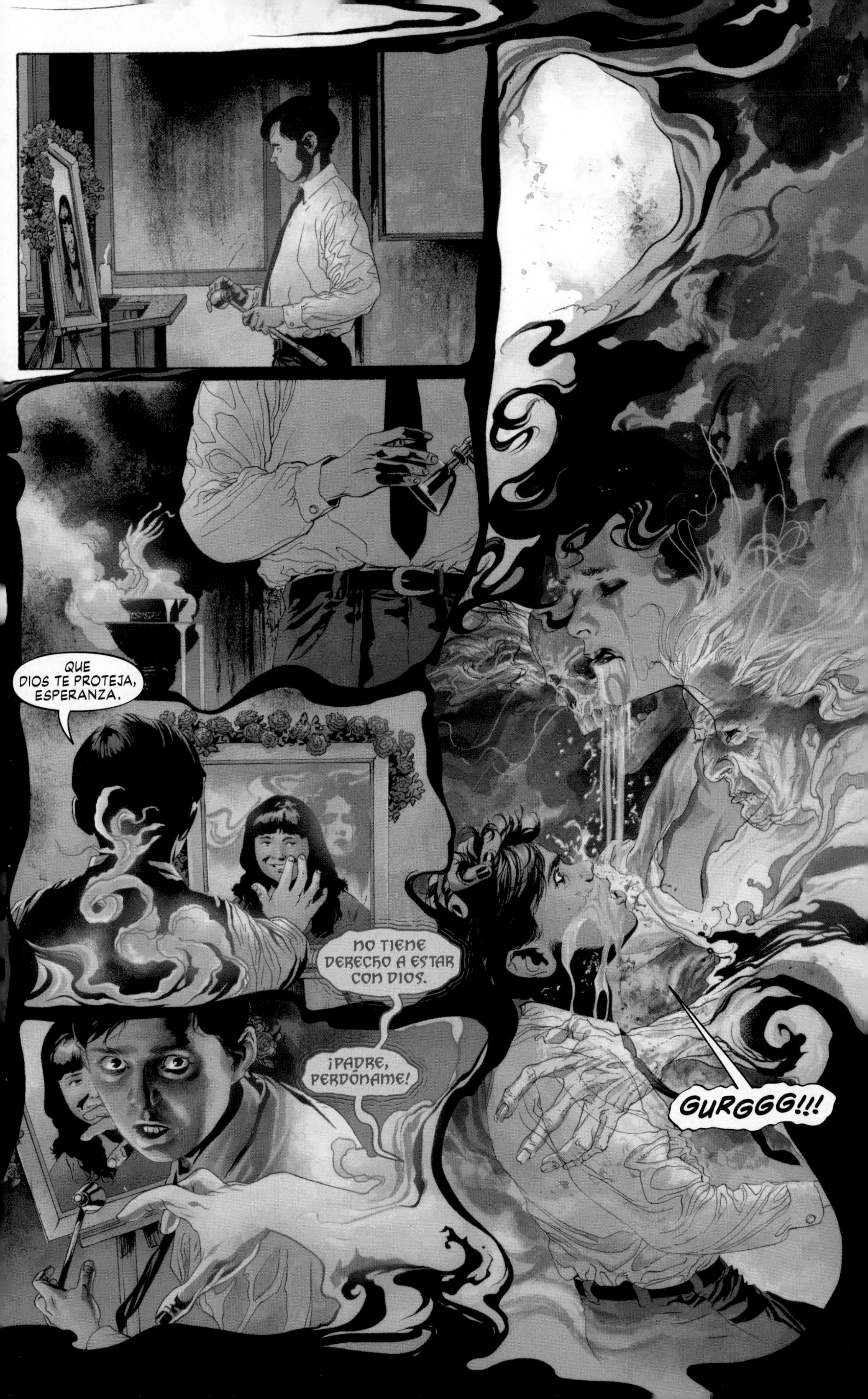
QUE DIOS TE PROTEJA, ESPERANZA.
NO TIENE DERECHO A ESTAR CON DIOS.
¡PADRE, PERDÓNAME!
GURGGG!!!

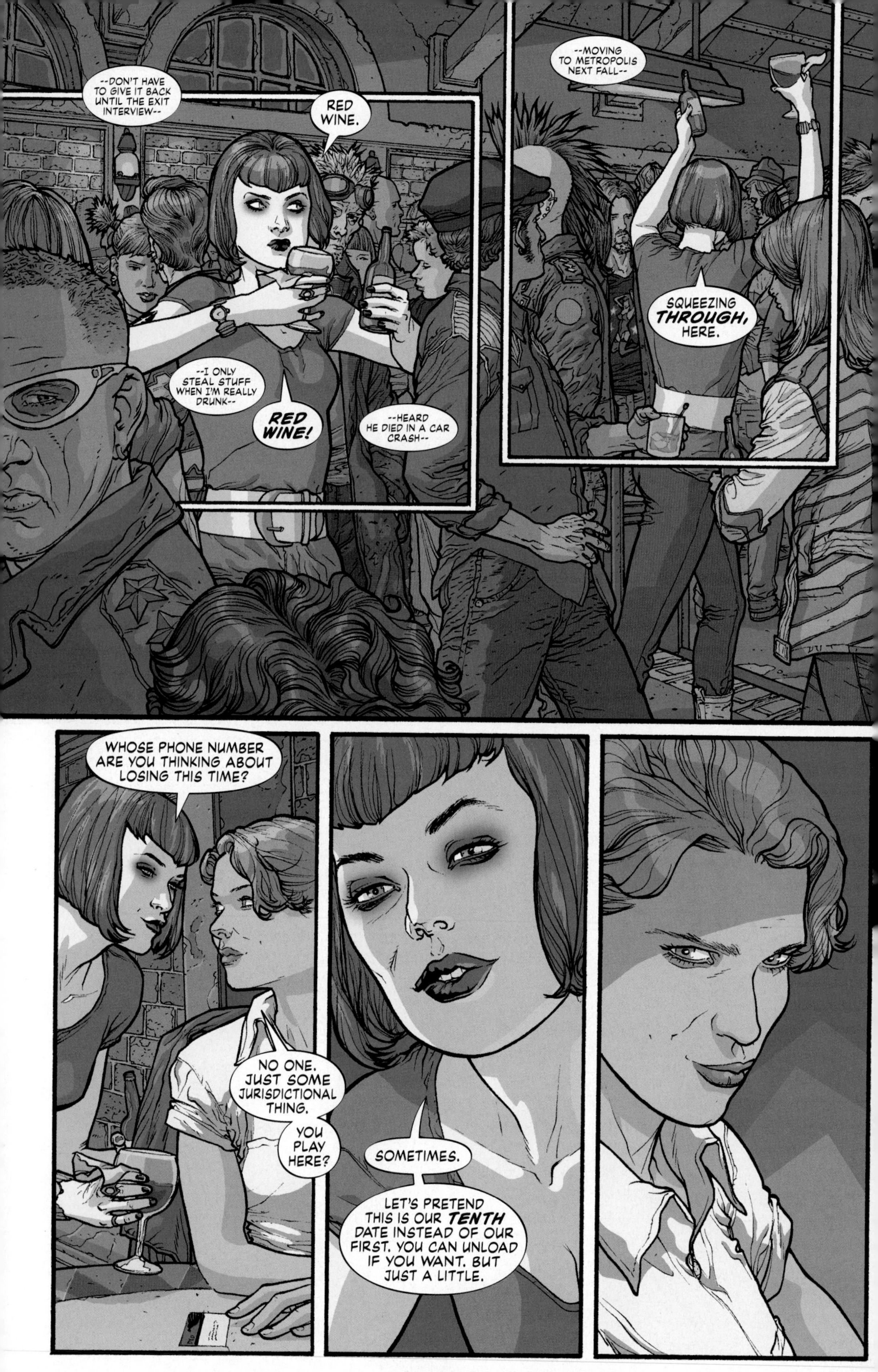
--DON'T HAVE TO GIVE IT BACK UNTIL THE EXIT INTERVIEW--
RED WINE.
--I ONLY STEAL STUFF WHEN I'M REALLY DRUNK--
RED WINE!
--HEARD HE DIED IN A CAR CRASH--
--MOVING TO METROPOLIS NEXT FALL--
SQUEEZING THROUGH, HERE.
WHOSE PHONE NUMBER ARE YOU THINKING ABOUT LOSING THIS TIME?
NO ONE. JUST SOME JURISDICTIONAL THING.
YOU PLAY HERE?
SOMETIMES.
LET'S PRETEND THIS IS OUR TENTH DATE INSTEAD OF OUR FIRST. YOU CAN UNLOAD IF YOU WANT. BUT JUST A LITTLE.

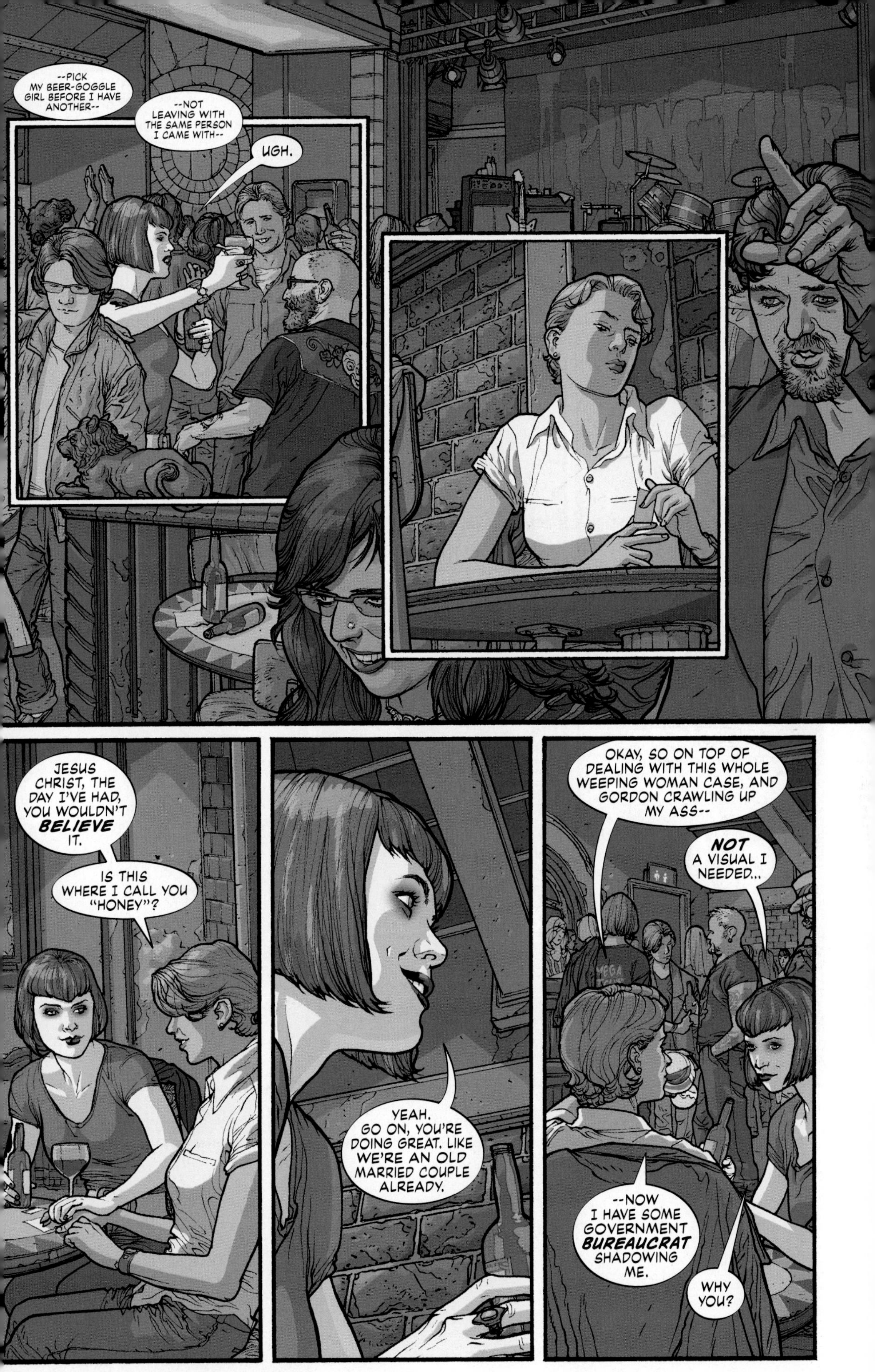
--PICK MY BEER-GOGGLE GIRL BEFORE I HAVE ANOTHER--
--NOT LEAVING WITH THE SAME PERSON I CAME WITH--
UGH.
JESUS CHRIST, THE DAY I'VE HAD, YOU WOULDN'T BELIEVE IT.
IS THIS WHERE I CALL YOU "HONEY"?
YEAH. GO ON, YOU'RE DOING GREAT. LIKE WE'RE AN OLD MARRIED COUPLE ALREADY.
OKAY, SO ON TOP OF DEALING WITH THIS WHOLE WEEPING WOMAN CASE, AND GORDON CRAWLING UP MY ASS--
NOT A VISUAL I NEEDED...
--NOW I HAVE SOME GOVERNMENT BUREAUCRAT SHADOWING ME.
WHY YOU?

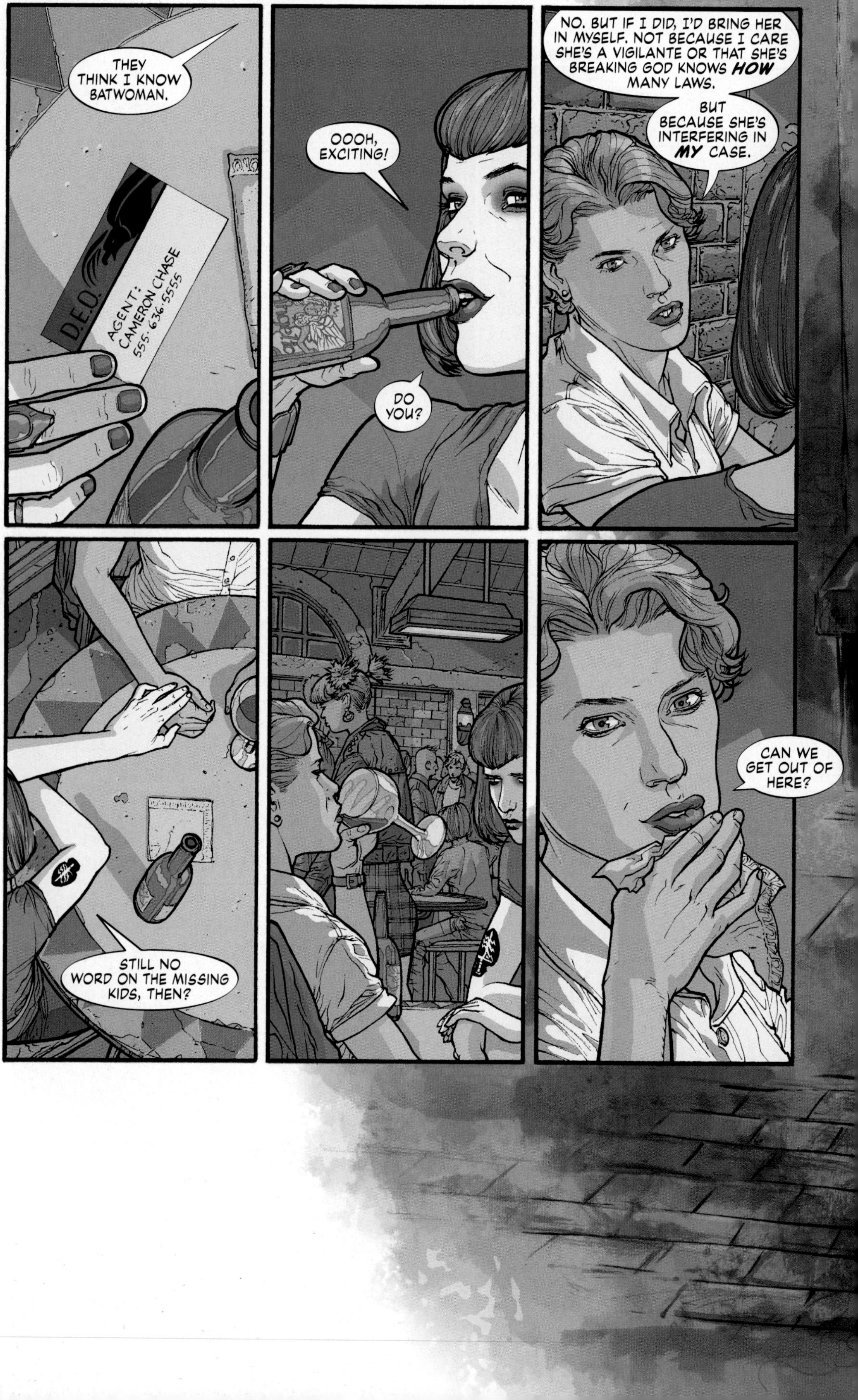
THEY THINK I KNOW BATWOMAN.
D.E.O.
AGENT: CAMERON CHASE 555·636·5555
OOOH, EXCITING!
DO YOU?
NO. BUT IF I DID, I'D BRING HER IN MYSELF. NOT BECAUSE I CARE SHE'S A VIGILANTE OR THAT SHE'S BREAKING GOD KNOWS **HOW** MANY LAWS.
BUT BECAUSE SHE'S INTERFERING IN **MY** CASE.
STILL NO WORD ON THE MISSING KIDS, THEN?
CAN WE GET OUT OF HERE?

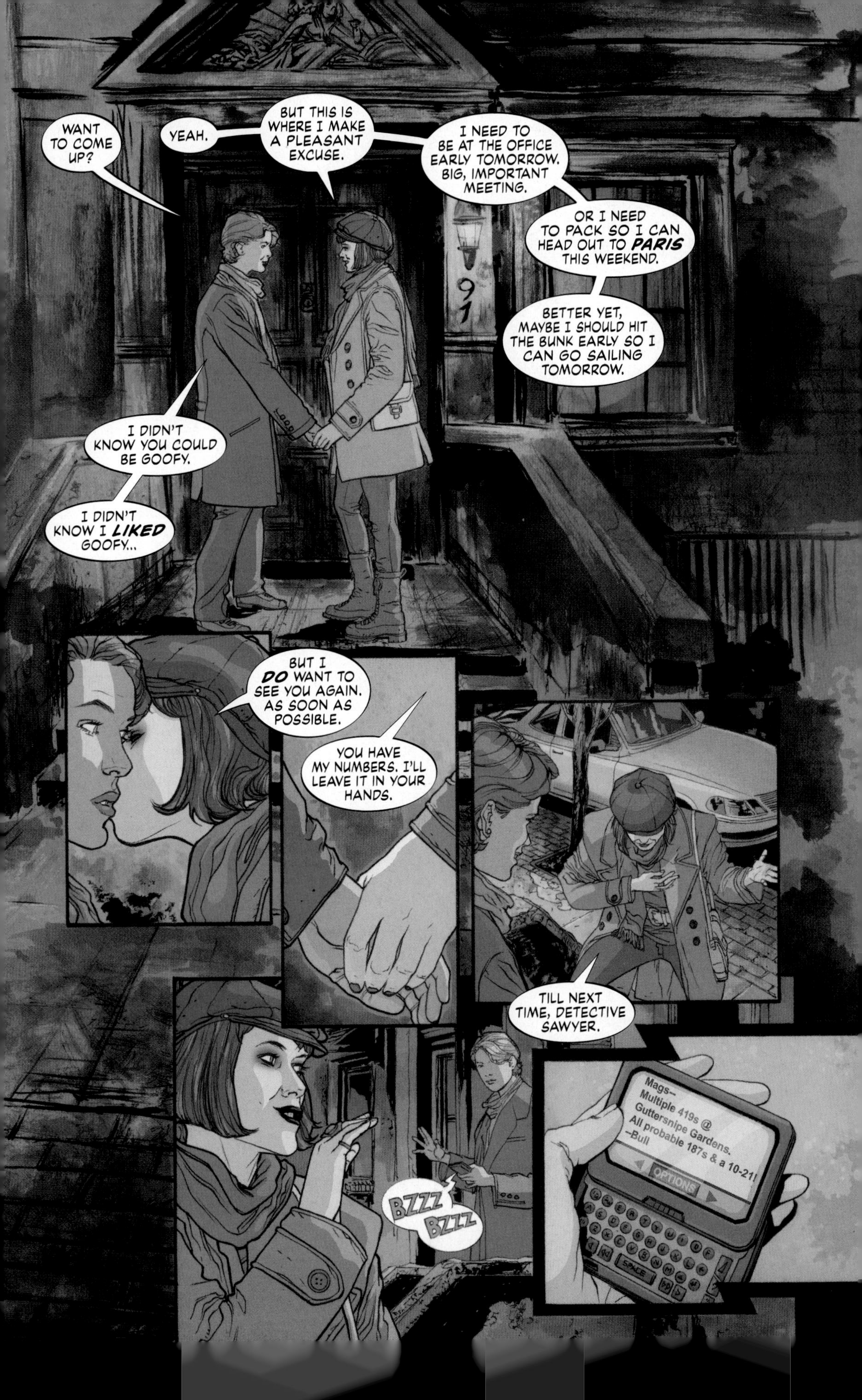
WANT TO COME UP?
YEAH.
BUT THIS IS WHERE I MAKE A PLEASANT EXCUSE.
I NEED TO BE AT THE OFFICE EARLY TOMORROW. BIG, IMPORTANT MEETING.
OR I NEED TO PACK SO I CAN HEAD OUT TO ***PARIS*** THIS WEEKEND.
BETTER YET, MAYBE I SHOULD HIT THE BUNK EARLY SO I CAN GO SAILING TOMORROW.
I DIDN'T KNOW YOU COULD BE GOOFY.
I DIDN'T KNOW I ***LIKED*** GOOFY...
BUT I ***DO*** WANT TO SEE YOU AGAIN. AS SOON AS POSSIBLE.
YOU HAVE MY NUMBERS. I'LL LEAVE IT IN YOUR HANDS.
TILL NEXT TIME, DETECTIVE SAWYER.
BZZZ BZZZ
Mags--
Multiple 419s @
Guttersnipe Gardens.
All probable 187s & a 10-21!
--Bull
OPTIONS
SPACE

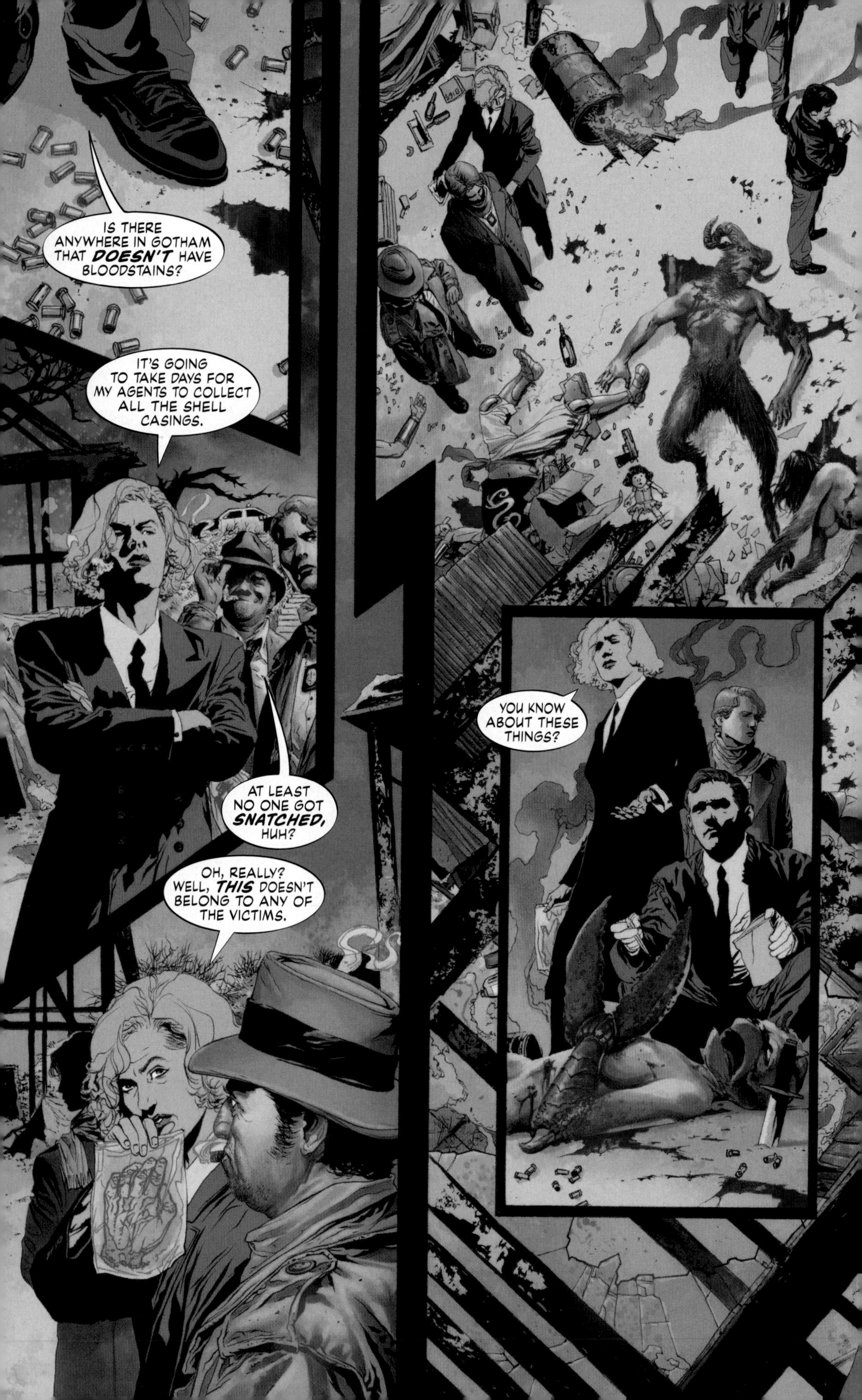
IS THERE ANYWHERE IN GOTHAM THAT DOESN'T HAVE BLOODSTAINS?
IT'S GOING TO TAKE DAYS FOR MY AGENTS TO COLLECT ALL THE SHELL CASINGS.
AT LEAST NO ONE GOT SNATCHED, HUH?
OH, REALLY? WELL, THIS DOESN'T BELONG TO ANY OF THE VICTIMS.
YOU KNOW ABOUT THESE THINGS?

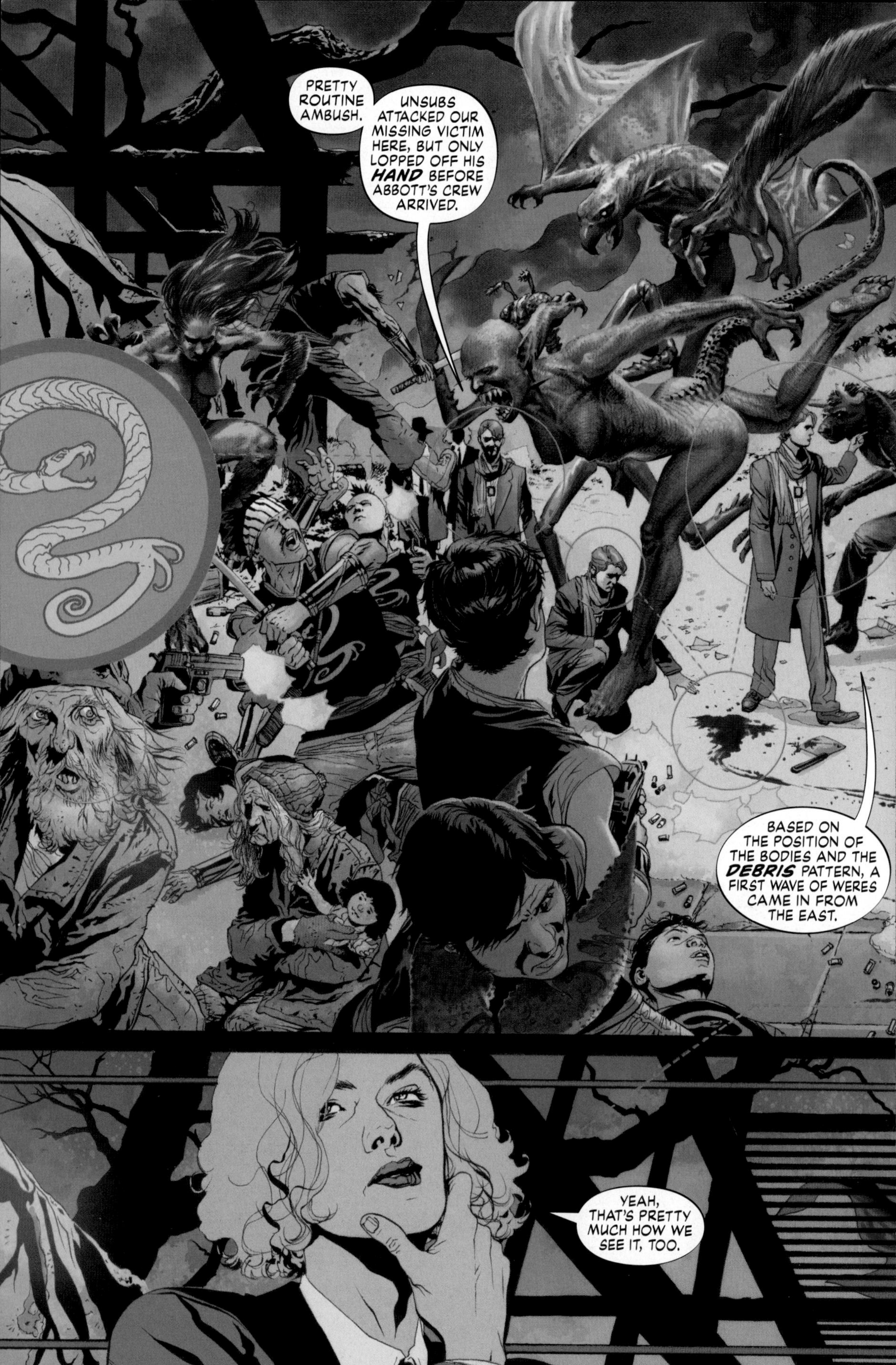
PRETTY ROUTINE AMBUSH.
UNSUBS ATTACKED OUR MISSING VICTIM HERE, BUT ONLY LOPPED OFF HIS HAND BEFORE ABBOTT'S CREW ARRIVED.
BASED ON THE POSITION OF THE BODIES AND THE DEBRIS PATTERN, A FIRST WAVE OF WERES CAME IN FROM THE EAST.
YEAH, THAT'S PRETTY MUCH HOW WE SEE IT, TOO.

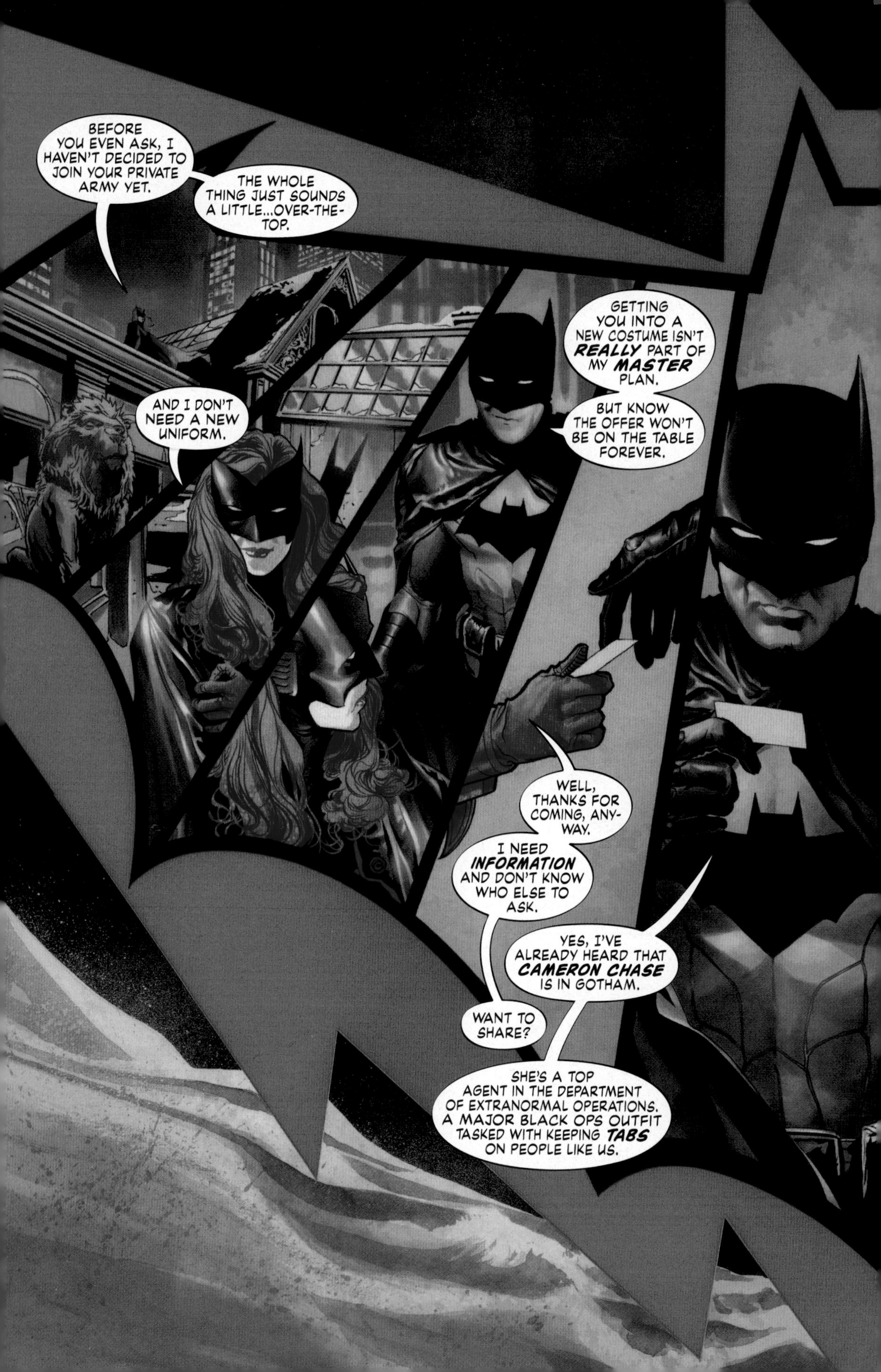

BEFORE YOU EVEN ASK, I HAVEN'T DECIDED TO JOIN YOUR PRIVATE ARMY YET.
THE WHOLE THING JUST SOUNDS A LITTLE...OVER-THE-TOP.
AND I DON'T NEED A NEW UNIFORM.
GETTING YOU INTO A NEW COSTUME ISN'T **REALLY** PART OF MY **MASTER** PLAN.
BUT KNOW THE OFFER WON'T BE ON THE TABLE FOREVER.
WELL, THANKS FOR COMING, ANYWAY.
I NEED **INFORMATION** AND DON'T KNOW WHO ELSE TO ASK.
WANT TO SHARE?
YES, I'VE ALREADY HEARD THAT **CAMERON CHASE** IS IN GOTHAM.
SHE'S A TOP AGENT IN THE DEPARTMENT OF EXTRANORMAL OPERATIONS. A MAJOR BLACK OPS OUTFIT TASKED WITH KEEPING **TABS** ON PEOPLE LIKE US.

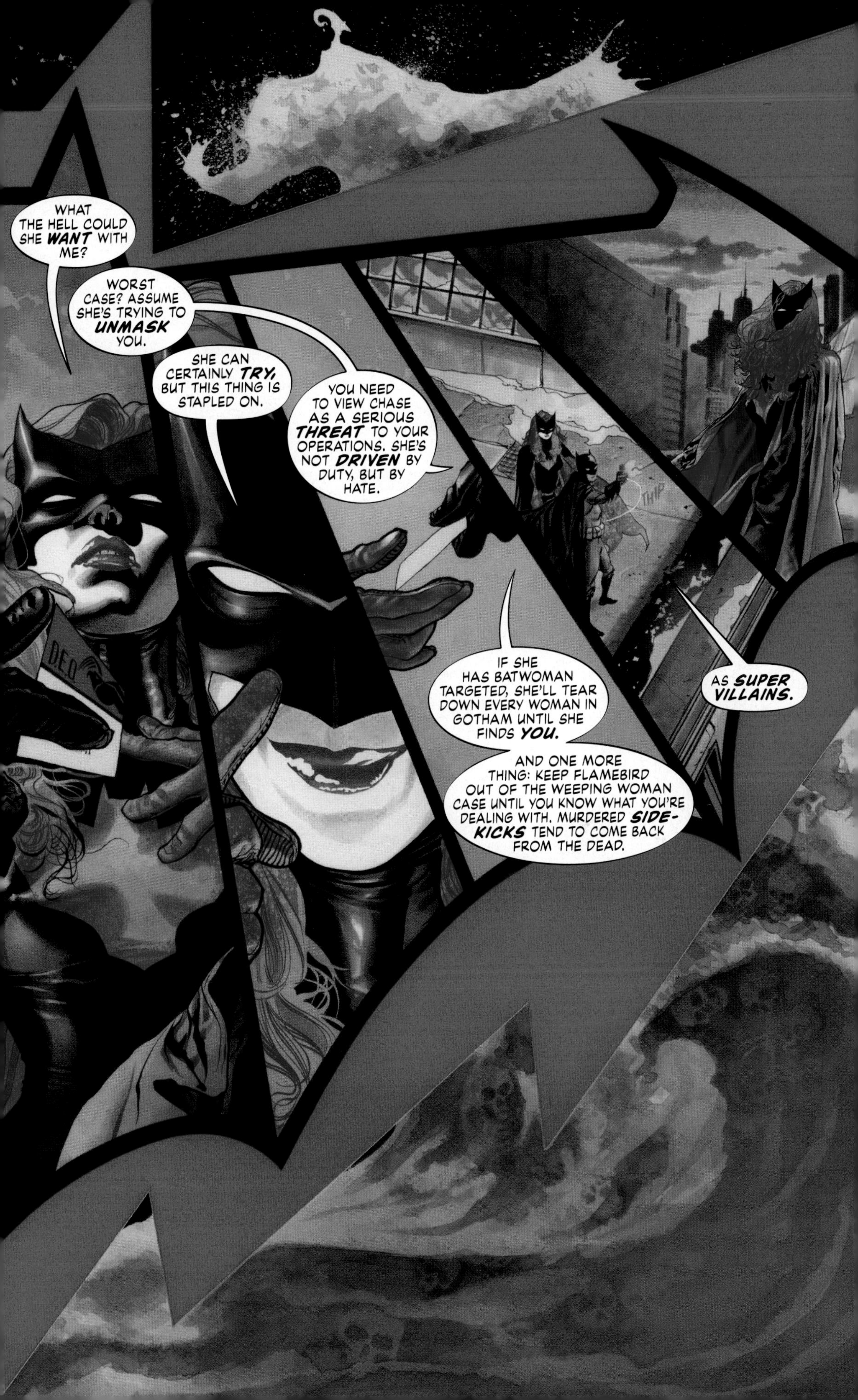
WHAT THE HELL COULD SHE WANT WITH ME?
WORST CASE? ASSUME SHE'S TRYING TO UNMASK YOU.
SHE CAN CERTAINLY TRY, BUT THIS THING IS STAPLED ON.
YOU NEED TO VIEW CHASE AS A SERIOUS THREAT TO YOUR OPERATIONS. SHE'S NOT DRIVEN BY DUTY, BUT BY HATE.
D.E.O.
THIP
IF SHE HAS BATWOMAN TARGETED, SHE'LL TEAR DOWN EVERY WOMAN IN GOTHAM UNTIL SHE FINDS YOU.
AND ONE MORE THING: KEEP FLAMEBIRD OUT OF THE WEEPING WOMAN CASE UNTIL YOU KNOW WHAT YOU'RE DEALING WITH. MURDERED SIDE-KICKS TEND TO COME BACK FROM THE DEAD.
AS SUPER VILLAINS.

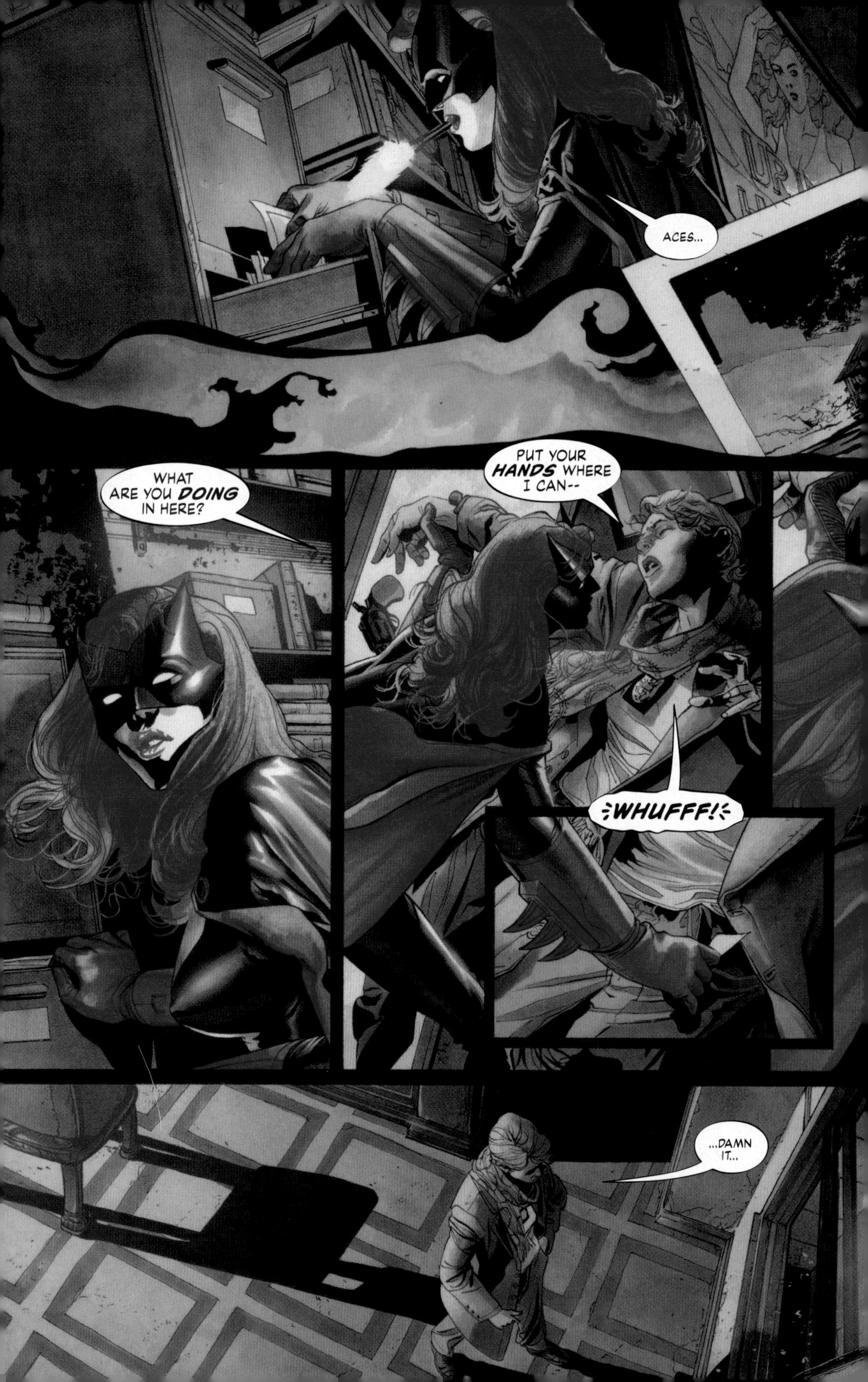
ACES...
WHAT ARE YOU *DOING* IN HERE?
PUT YOUR *HANDS* WHERE I CAN--
WHUFFF!
...DAMN IT...

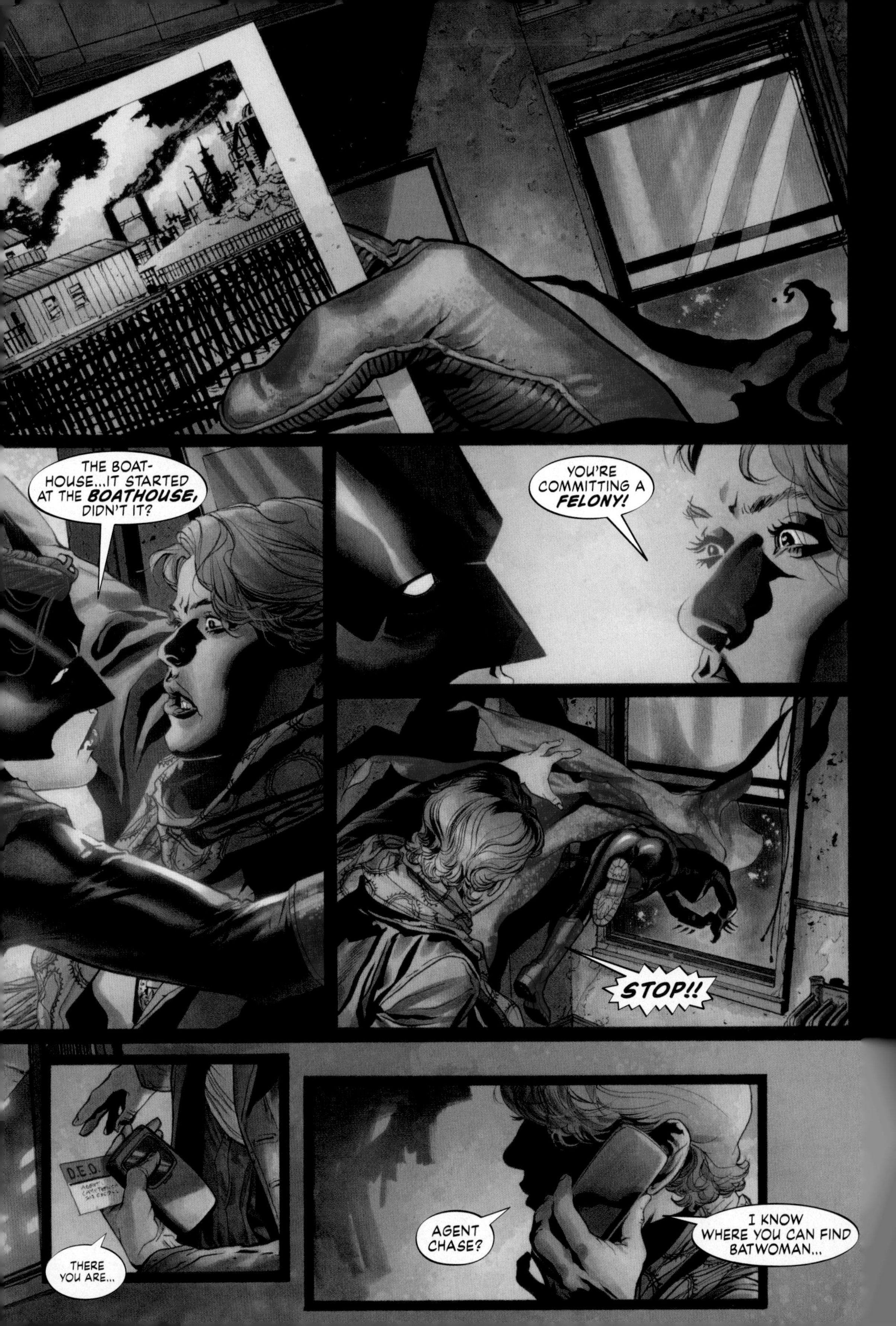
THE BOAT-HOUSE...IT STARTED AT THE BOATHOUSE, DIDN'T IT?
YOU'RE COMMITTING A FELONY!
STOP!!
D.E.O.
THERE YOU ARE...
AGENT CHASE?
I KNOW WHERE YOU CAN FIND BATWOMAN...

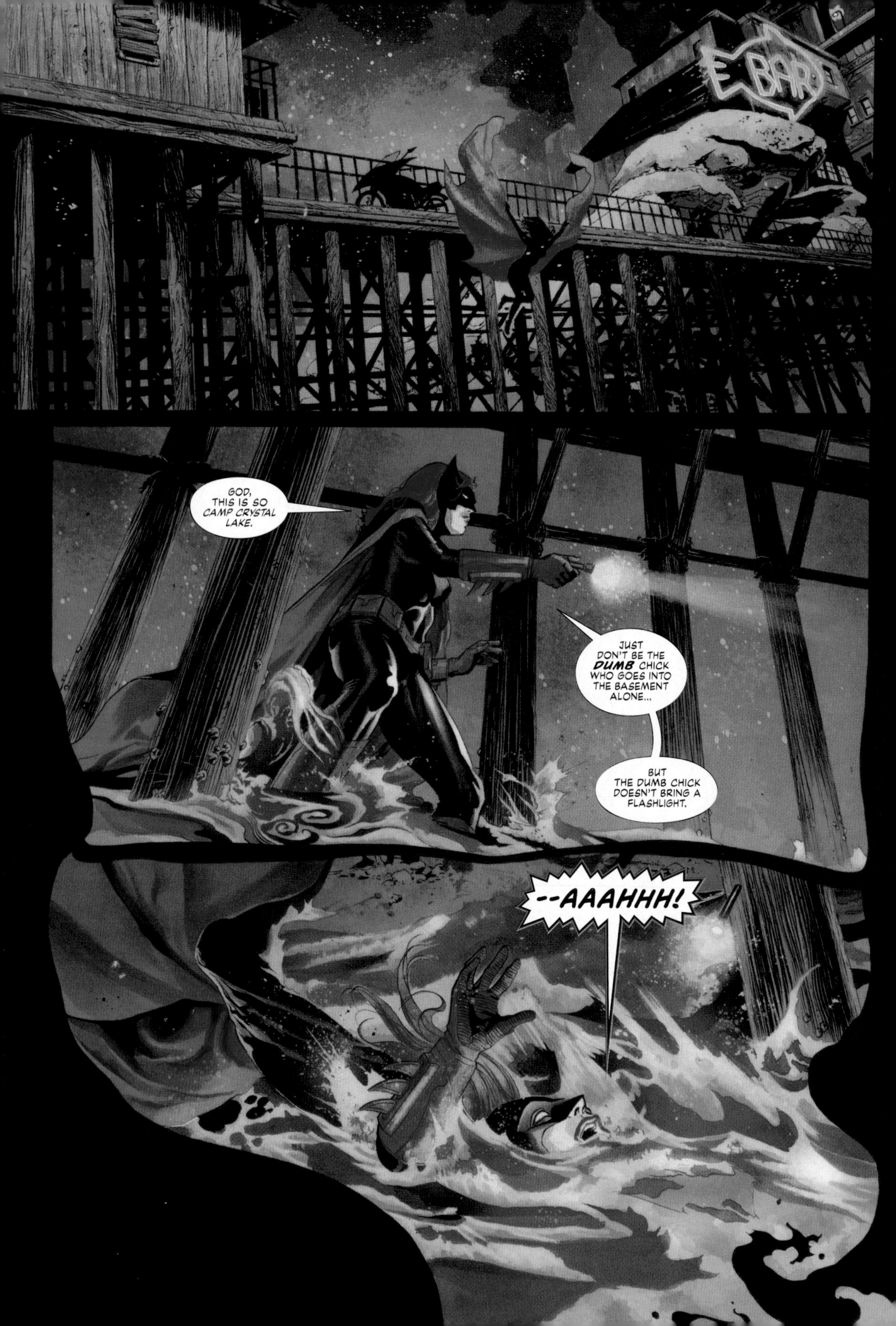

BAR
GOD, THIS IS SO CAMP CRYSTAL LAKE.
JUST DON'T BE THE DUMB CHICK WHO GOES INTO THE BASEMENT ALONE...
BUT THE DUMB CHICK DOESN'T BRING A FLASHLIGHT.
--AAAHHH!

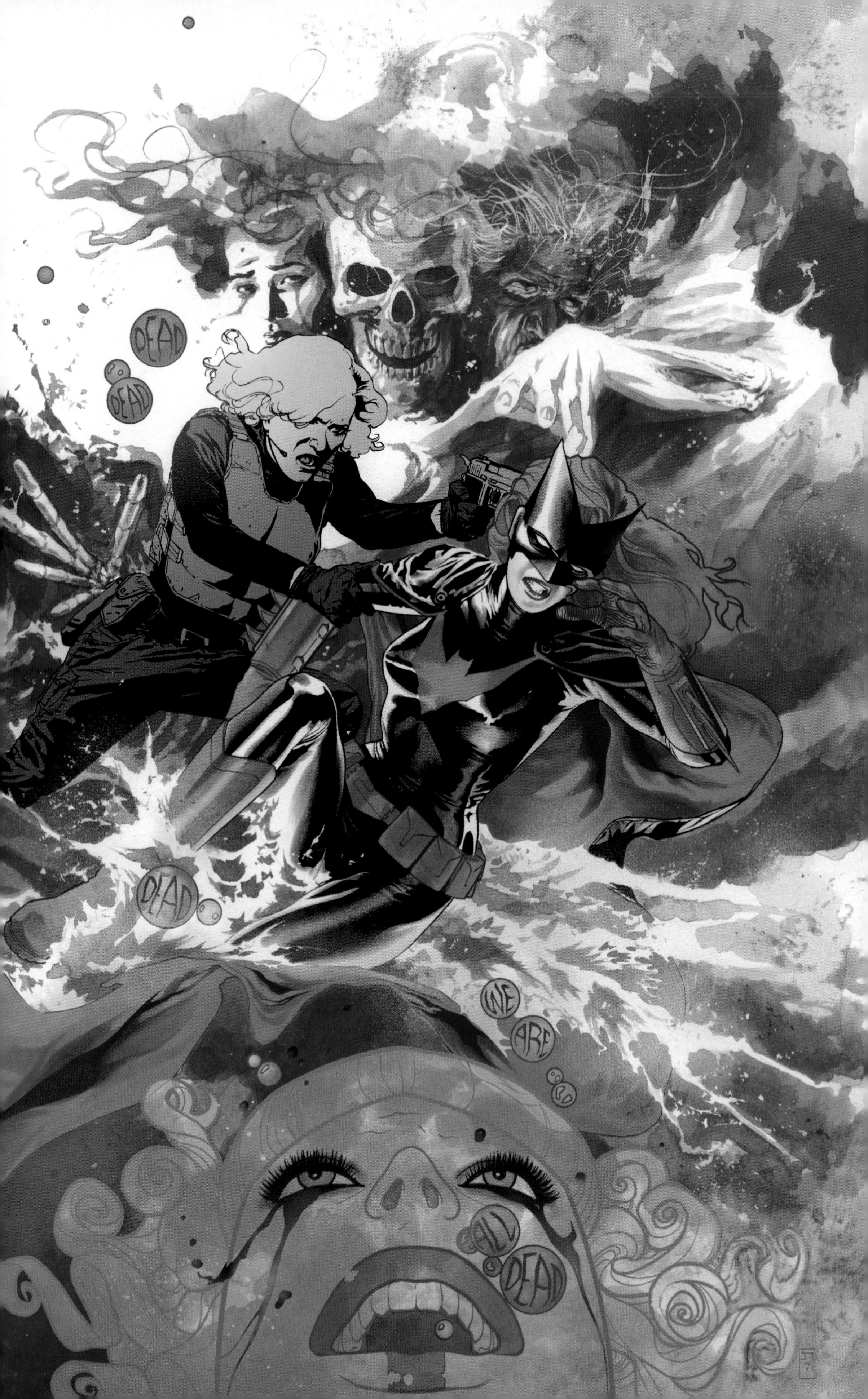
DEAD
DEAD
DEAD
WE
ARE
ALL
DEAD

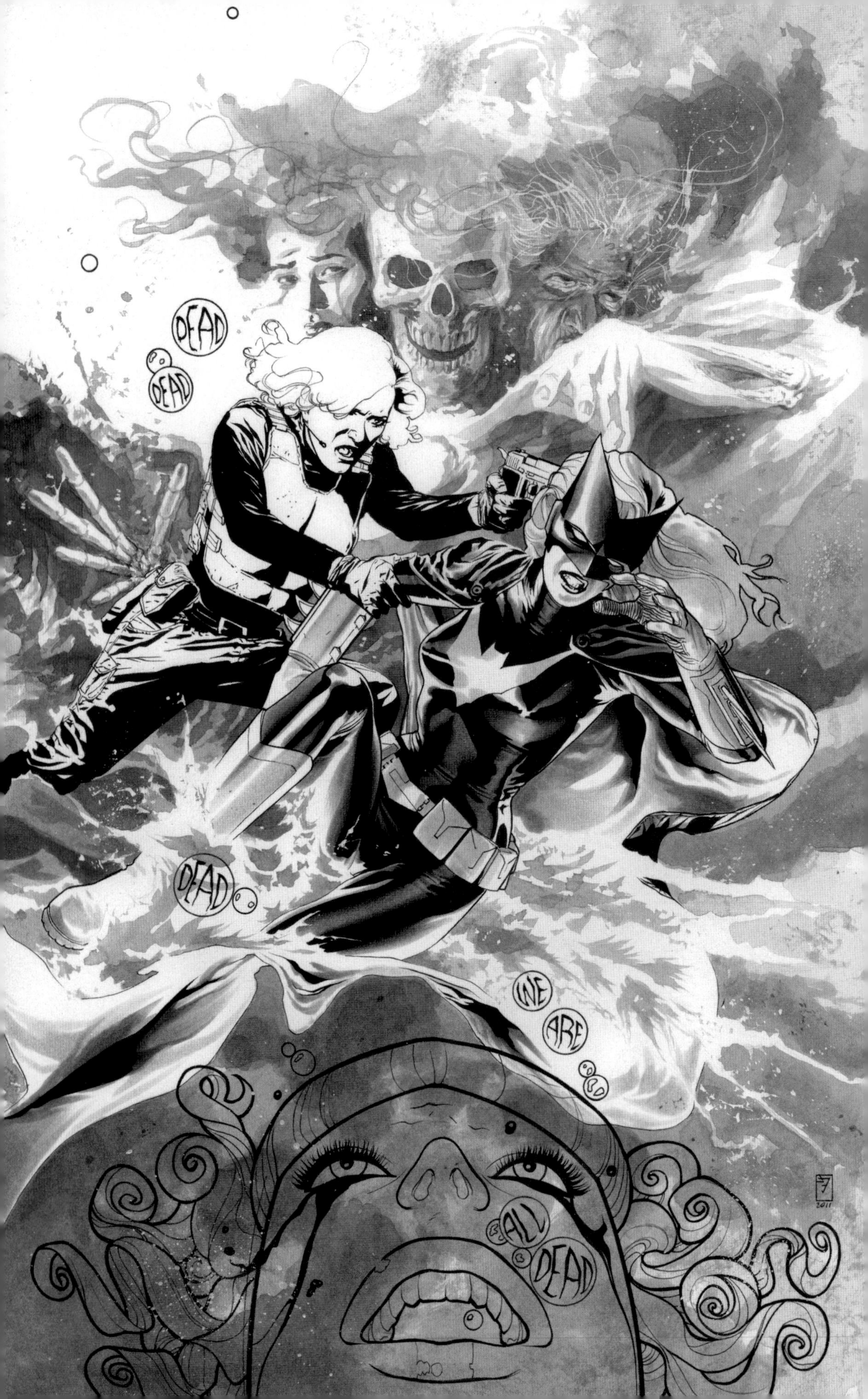

DEAD
DEAD
DEAD
WE
ARE
ALL
DEAD

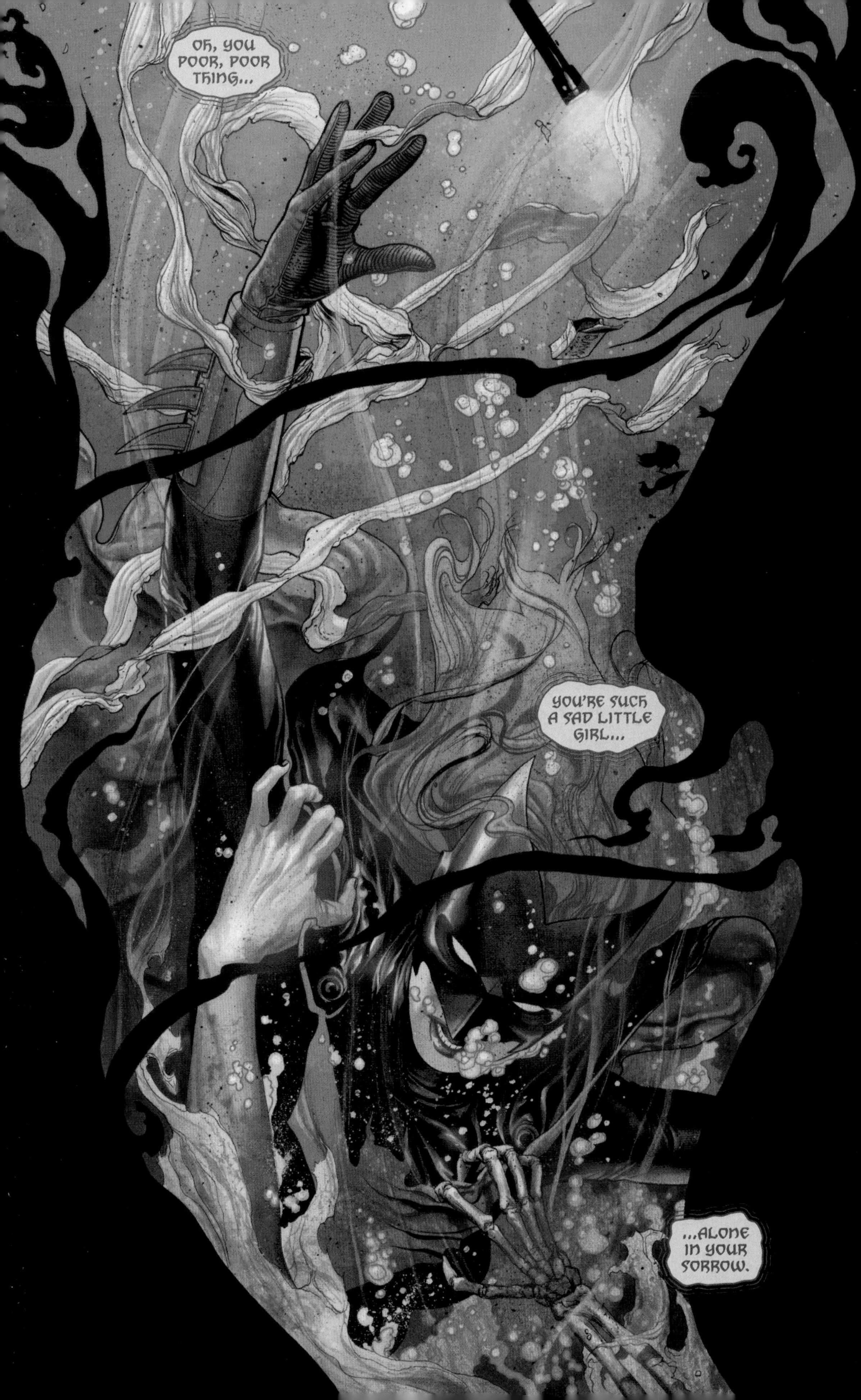
OH, YOU POOR, POOR THING...
YOU'RE SUCH A SAD LITTLE GIRL...
...ALONE IN YOUR SORROW.

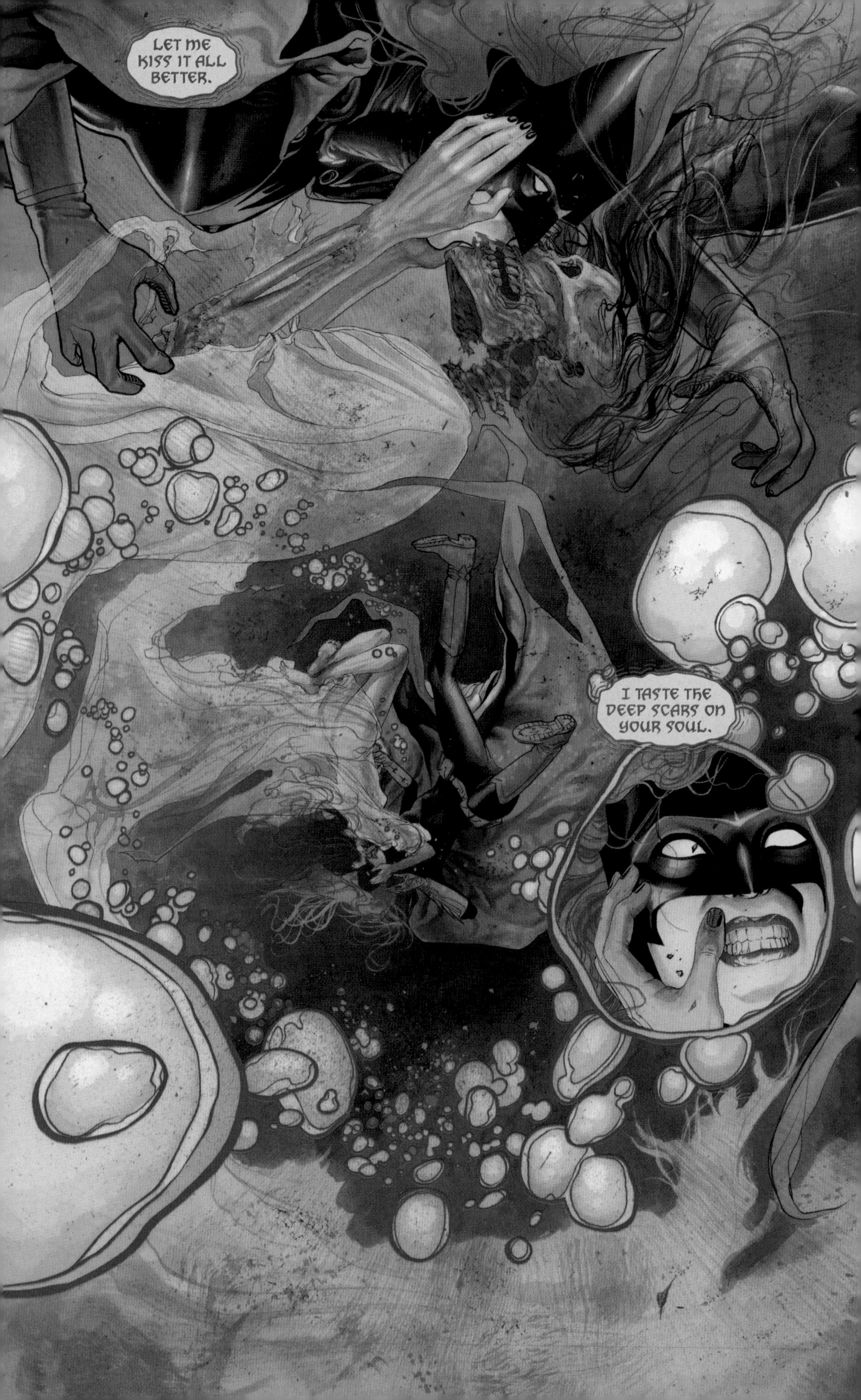
LET ME KISS IT ALL BETTER.
I TASTE THE DEEP SCARS ON YOUR SOUL.

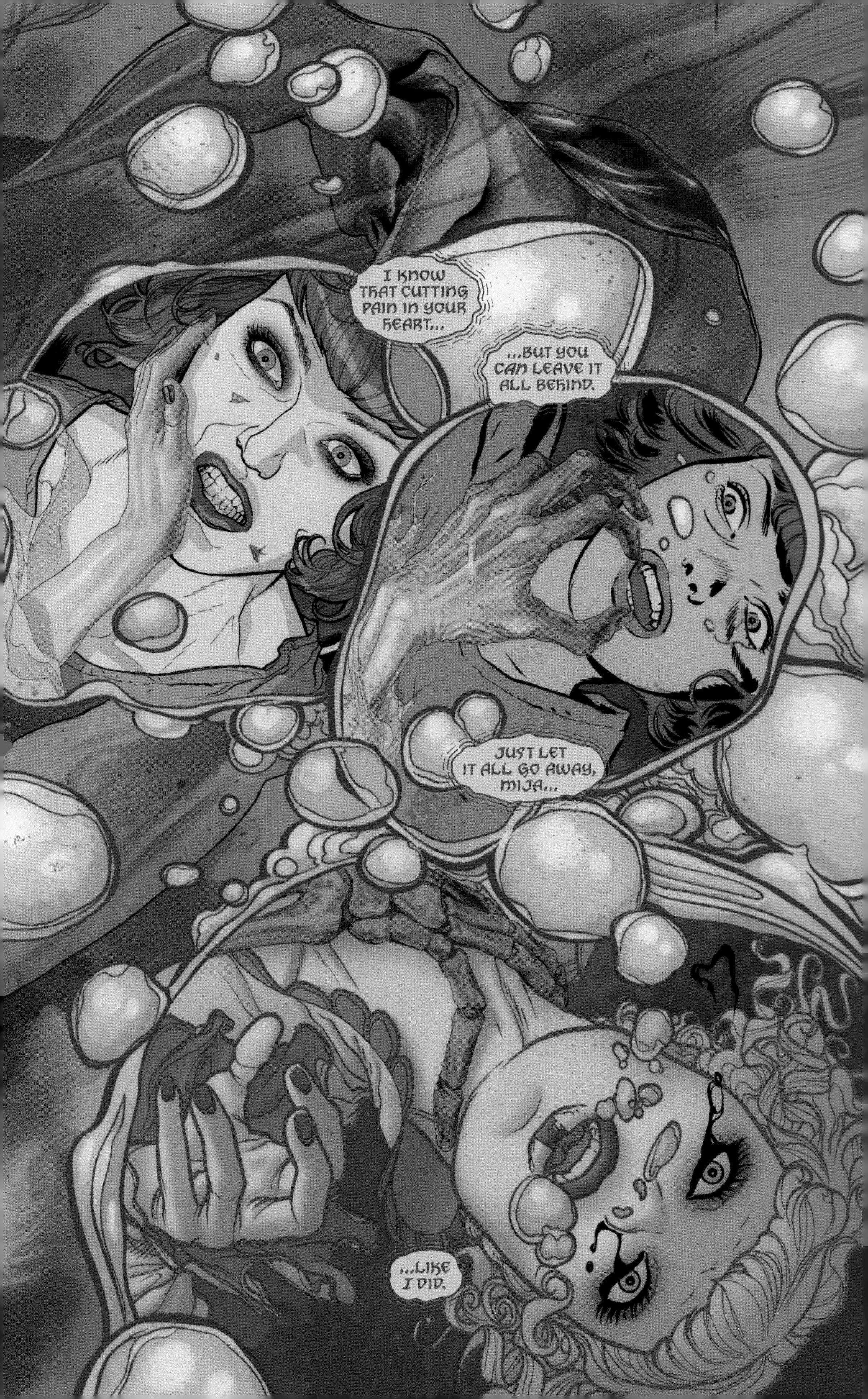
I KNOW THAT CUTTING PAIN IN YOUR HEART...
...BUT YOU CAN LEAVE IT ALL BEHIND.
JUST LET IT ALL GO AWAY, MIJA...
...LIKE I DID.

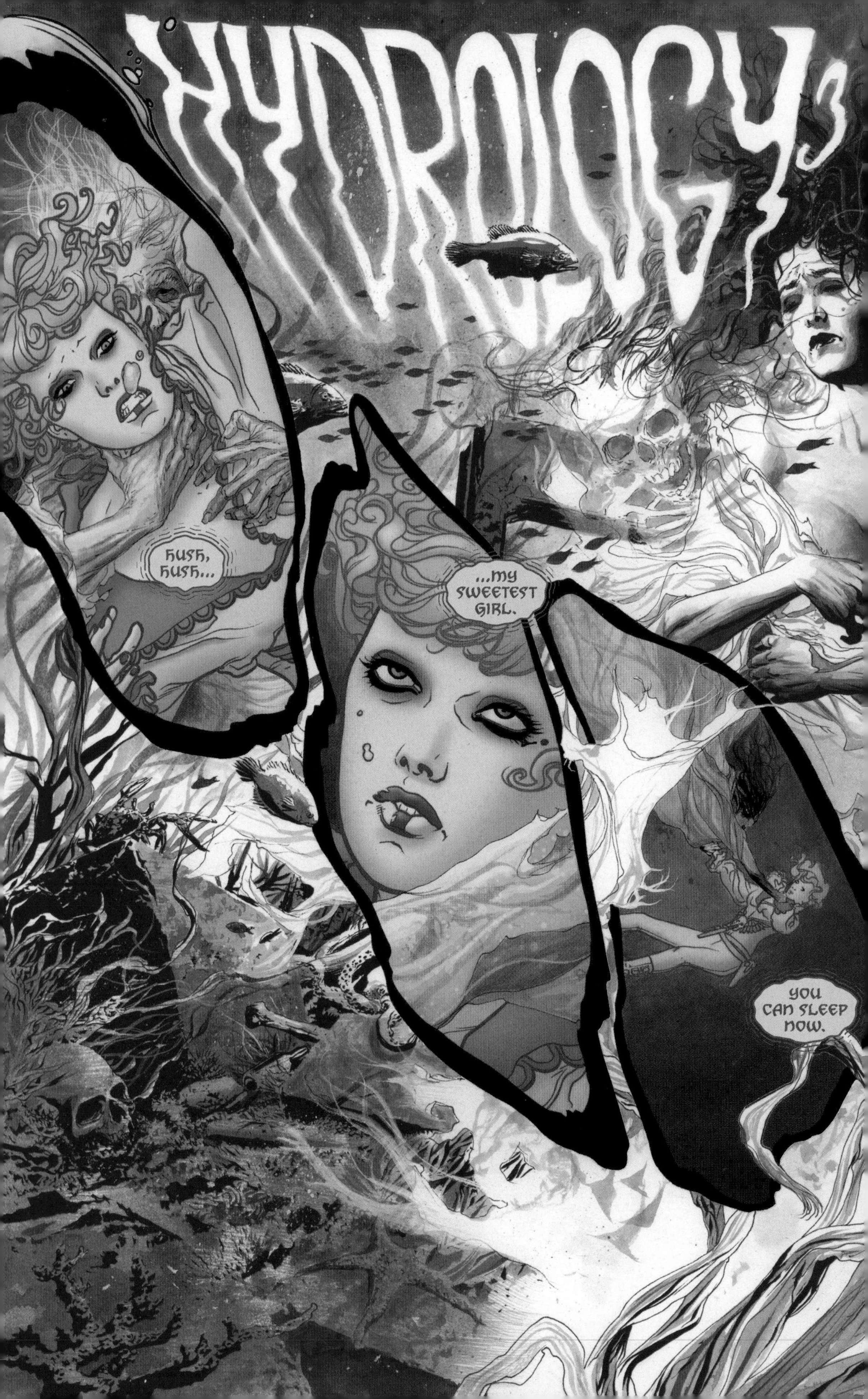
HYDROLOGY 3
HUSH, HUSH...
...MY SWEETEST GIRL.
YOU CAN SLEEP NOW.

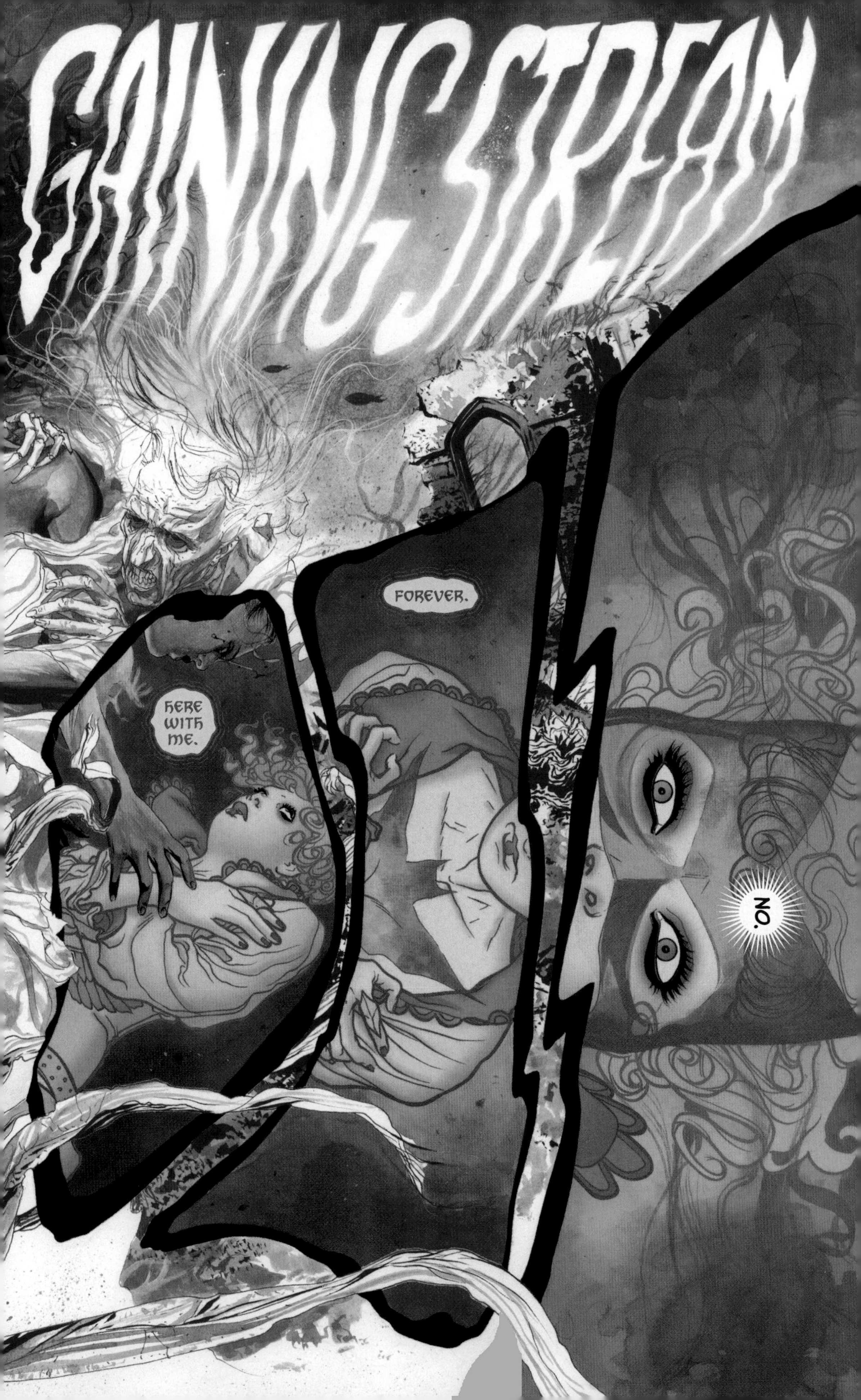
GAINING STREAM
HERE WITH ME.
FOREVER.
NO.

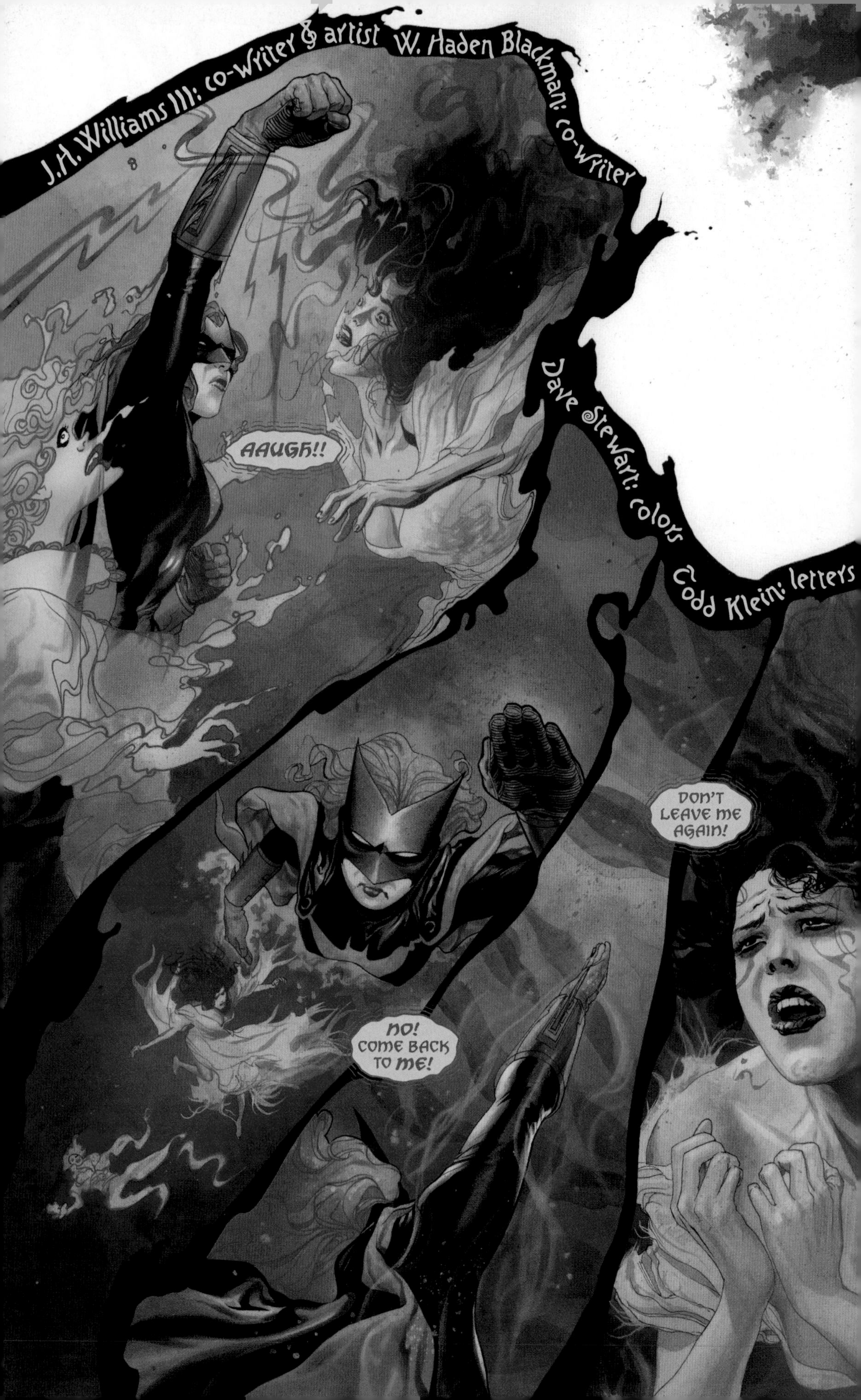
J.H. Williams III: co-writer & artist
W. Haden Blackman: co-writer
Dave Stewart: colors
Todd Klein: letters
AAUGH!!
DON'T LEAVE ME AGAIN!
NO! COME BACK TO ME!

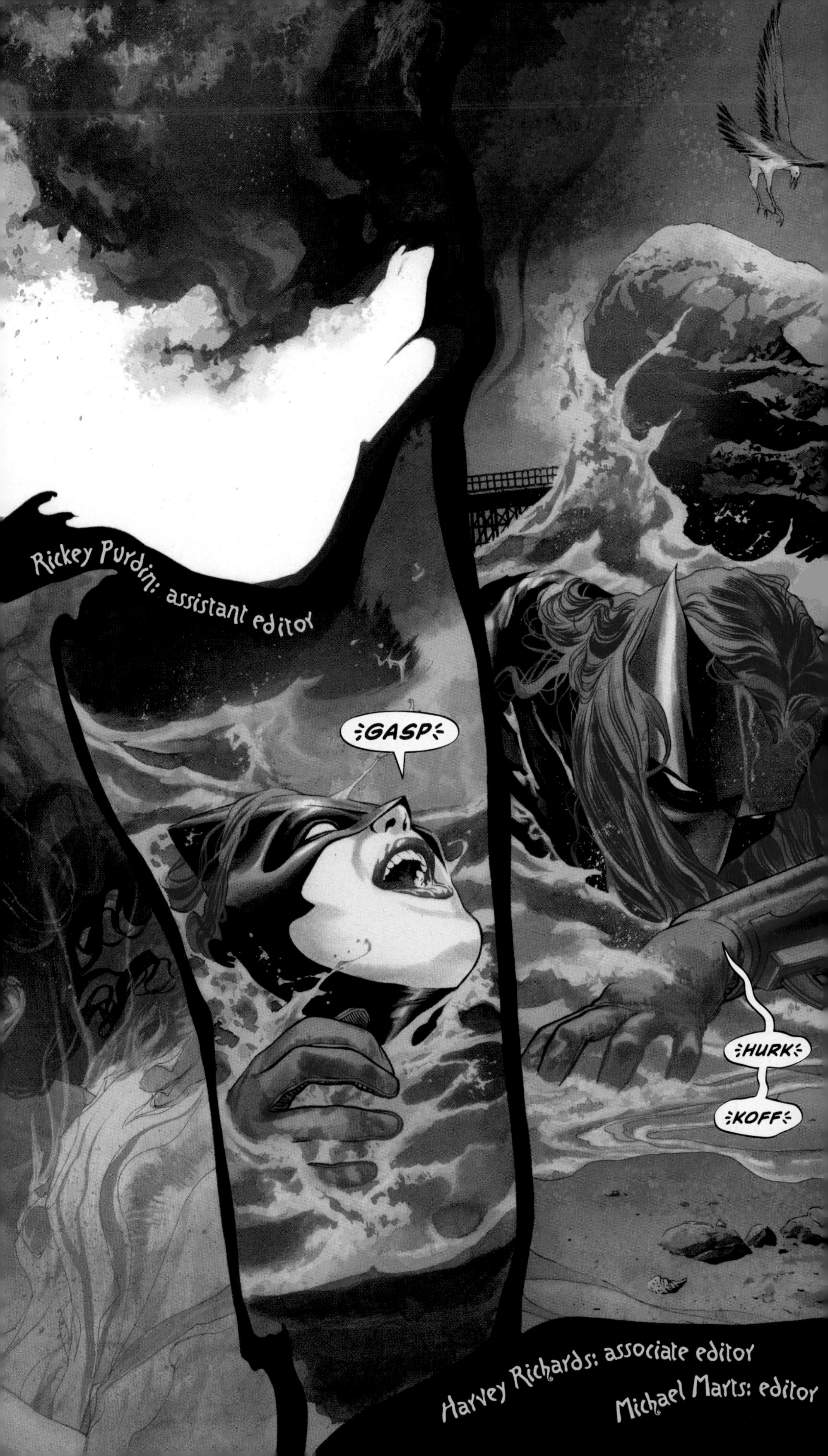
Rickey Purdin: assistant editor
GASP
HURK
KOFF
Harvey Richards: associate editor
Michael Marts: editor

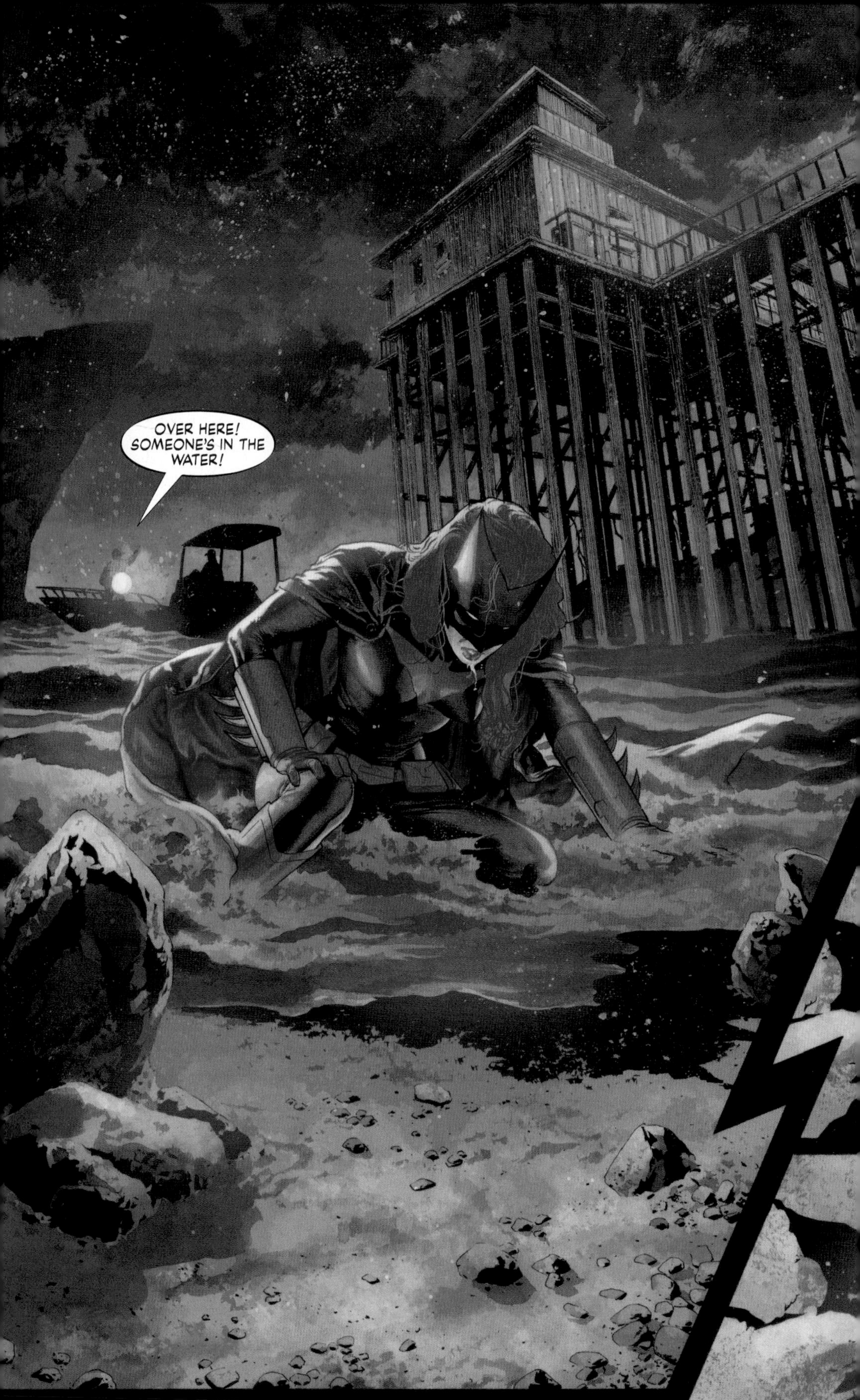
OVER HERE! SOMEONE'S IN THE WATER!

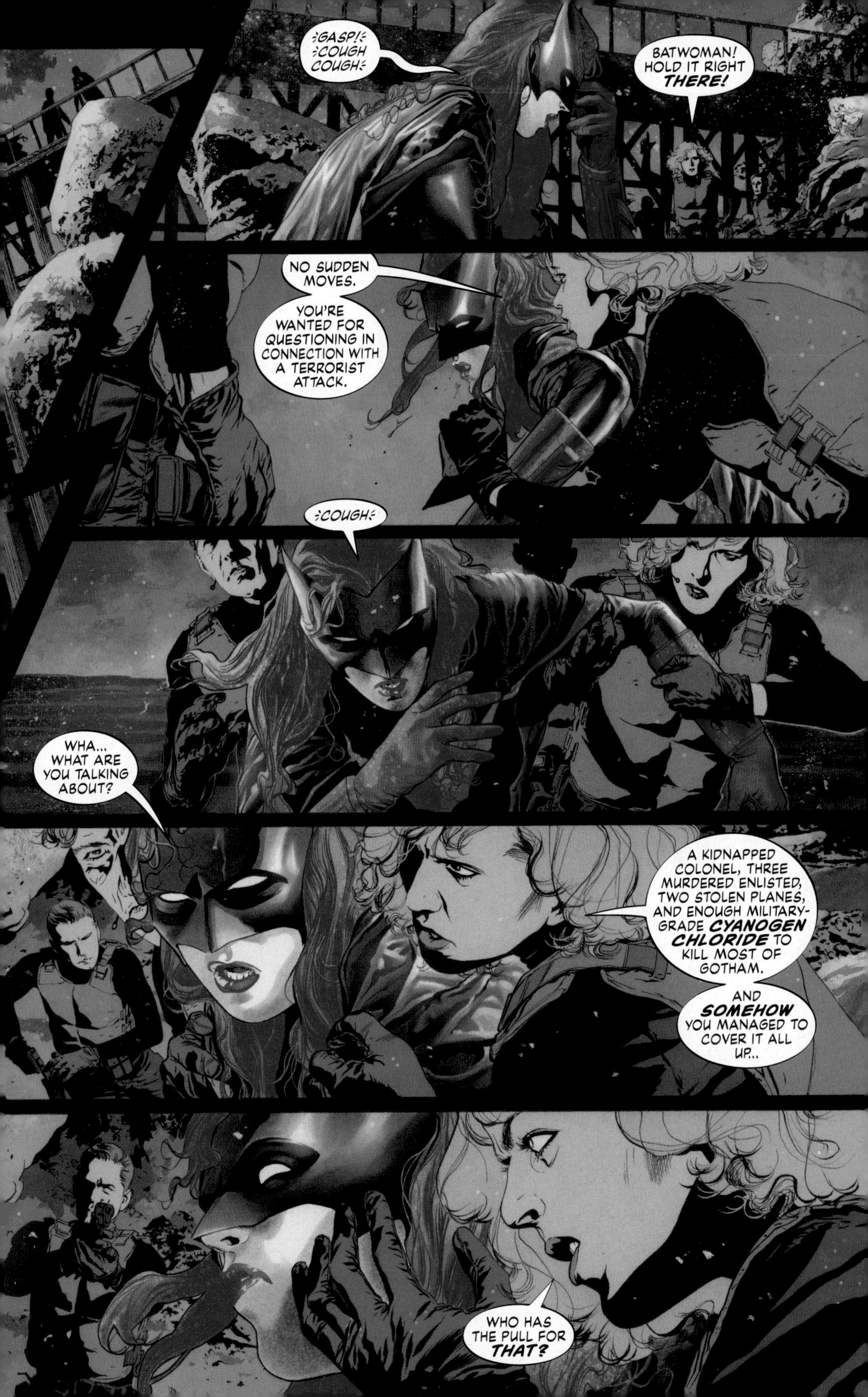
GASP! COUGH COUGH
BATWOMAN! HOLD IT RIGHT THERE!
NO SUDDEN MOVES.
YOU'RE WANTED FOR QUESTIONING IN CONNECTION WITH A TERRORIST ATTACK.
COUGH
WHA... WHAT ARE YOU TALKING ABOUT?
A KIDNAPPED COLONEL, THREE MURDERED ENLISTED, TWO STOLEN PLANES, AND ENOUGH MILITARY-GRADE CYANOGEN CHLORIDE TO KILL MOST OF GOTHAM.
AND SOMEHOW YOU MANAGED TO COVER IT ALL UP...
WHO HAS THE PULL FOR THAT?

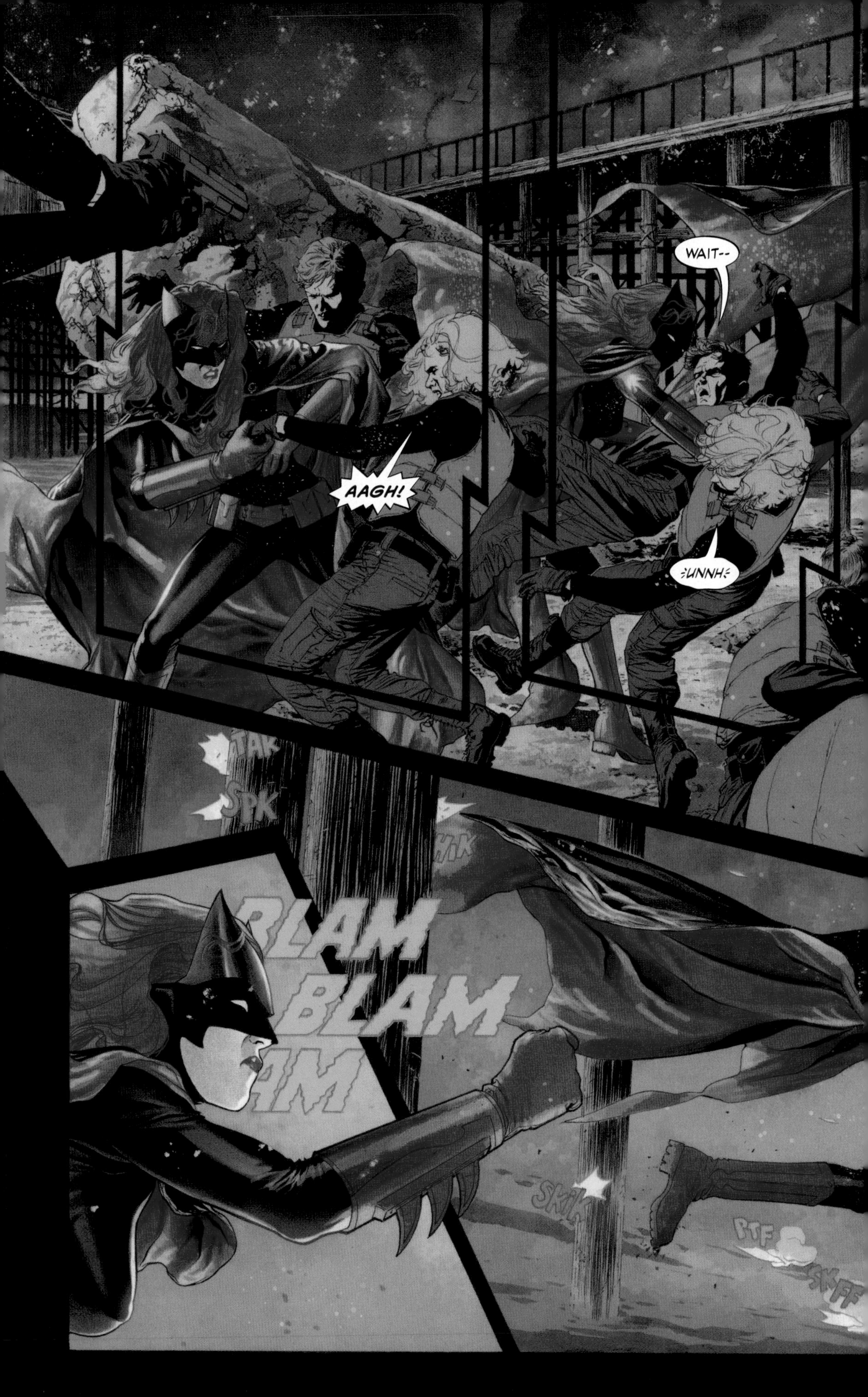
WAIT--
AAGH!
UNNH
TAK
SPK
SHIK
BLAM
BLAM
AM
SKIK
PTF
SKFF

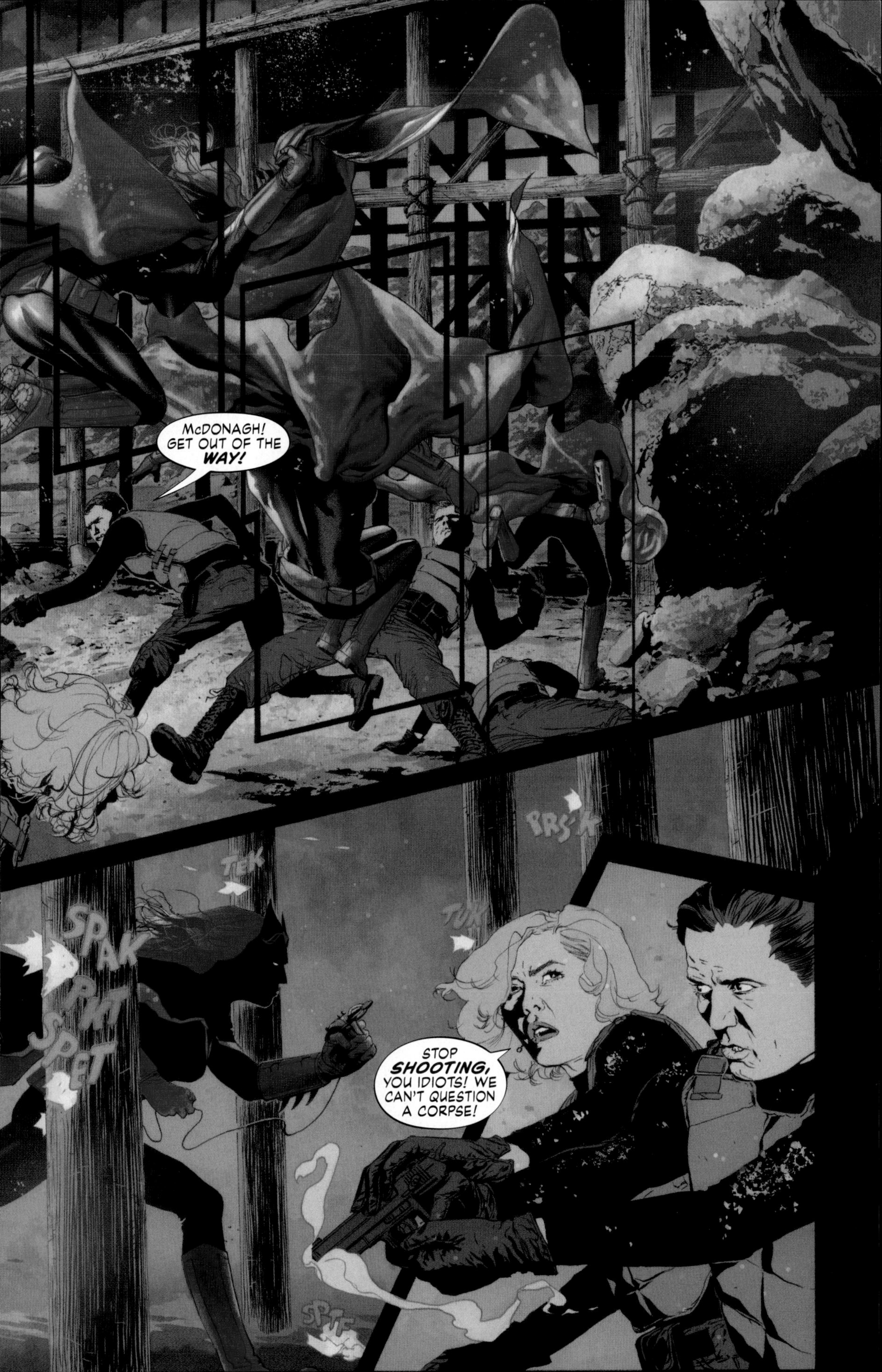
McDONAGH! GET OUT OF THE **WAY!**
BRS-K
TEK
TUK
SPAK
PWT
SPET
STOP **SHOOTING,** YOU IDIOTS! WE CAN'T QUESTION A CORPSE!
SPTT

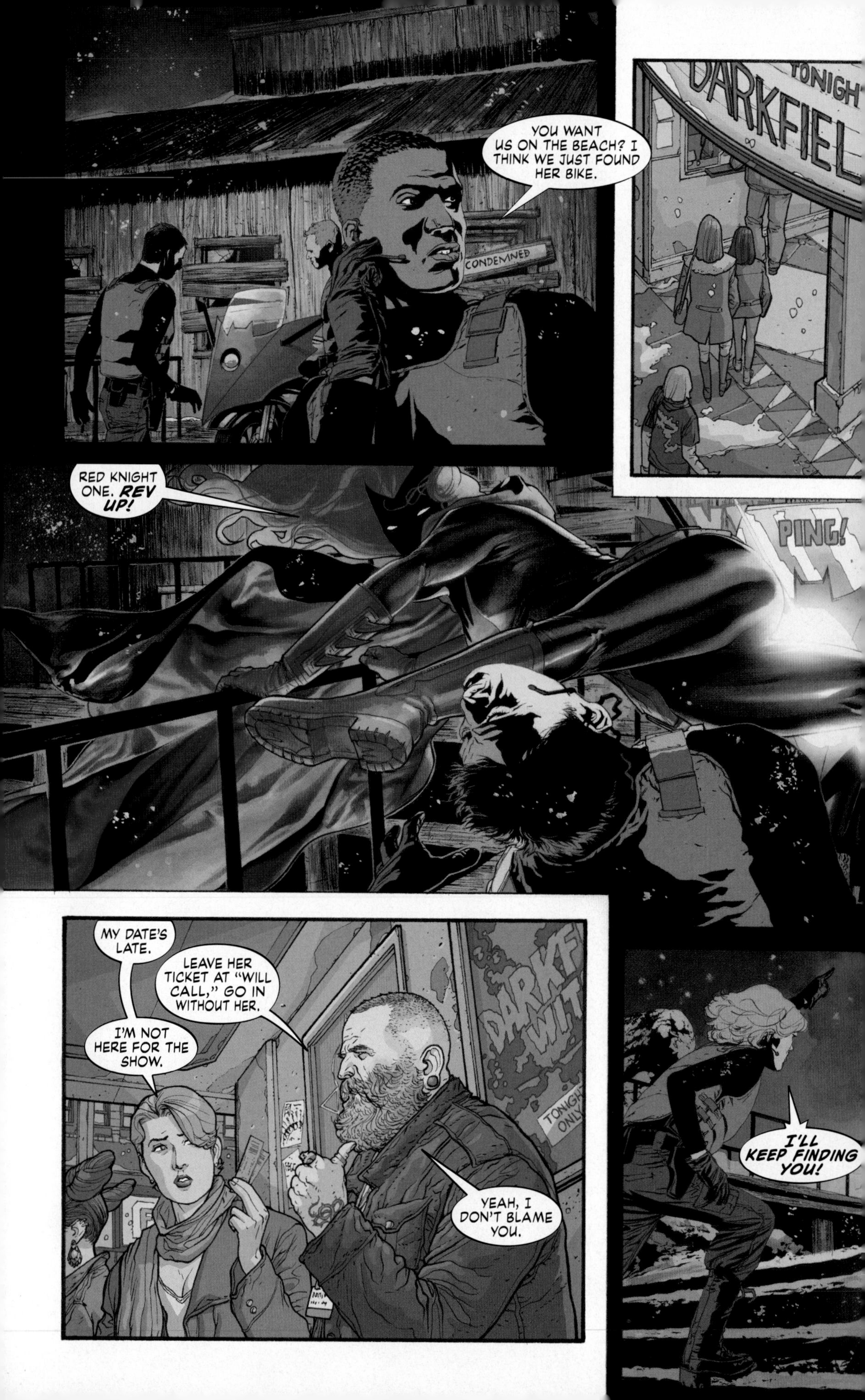
YOU WANT US ON THE BEACH? I THINK WE JUST FOUND HER BIKE.
CONDEMNED
TONIGH
DARKFIEL
RED KNIGHT ONE. REV UP!
PING!
MY DATE'S LATE.
LEAVE HER TICKET AT "WILL CALL," GO IN WITHOUT HER.
I'M NOT HERE FOR THE SHOW.
YEAH, I DON'T BLAME YOU.
TONIGHT ONLY
I'LL KEEP FINDING YOU!

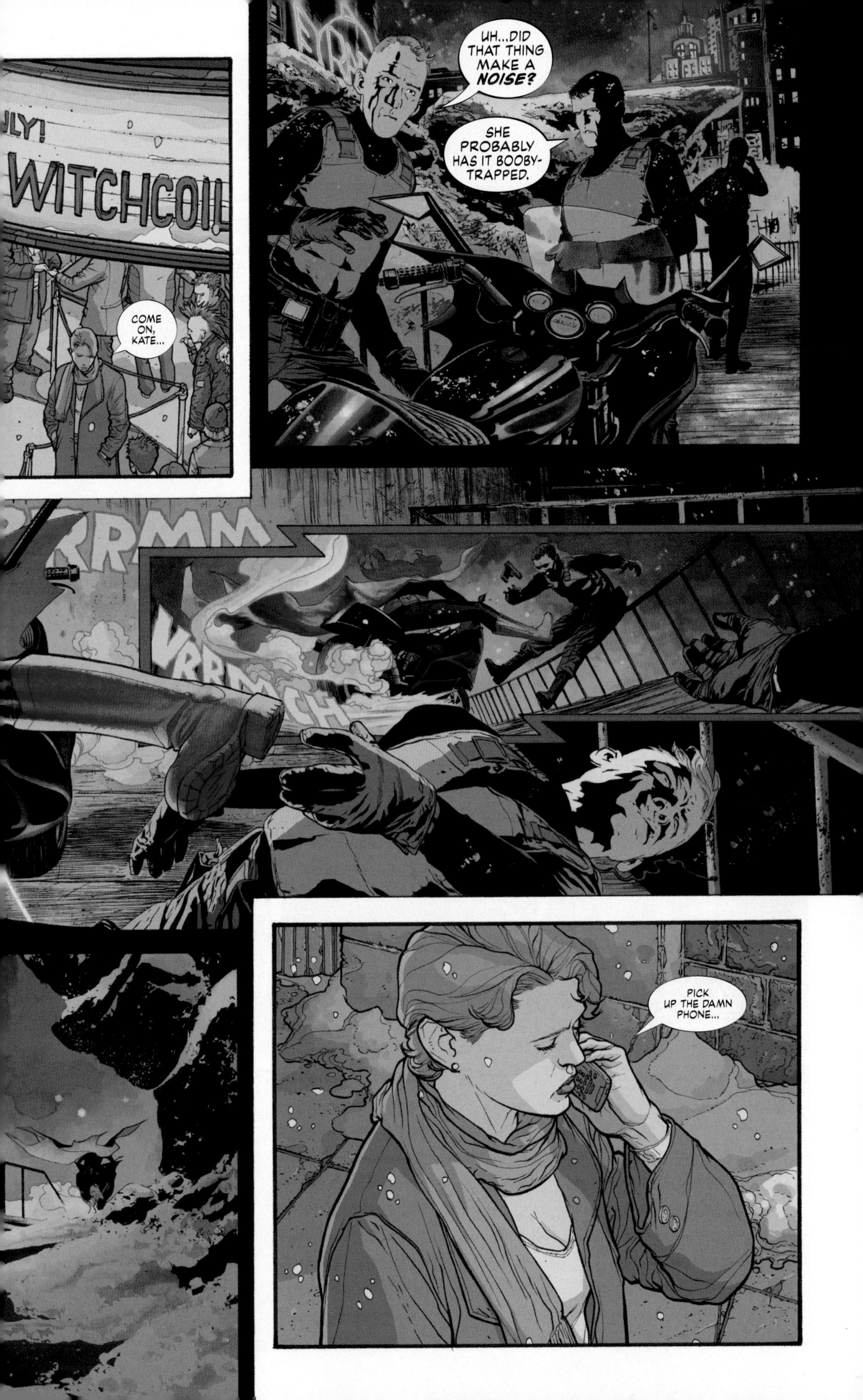

NLY!
WITCHCOIL
COME ON, KATE...
UH...DID THAT THING MAKE A NOISE?
SHE PROBABLY HAS IT BOOBY-TRAPPED.
RRMM
VRRMCH
PICK UP THE DAMN PHONE...

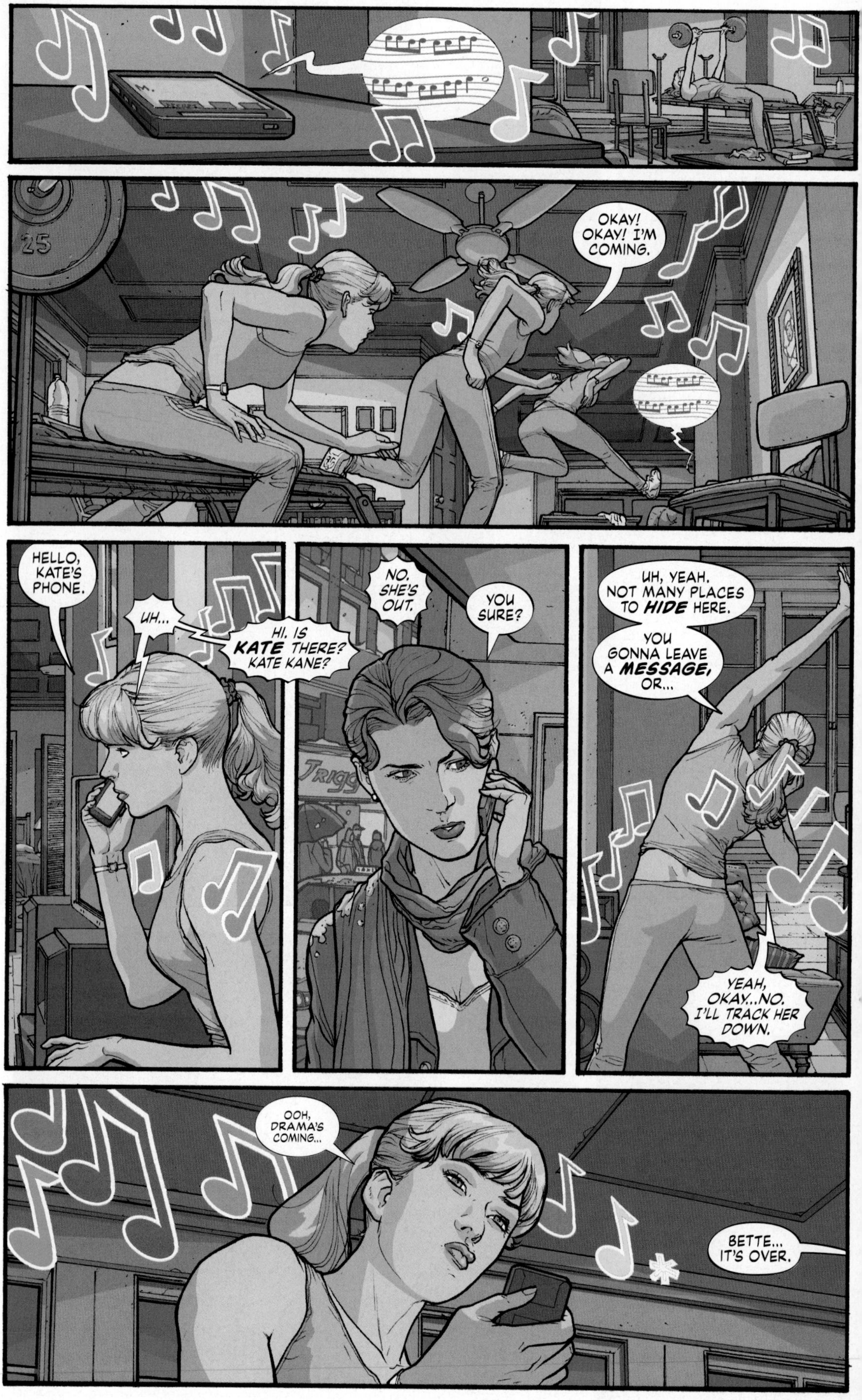
OKAY! OKAY! I'M COMING.
HELLO, KATE'S PHONE.
UH...
HI. IS KATE THERE? KATE KANE?
NO. SHE'S OUT.
YOU SURE?
UH, YEAH. NOT MANY PLACES TO HIDE HERE.
YOU GONNA LEAVE A MESSAGE, OR...
YEAH, OKAY...NO. I'LL TRACK HER DOWN.
OOH, DRAMA'S COMING...
BETTE... IT'S OVER.

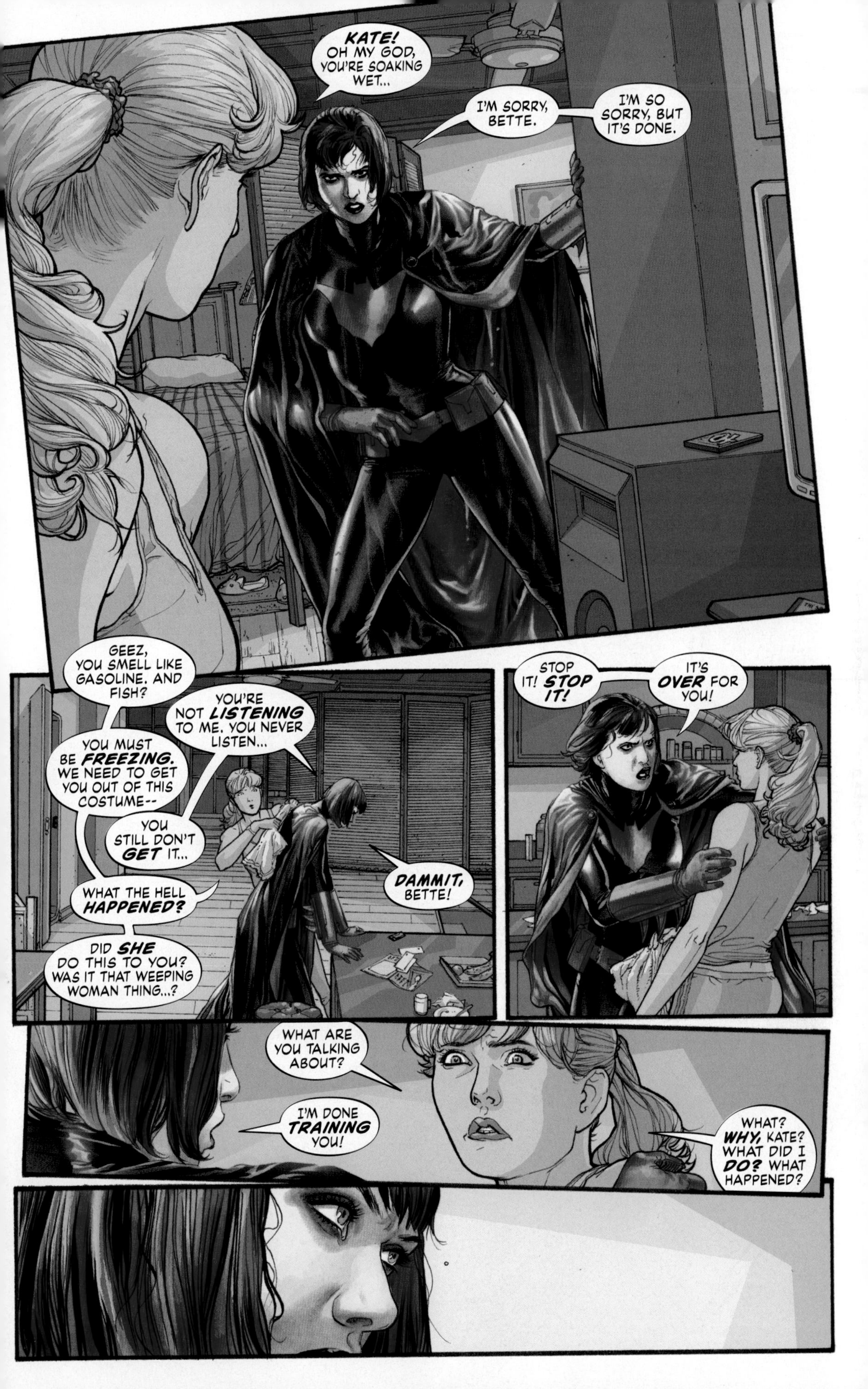
KATE! OH MY GOD, YOU'RE SOAKING WET...
I'M SORRY, BETTE.
I'M SO SORRY, BUT IT'S DONE.
GEEZ, YOU SMELL LIKE GASOLINE. AND FISH?
YOU'RE NOT LISTENING TO ME. YOU NEVER LISTEN...
YOU MUST BE FREEZING. WE NEED TO GET YOU OUT OF THIS COSTUME--
YOU STILL DON'T GET IT...
WHAT THE HELL HAPPENED?
DAMMIT, BETTE!
DID SHE DO THIS TO YOU? WAS IT THAT WEEPING WOMAN THING...?
STOP IT! STOP IT!
IT'S OVER FOR YOU!
WHAT ARE YOU TALKING ABOUT?
I'M DONE TRAINING YOU!
WHAT? WHY, KATE? WHAT DID I DO? WHAT HAPPENED?

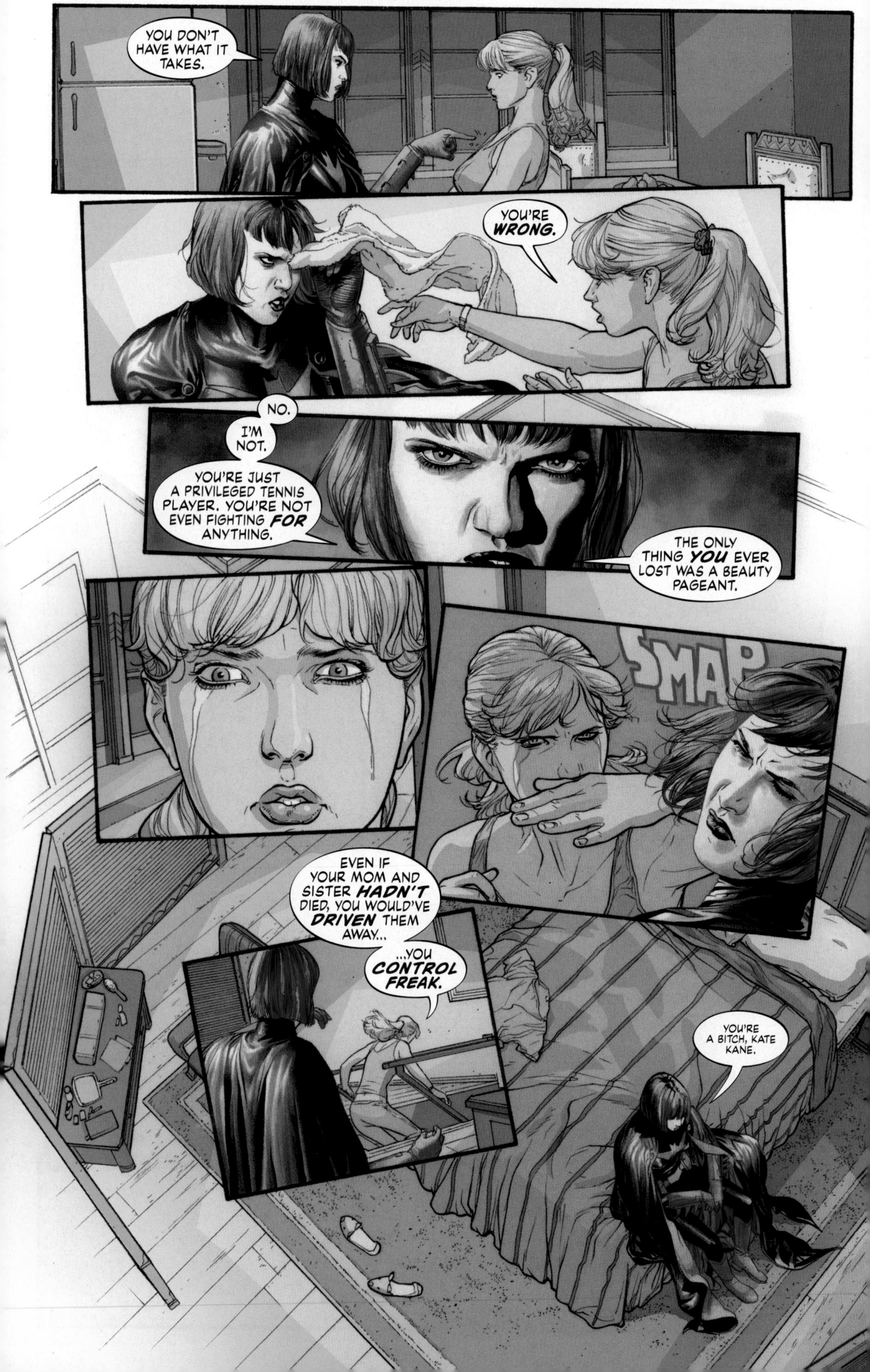
YOU DON'T HAVE WHAT IT TAKES.
YOU'RE WRONG.
NO.
I'M NOT.
YOU'RE JUST A PRIVILEGED TENNIS PLAYER. YOU'RE NOT EVEN FIGHTING FOR ANYTHING.
THE ONLY THING YOU EVER LOST WAS A BEAUTY PAGEANT.
SMAP
EVEN IF YOUR MOM AND SISTER HADN'T DIED, YOU WOULD'VE DRIVEN THEM AWAY...
...YOU CONTROL FREAK.
YOU'RE A BITCH, KATE KANE.

THIS POOL IS FOR ENLISTED ONLY, MA'AM.

MY *VICODIN* IS STARTING TO WEAR OFF, COLONEL, SO I DON'T HAVE TIME FOR YOU TO BE *CUTE* WITH ME.

JUST ANSWER MY DAMN *QUESTIONS*.

SIR.

WITH ALL DUE RESPECT, MA'AM, UNLESS YOU HAVE A *GENERAL* WITH YOU, I CANNOT BE COMPELLED TO TELL YOU ANYTHING.

YOU WERE KIDNAPPED A FEW MONTHS AGO BY A TERRORIST, *CORRECT?* AND *RESCUED* BY THE BATWOMAN?

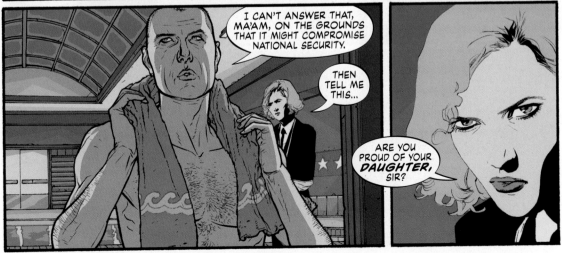

I CAN'T ANSWER THAT, MA'AM, ON THE GROUNDS THAT IT MIGHT COMPROMISE NATIONAL SECURITY.

THEN TELL ME THIS...

ARE YOU PROUD OF YOUR *DAUGHTER,* SIR?

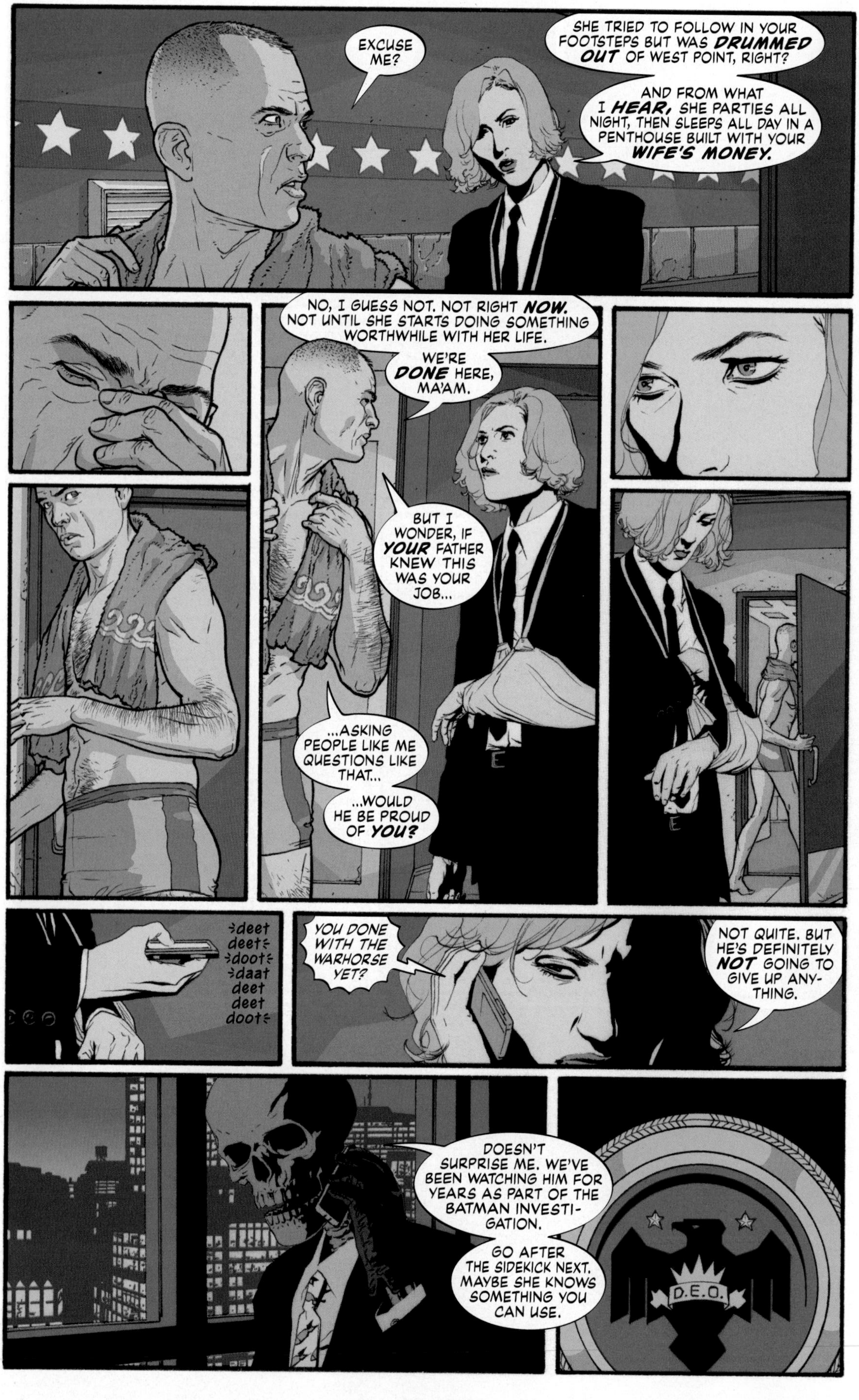
EXCUSE ME?
SHE TRIED TO FOLLOW IN YOUR FOOTSTEPS BUT WAS DRUMMED OUT OF WEST POINT, RIGHT?
AND FROM WHAT I HEAR, SHE PARTIES ALL NIGHT, THEN SLEEPS ALL DAY IN A PENTHOUSE BUILT WITH YOUR WIFE'S MONEY.
NO, I GUESS NOT. NOT RIGHT NOW. NOT UNTIL SHE STARTS DOING SOMETHING WORTHWHILE WITH HER LIFE.
WE'RE DONE HERE, MA'AM.
BUT I WONDER, IF YOUR FATHER KNEW THIS WAS YOUR JOB...
...ASKING PEOPLE LIKE ME QUESTIONS LIKE THAT...
...WOULD HE BE PROUD OF YOU?
deet deet doot daat deet deet doot
YOU DONE WITH THE WARHORSE YET?
NOT QUITE. BUT HE'S DEFINITELY NOT GOING TO GIVE UP ANY-THING.
DOESN'T SURPRISE ME. WE'VE BEEN WATCHING HIM FOR YEARS AS PART OF THE BATMAN INVESTI-GATION.
GO AFTER THE SIDEKICK NEXT. MAYBE SHE KNOWS SOMETHING YOU CAN USE.
D.E.O.

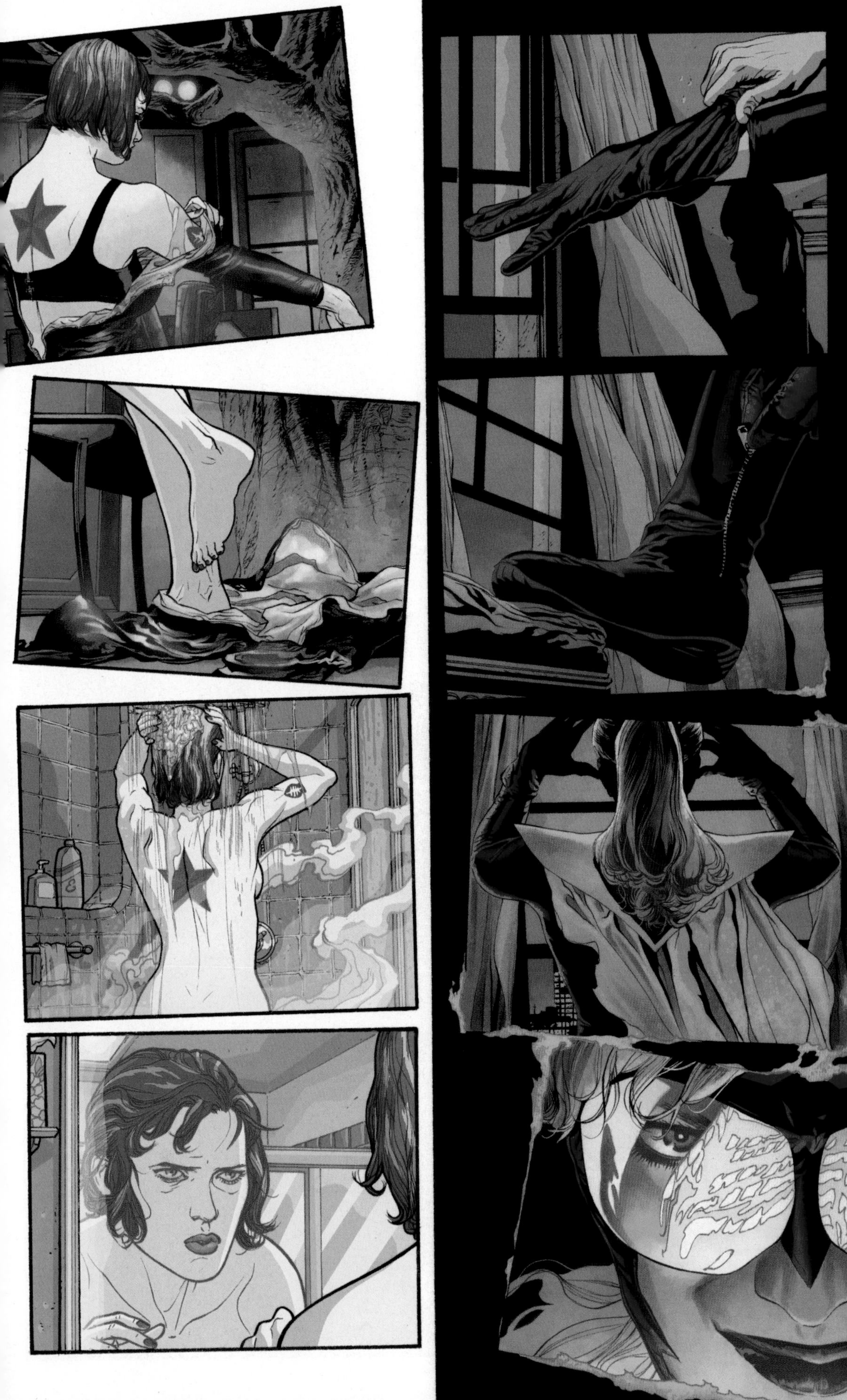

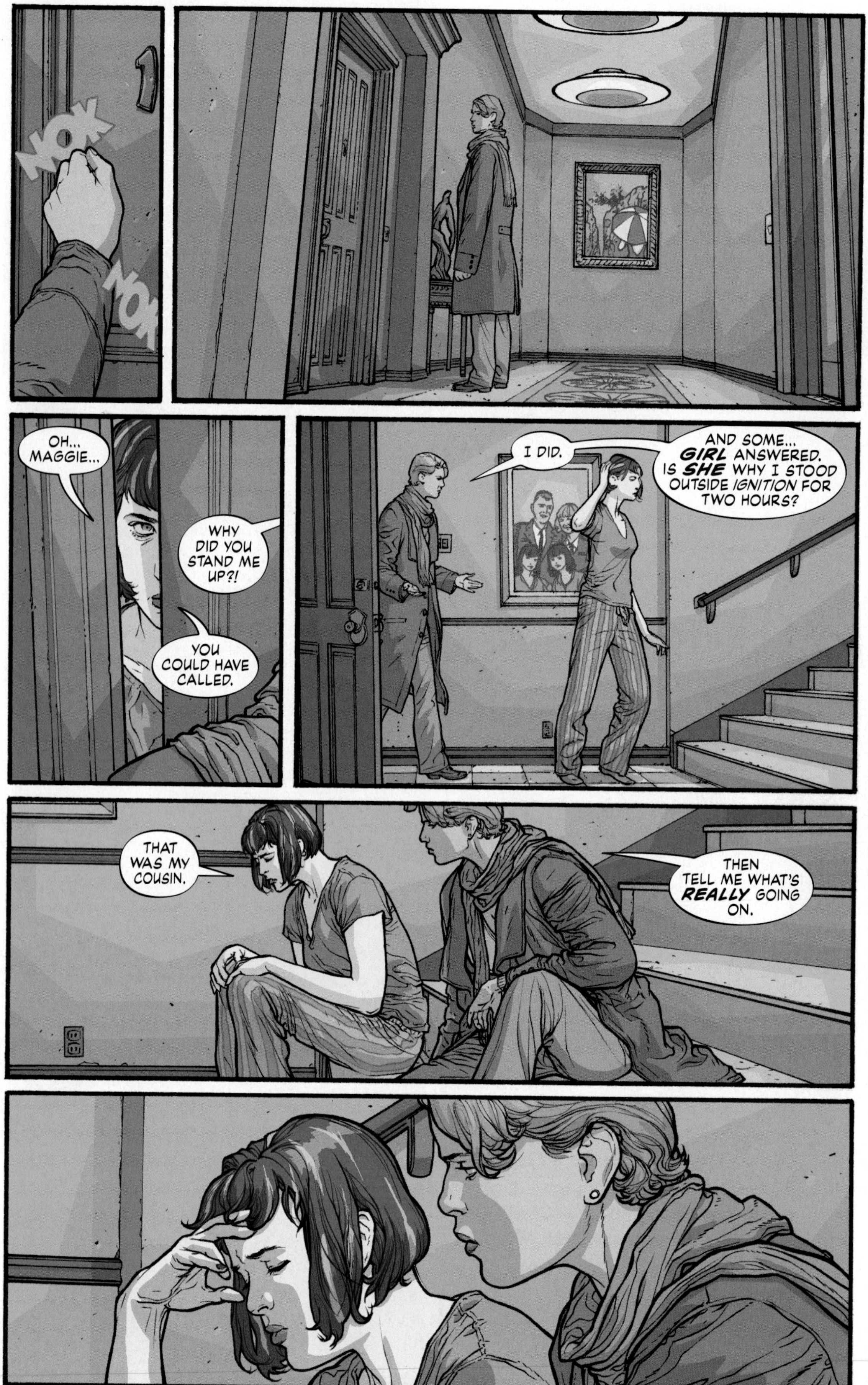
NOK
NOK
OH... MAGGIE...
WHY DID YOU STAND ME UP?!
YOU COULD HAVE CALLED.
I DID.
AND SOME... GIRL ANSWERED. IS SHE WHY I STOOD OUTSIDE IGNITION FOR TWO HOURS?
THAT WAS MY COUSIN.
THEN TELL ME WHAT'S REALLY GOING ON.

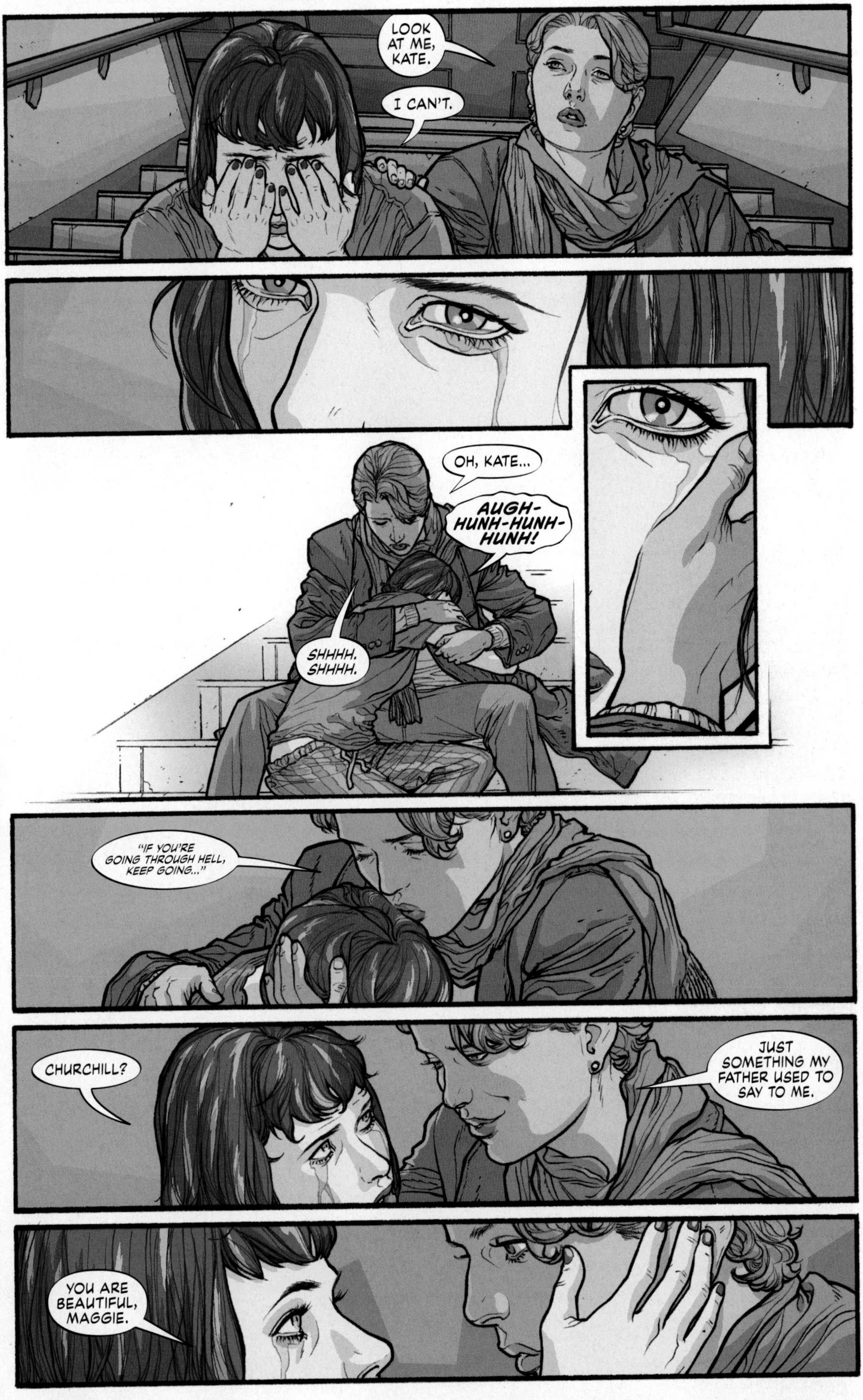

LOOK AT ME, KATE.
I CAN'T.
OH, KATE...
AUGH-HUNH-HUNH-HUNH!
SHHHH. SHHHH.
"IF YOU'RE GOING THROUGH HELL, KEEP GOING..."
CHURCHILL?
JUST SOMETHING MY FATHER USED TO SAY TO ME.
YOU ARE BEAUTIFUL, MAGGIE.

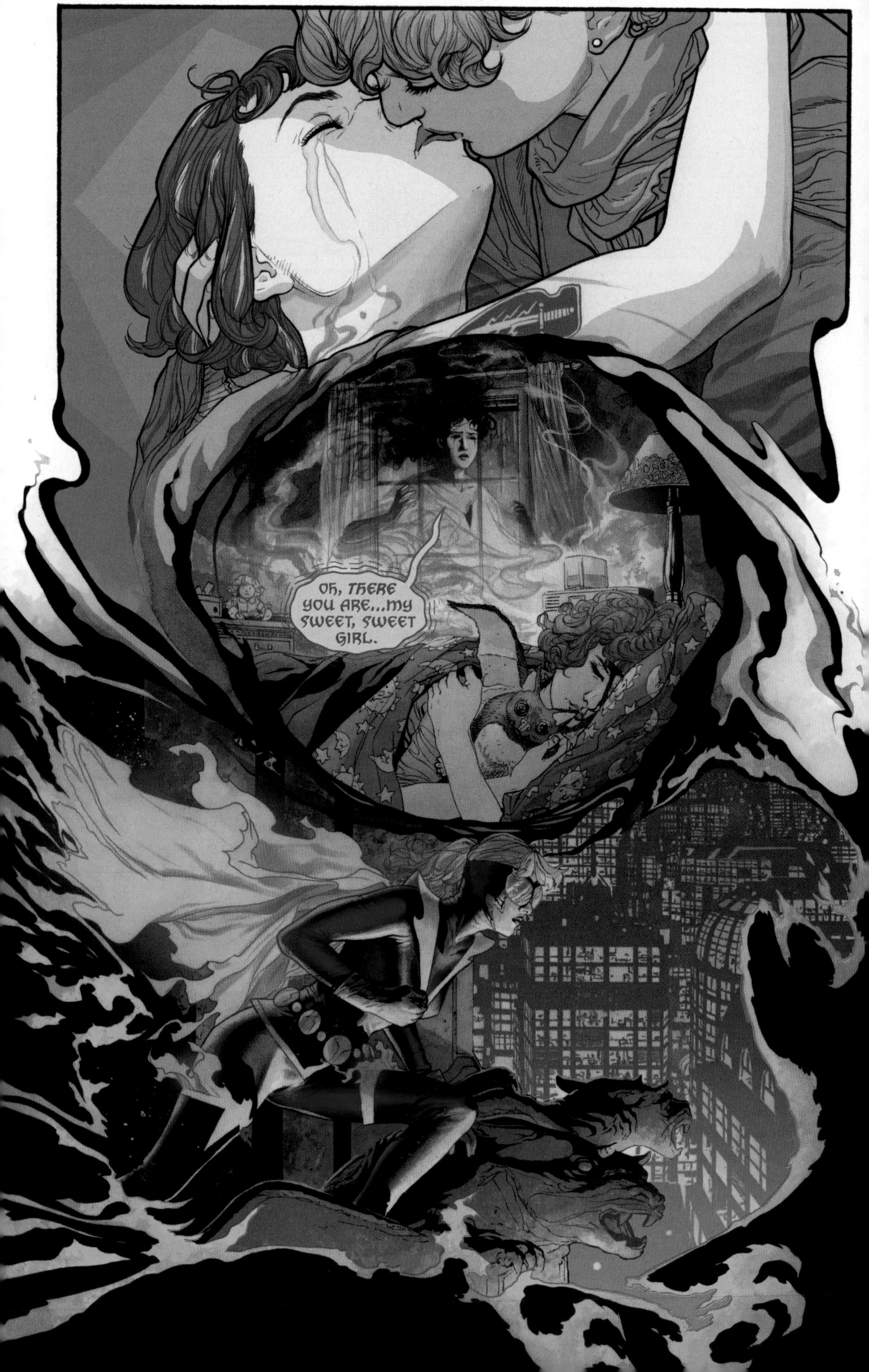
OH, THERE YOU ARE...MY SWEET, SWEET GIRL.

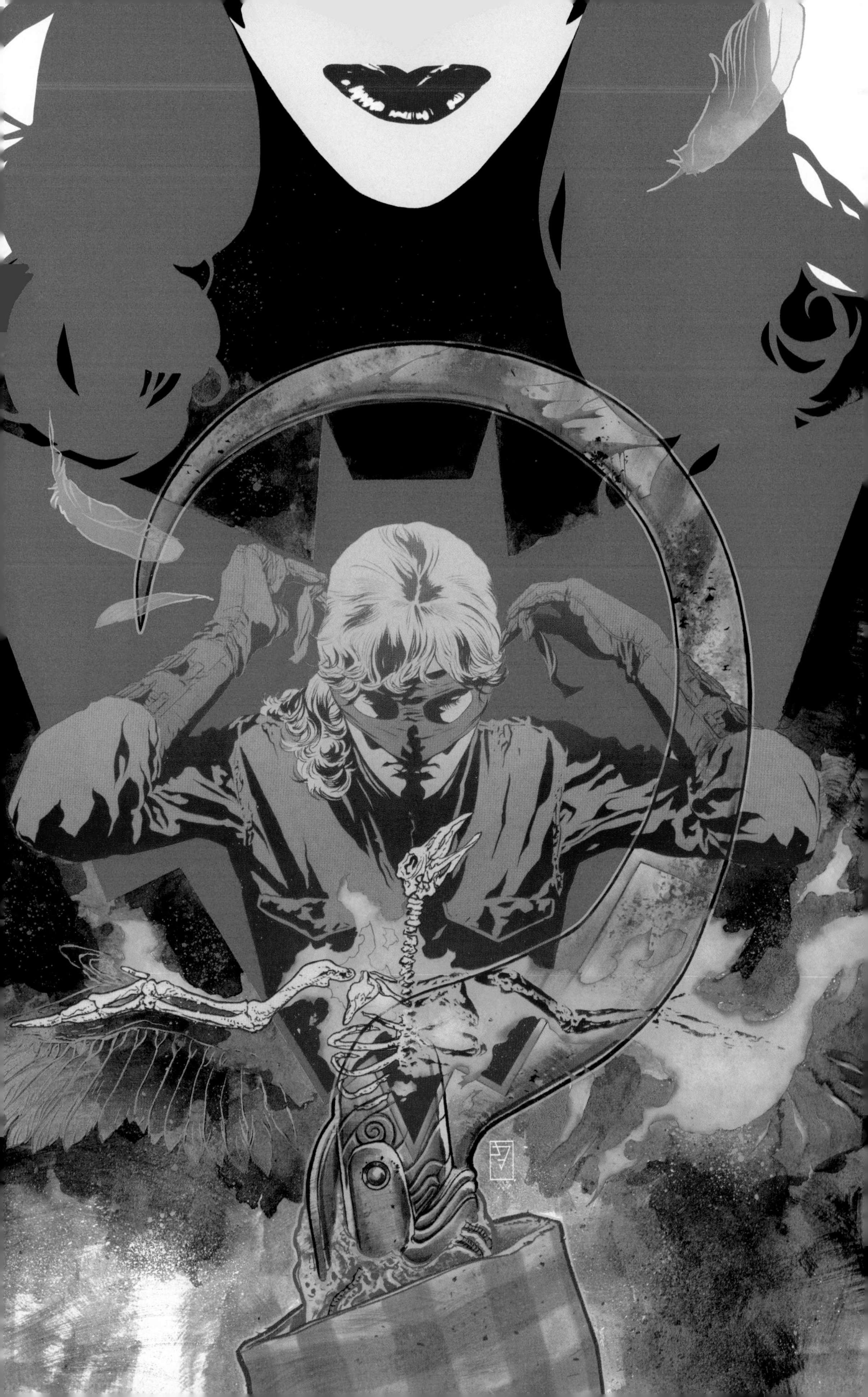

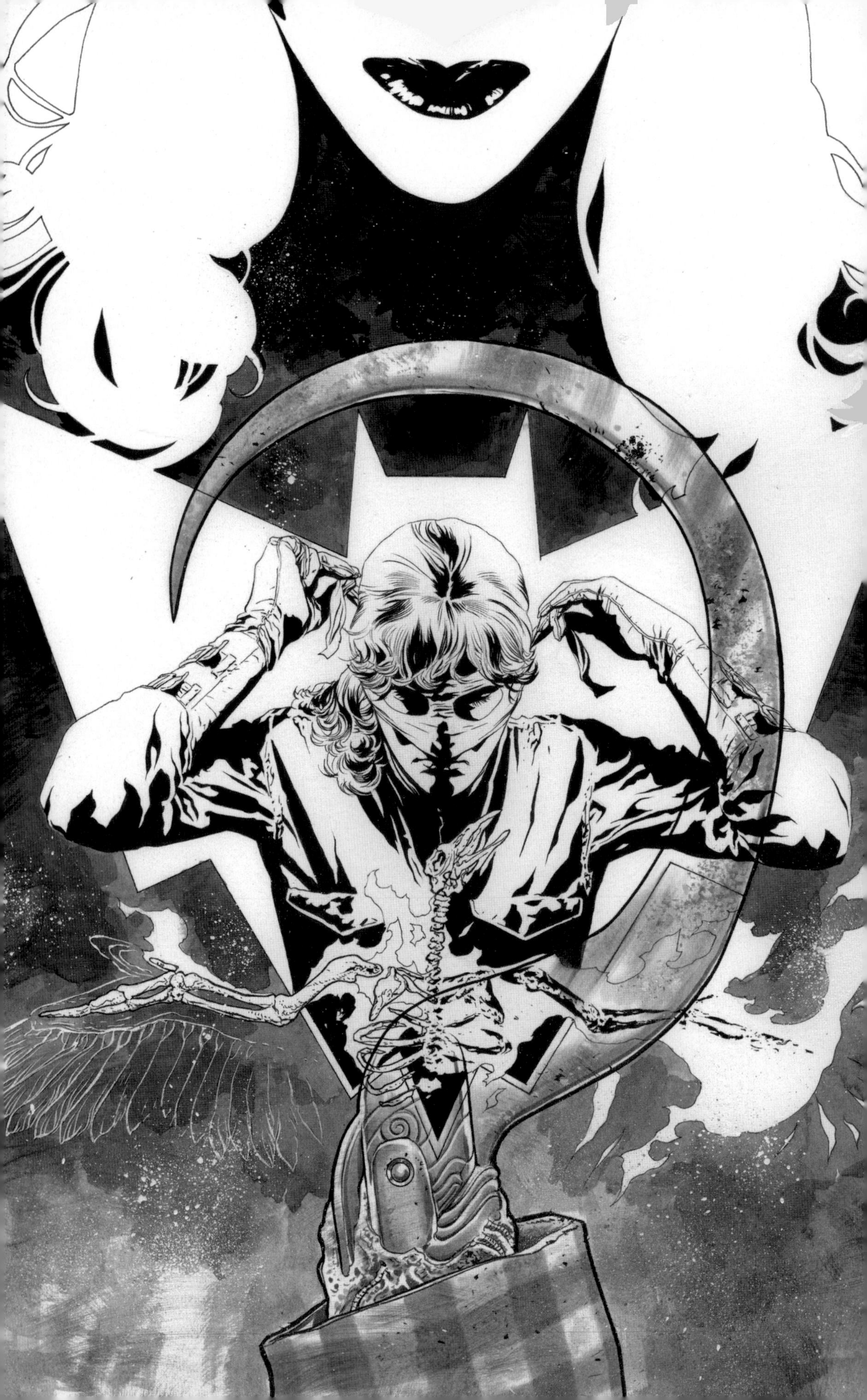

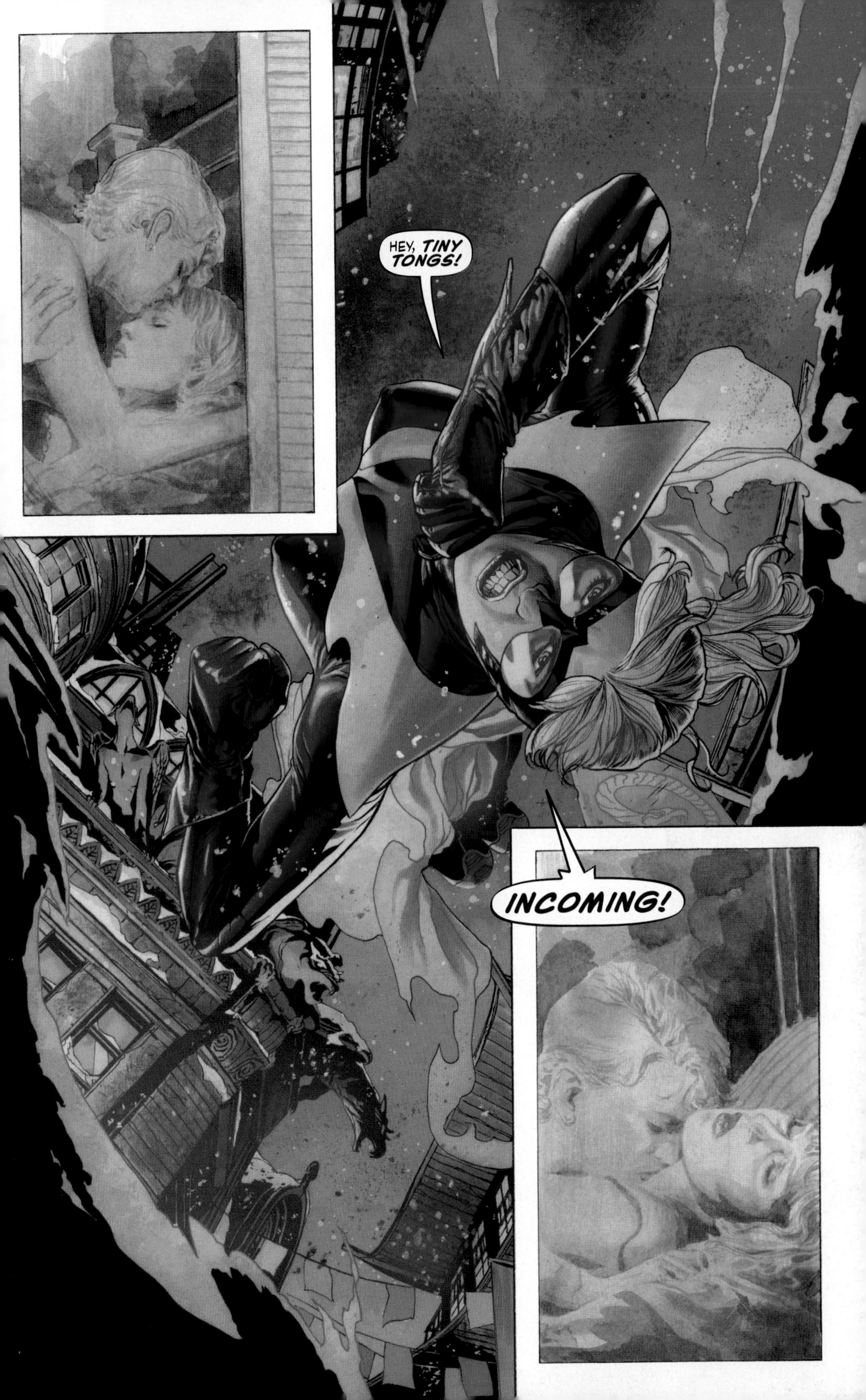
HEY, *TINY TONGS!*
INCOMING!

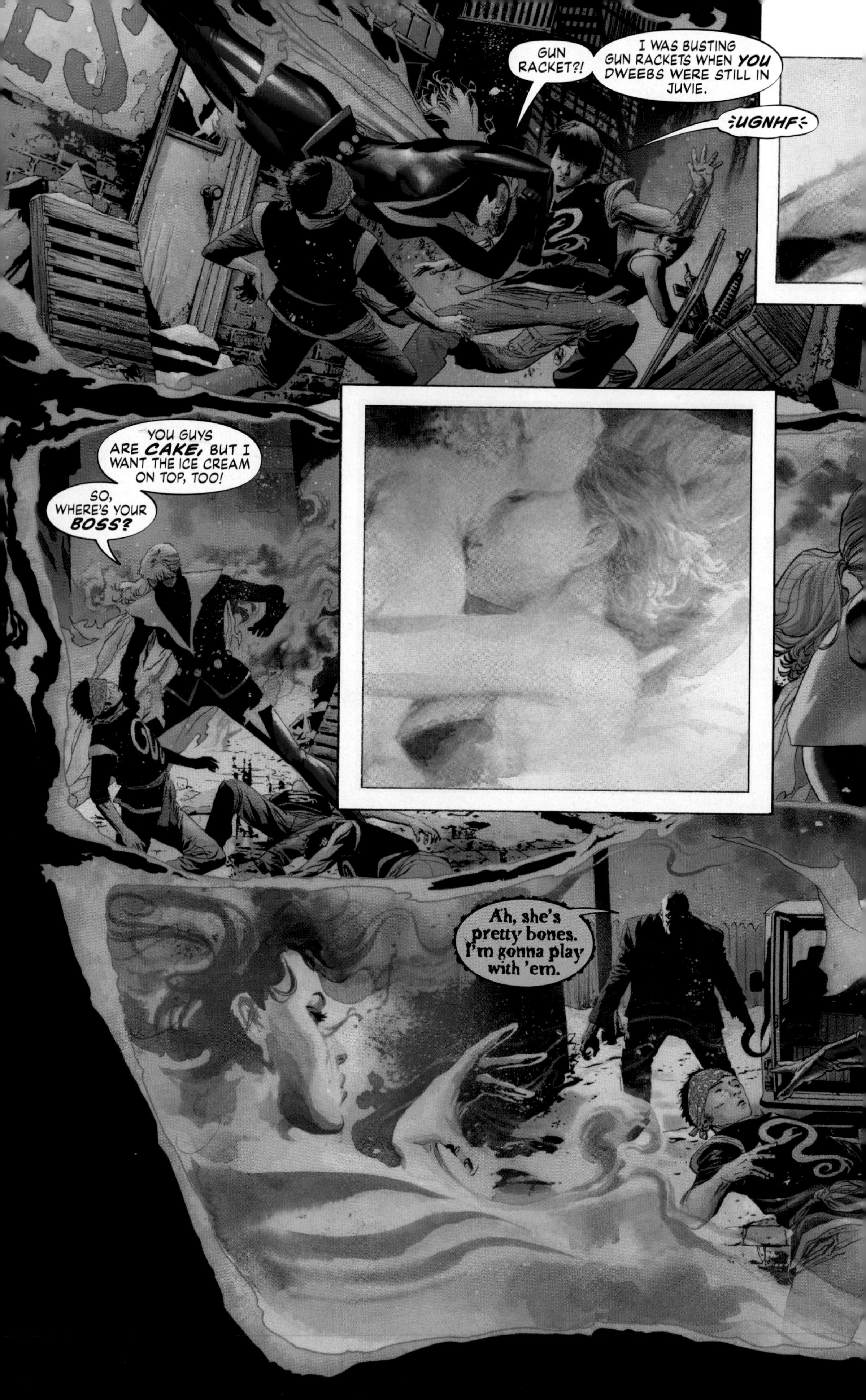

GUN RACKET?!
I WAS BUSTING GUN RACKETS WHEN YOU DWEEBS WERE STILL IN JUVIE.
UGNHF
YOU GUYS ARE CAKE, BUT I WANT THE ICE CREAM ON TOP, TOO!
SO, WHERE'S YOUR BOSS?
Ah, she's pretty bones. I'm gonna play with 'em.

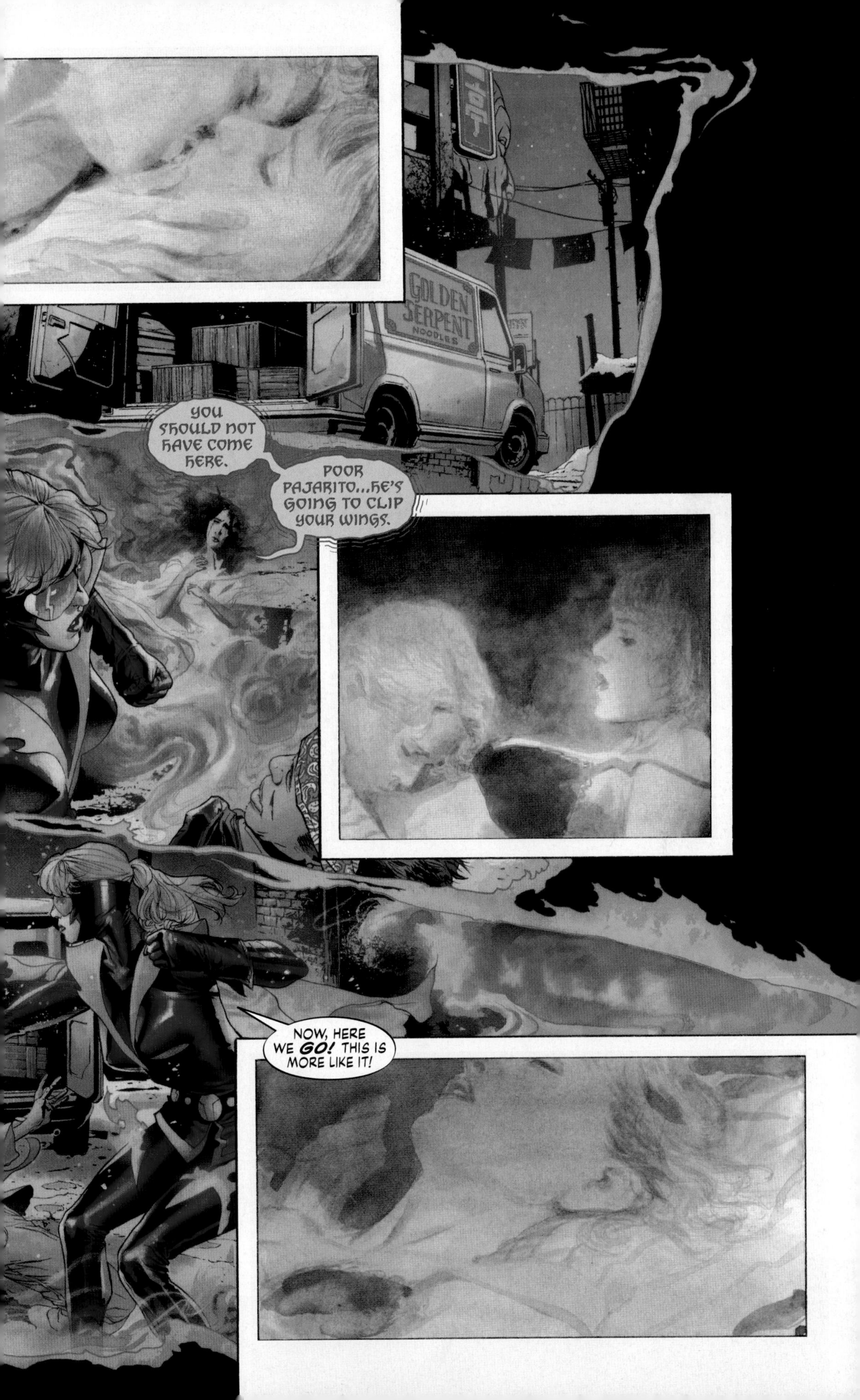
GOLDEN SERPENT NOODLES
YOU SHOULD NOT HAVE COME HERE.
POOR PAJARITO...HE'S GOING TO CLIP YOUR WINGS.
NOW, HERE WE GO! THIS IS MORE LIKE IT!

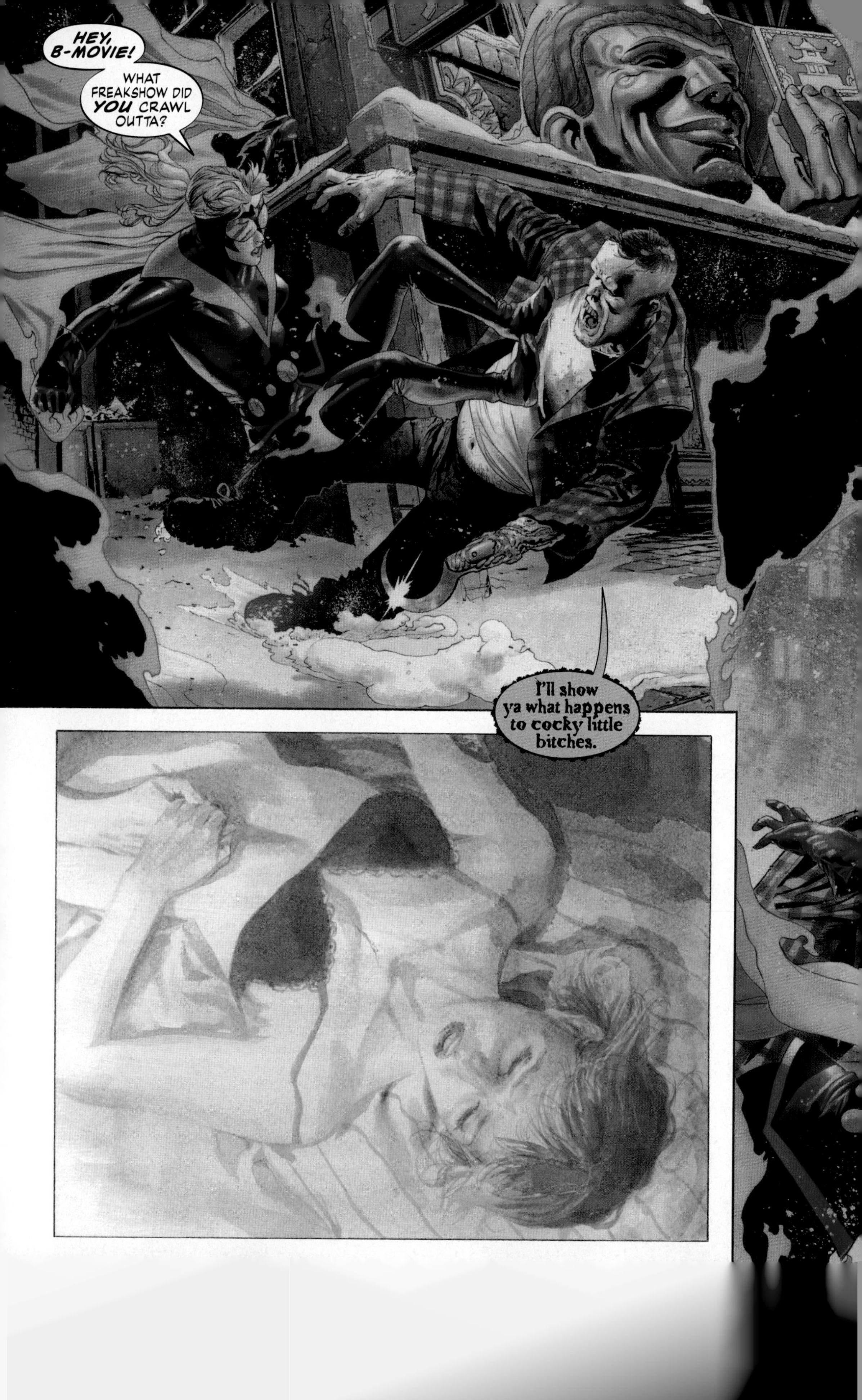
HEY, B-MOVIE!
WHAT FREAKSHOW DID YOU CRAWL OUTTA?
I'll show ya what happens to cocky little bitches.

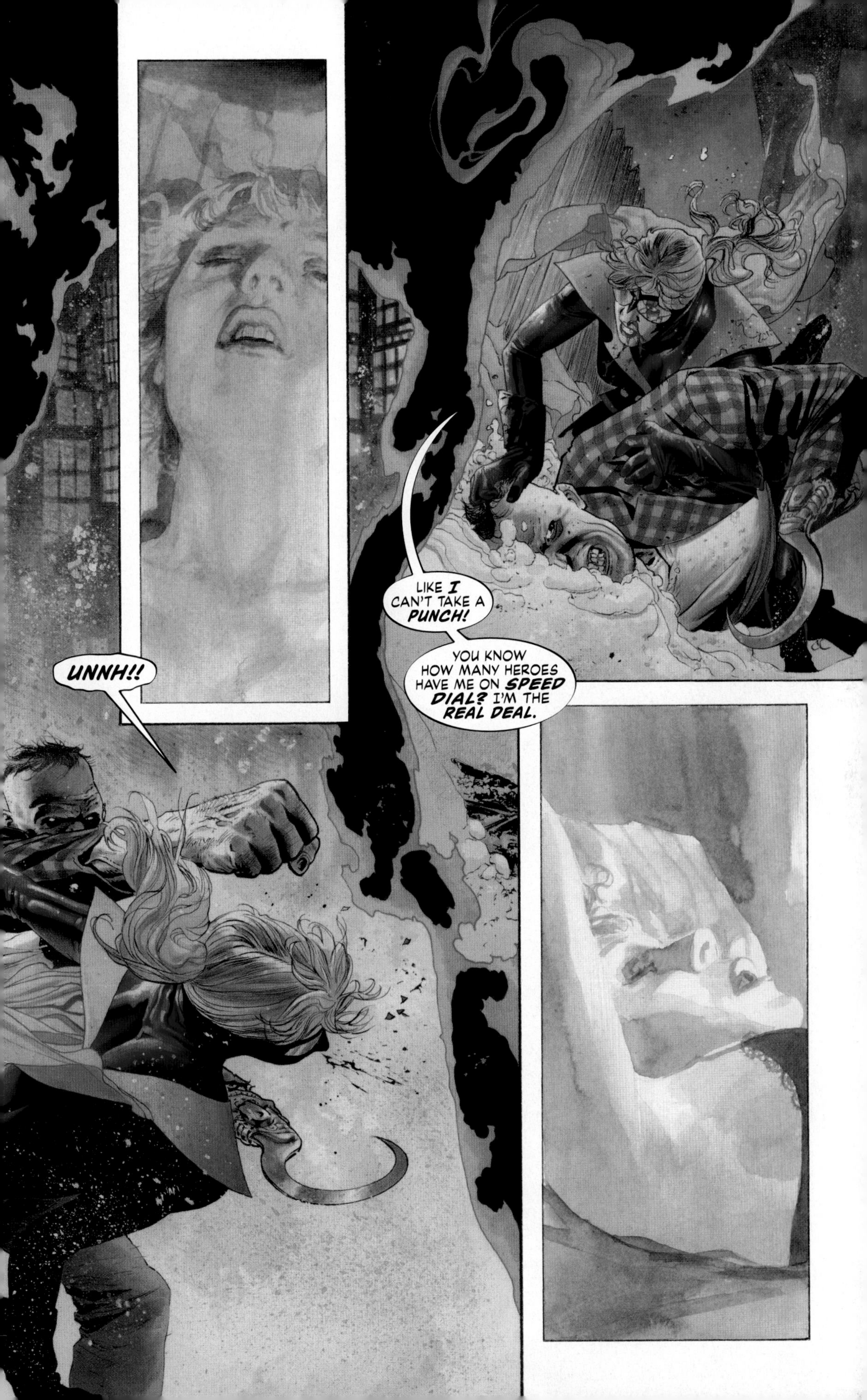
LIKE I CAN'T TAKE A PUNCH!
YOU KNOW HOW MANY HEROES HAVE ME ON SPEED DIAL? I'M THE REAL DEAL.
UNNH!!

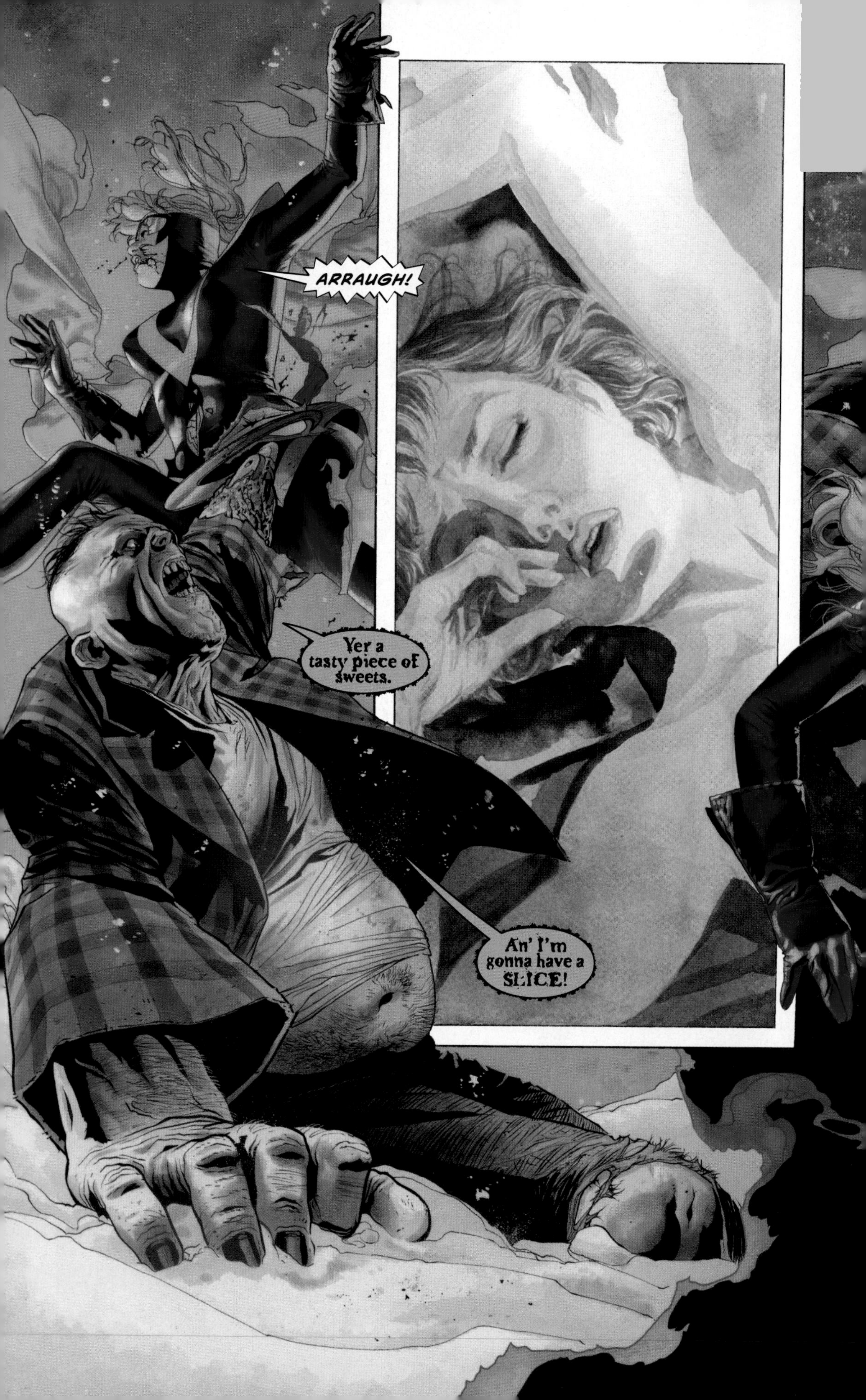
ARRAUGH!
Yer a tasty piece of sweets.
An' I'm gonna have a SLICE!

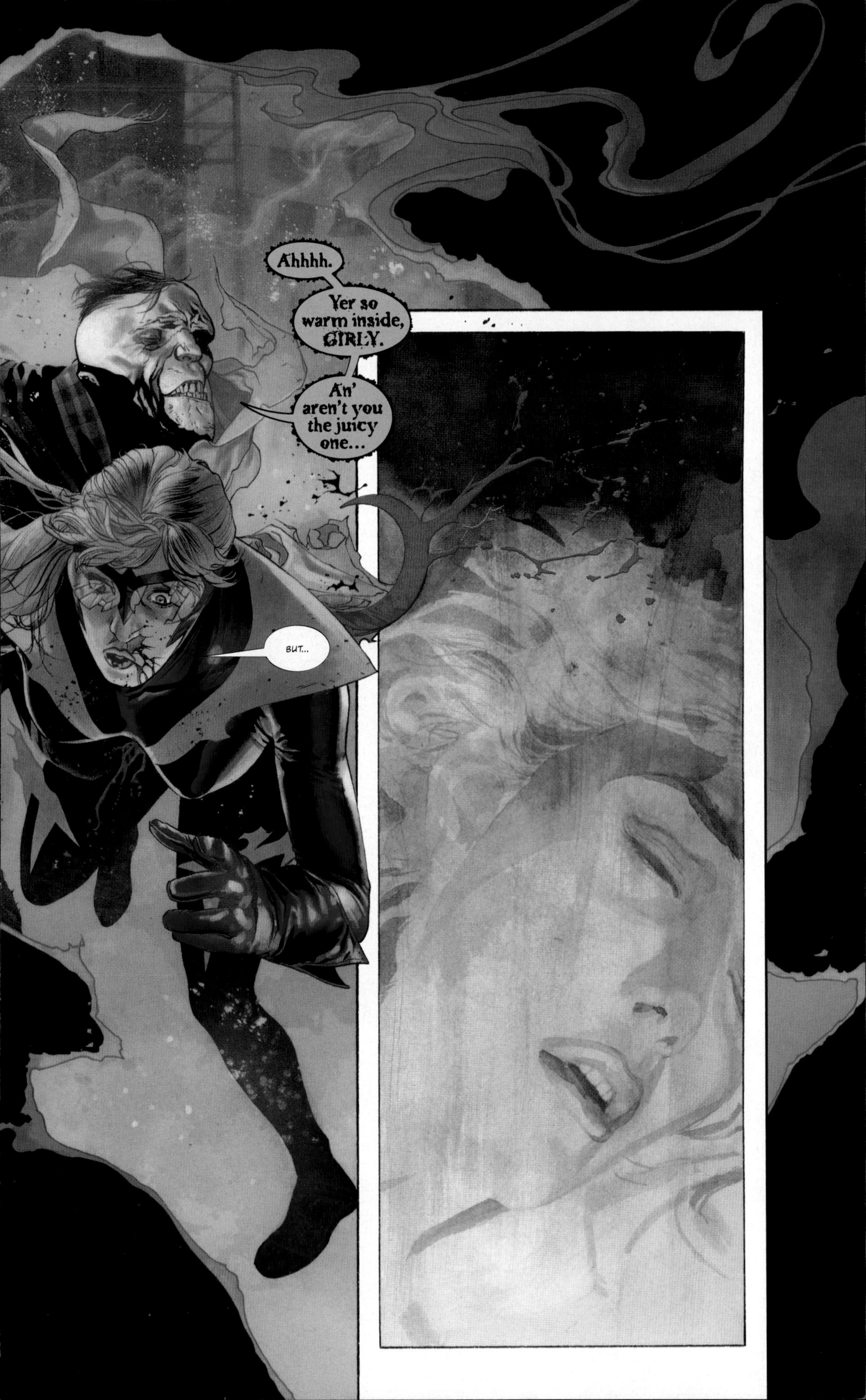
Ahhhh.
Yer so warm inside, GIRLY.
An' aren't you the juicy one...
BUT...

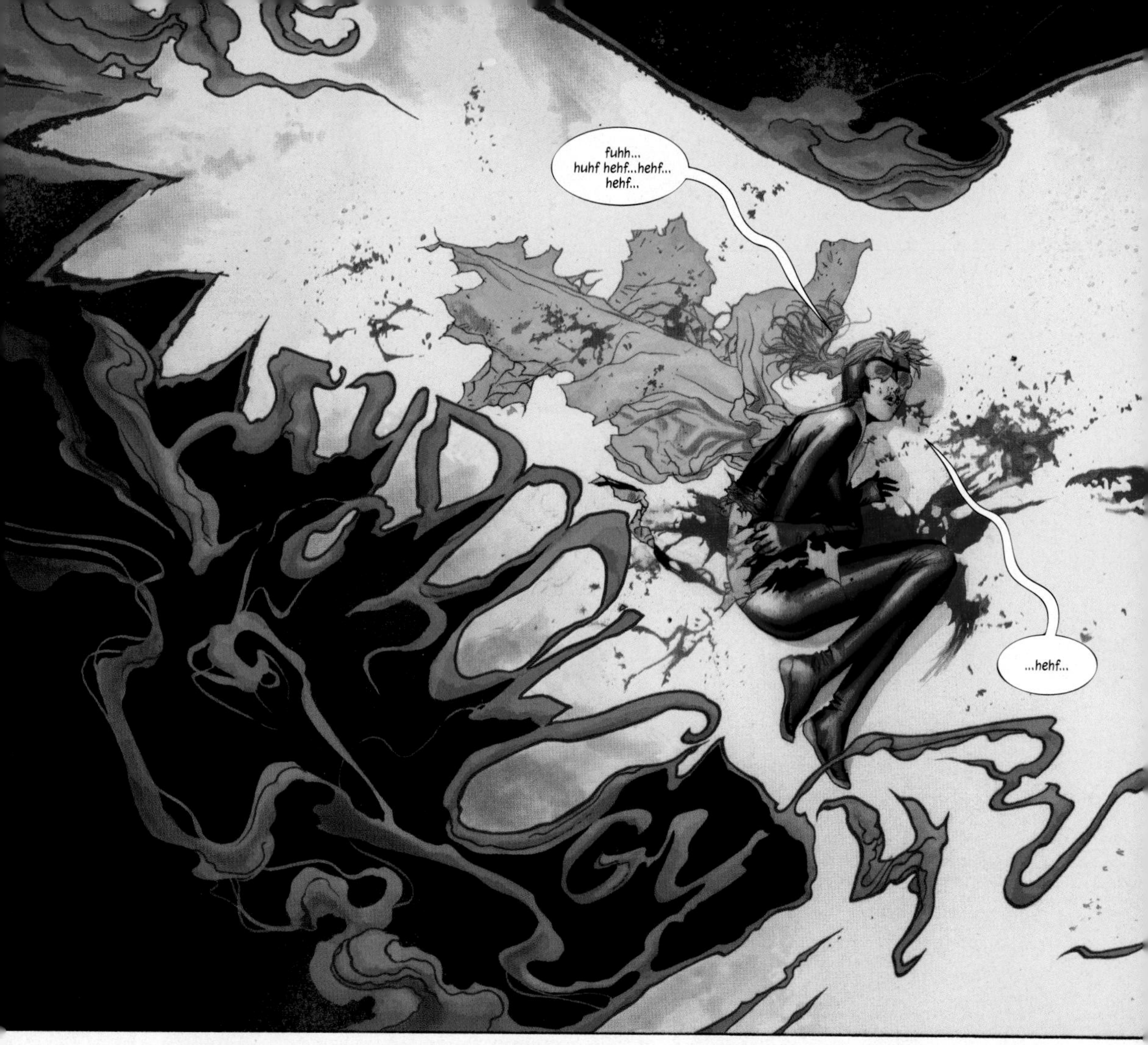
fuhh... huhf hehf...hehf... hehf...
...hehf...

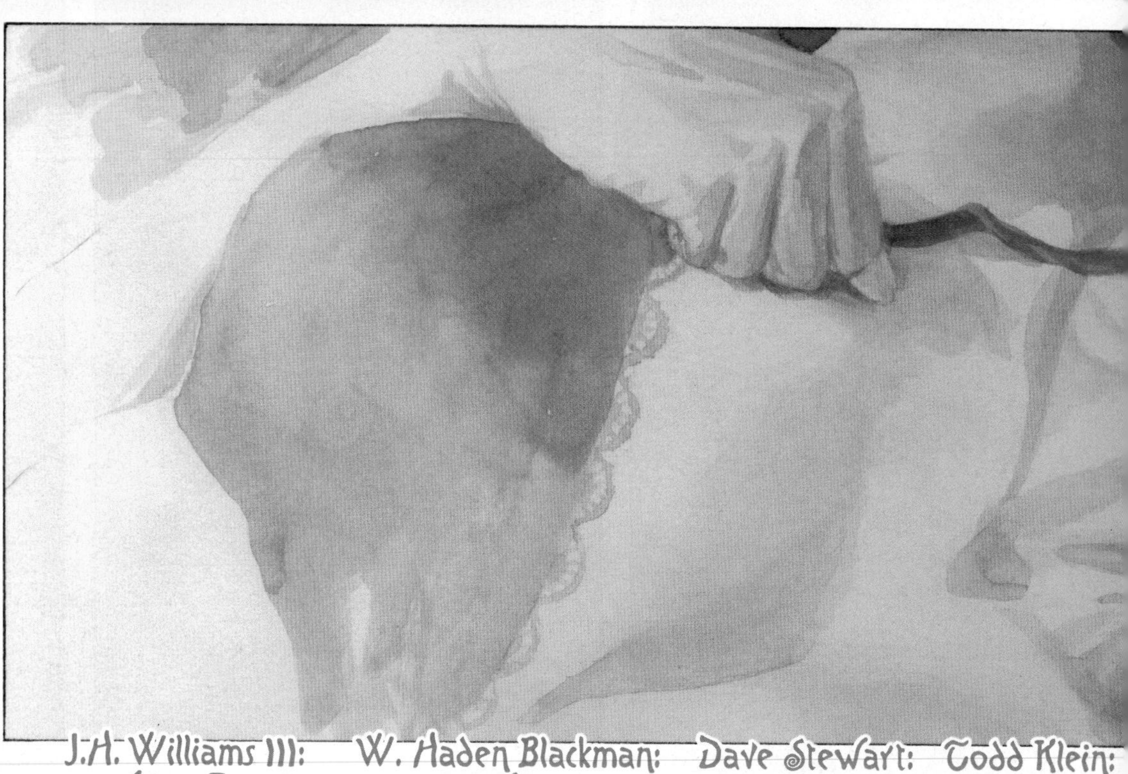

J.H. Williams III: co-writer & artist
W. Haden Blackman: co-writer
Dave Stewart: colors
Todd Klein: letters

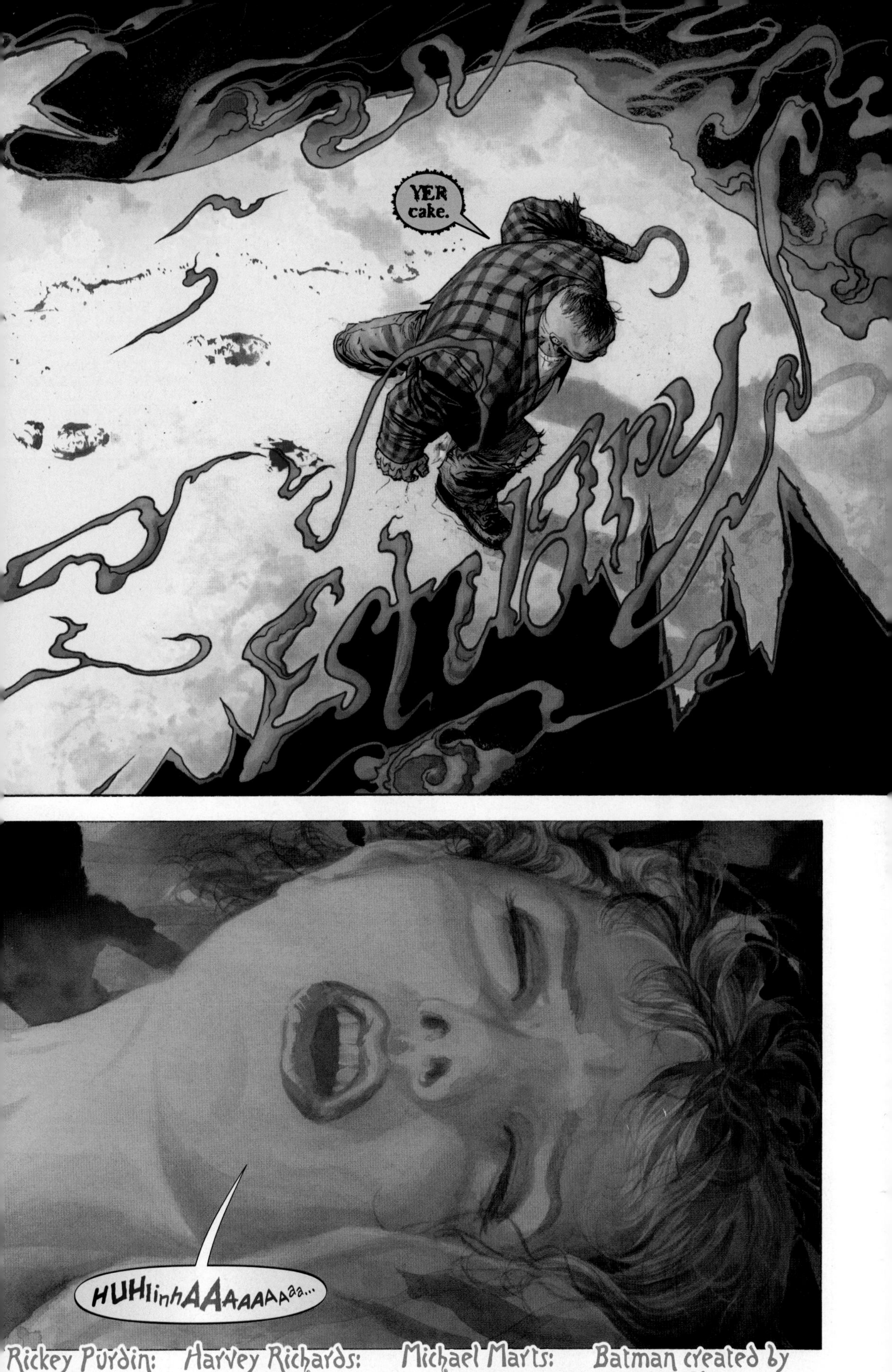
YER cake.
Estuary
HUHIinhAAAAAAAaa...

Rickey Purdin: asst. ed. Harvey Richards: assoc. ed. Michael Marts: editor Batman created by Bob Kane

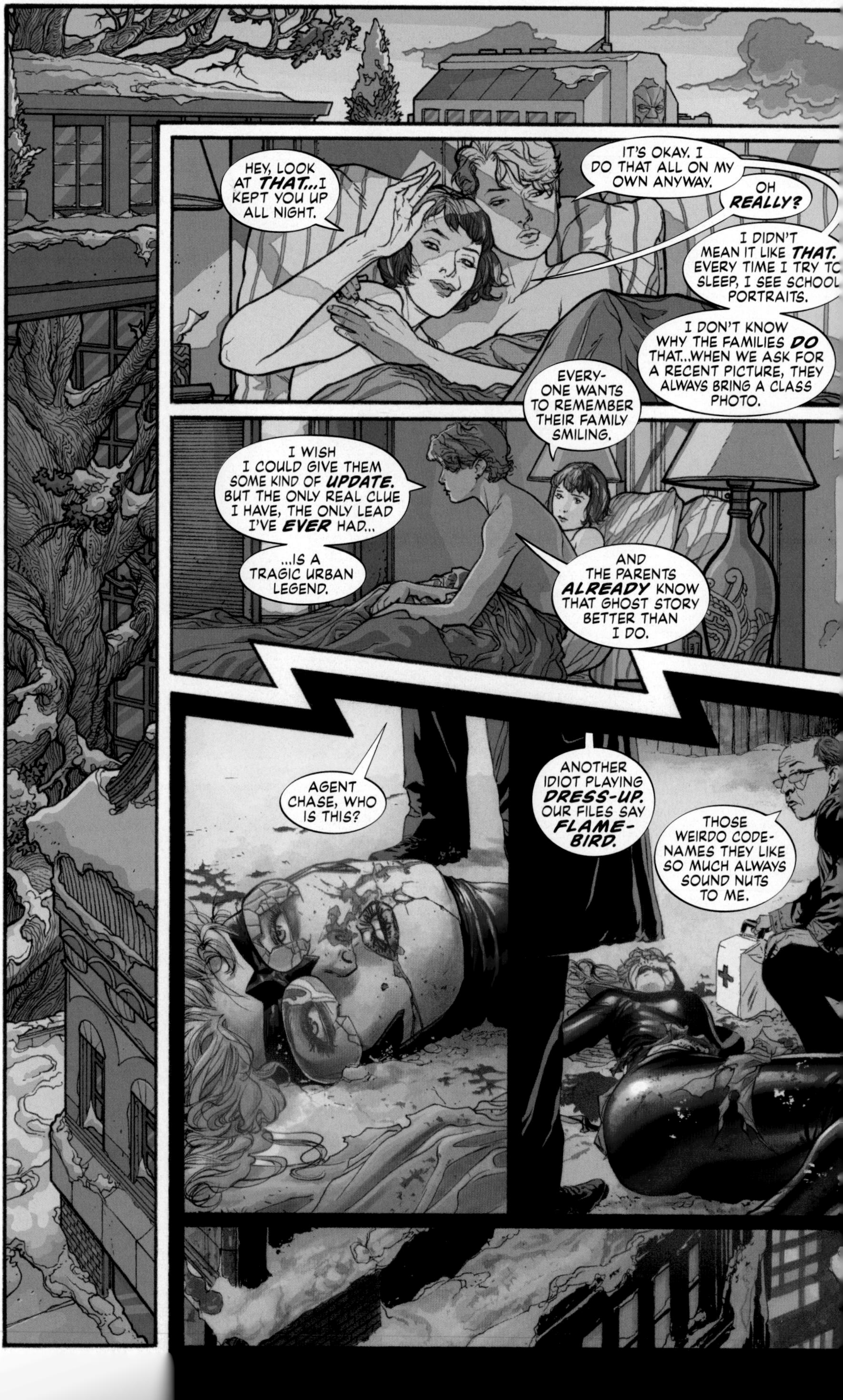
HEY, LOOK AT THAT...I KEPT YOU UP ALL NIGHT.
IT'S OKAY. I DO THAT ALL ON MY OWN ANYWAY.
OH REALLY?
I DIDN'T MEAN IT LIKE THAT. EVERY TIME I TRY TO SLEEP, I SEE SCHOOL PORTRAITS.
I DON'T KNOW WHY THE FAMILIES DO THAT...WHEN WE ASK FOR A RECENT PICTURE, THEY ALWAYS BRING A CLASS PHOTO.
EVERY-ONE WANTS TO REMEMBER THEIR FAMILY SMILING.
I WISH I COULD GIVE THEM SOME KIND OF UPDATE. BUT THE ONLY REAL CLUE I HAVE, THE ONLY LEAD I'VE EVER HAD...
...IS A TRAGIC URBAN LEGEND.
AND THE PARENTS ALREADY KNOW THAT GHOST STORY BETTER THAN I DO.
AGENT CHASE, WHO IS THIS?
ANOTHER IDIOT PLAYING DRESS-UP. OUR FILES SAY FLAME-BIRD.
THOSE WEIRDO CODE-NAMES THEY LIKE SO MUCH ALWAYS SOUND NUTS TO ME.

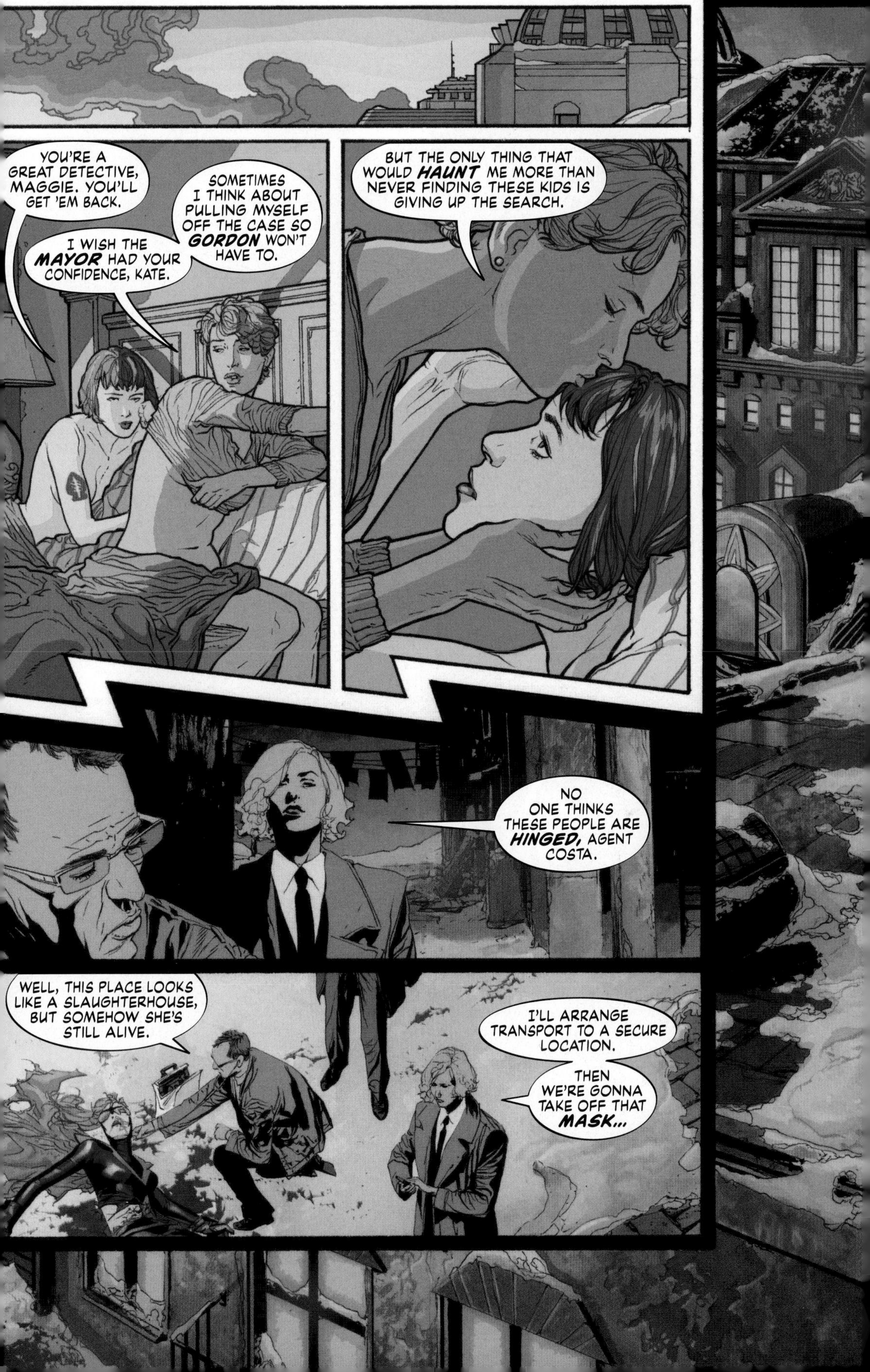
YOU'RE A GREAT DETECTIVE, MAGGIE. YOU'LL GET 'EM BACK.
I WISH THE MAYOR HAD YOUR CONFIDENCE, KATE.
SOMETIMES I THINK ABOUT PULLING MYSELF OFF THE CASE SO GORDON WON'T HAVE TO.
BUT THE ONLY THING THAT WOULD HAUNT ME MORE THAN NEVER FINDING THESE KIDS IS GIVING UP THE SEARCH.
NO ONE THINKS THESE PEOPLE ARE HINGED, AGENT COSTA.
WELL, THIS PLACE LOOKS LIKE A SLAUGHTERHOUSE, BUT SOMEHOW SHE'S STILL ALIVE.
I'LL ARRANGE TRANSPORT TO A SECURE LOCATION.
THEN WE'RE GONNA TAKE OFF THAT MASK...

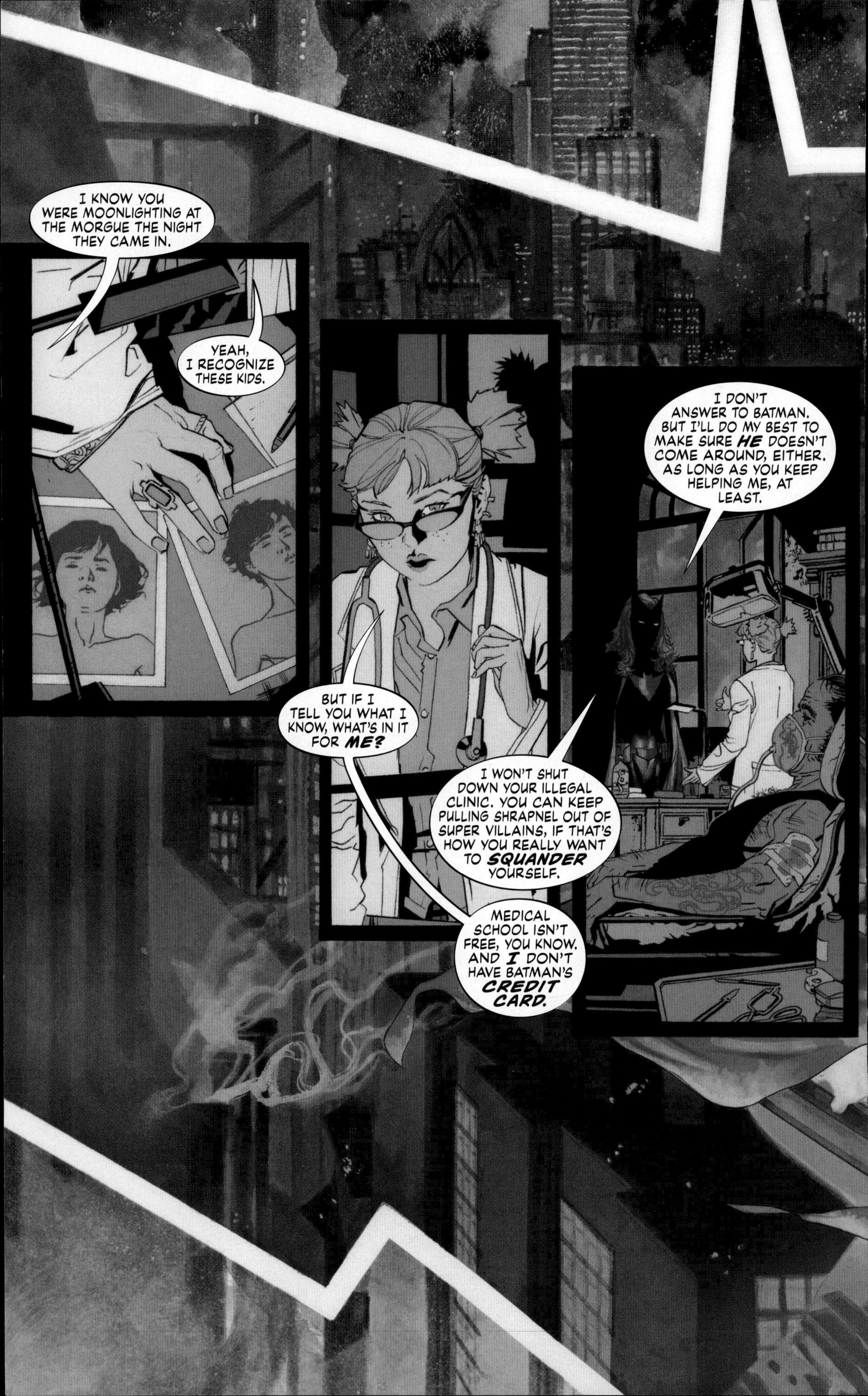
I KNOW YOU WERE MOONLIGHTING AT THE MORGUE THE NIGHT THEY CAME IN.
YEAH, I RECOGNIZE THESE KIDS.
BUT IF I TELL YOU WHAT I KNOW, WHAT'S IN IT FOR ME?
MEDICAL SCHOOL ISN'T FREE, YOU KNOW. AND I DON'T HAVE BATMAN'S CREDIT CARD.
I WON'T SHUT DOWN YOUR ILLEGAL CLINIC. YOU CAN KEEP PULLING SHRAPNEL OUT OF SUPER VILLAINS, IF THAT'S HOW YOU REALLY WANT TO SQUANDER YOURSELF.
I DON'T ANSWER TO BATMAN. BUT I'LL DO MY BEST TO MAKE SURE HE DOESN'T COME AROUND, EITHER. AS LONG AS YOU KEEP HELPING ME, AT LEAST.

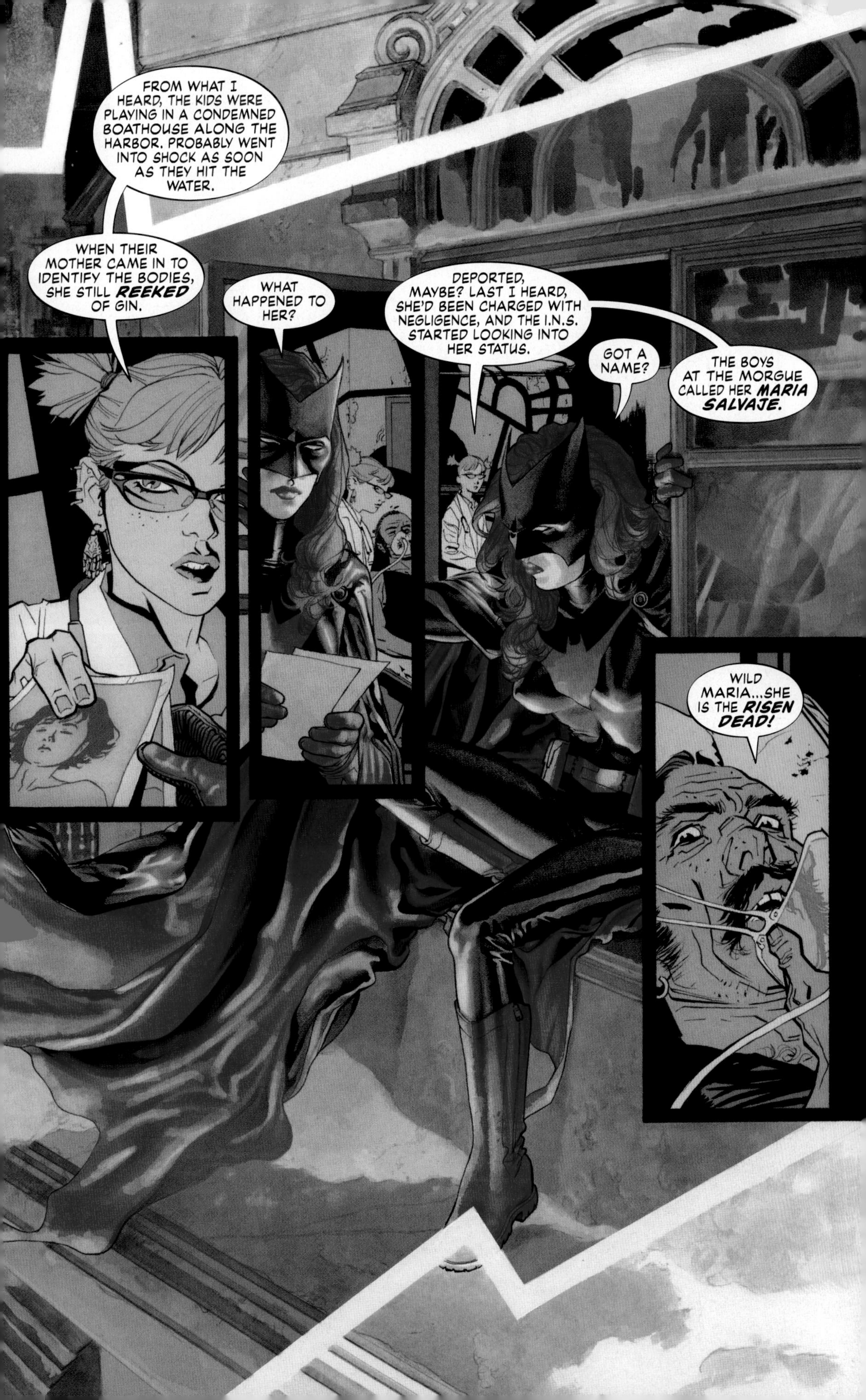
FROM WHAT I HEARD, THE KIDS WERE PLAYING IN A CONDEMNED BOATHOUSE ALONG THE HARBOR. PROBABLY WENT INTO SHOCK AS SOON AS THEY HIT THE WATER.
WHEN THEIR MOTHER CAME IN TO IDENTIFY THE BODIES, SHE STILL REEKED OF GIN.
WHAT HAPPENED TO HER?
DEPORTED, MAYBE? LAST I HEARD, SHE'D BEEN CHARGED WITH NEGLIGENCE, AND THE I.N.S. STARTED LOOKING INTO HER STATUS.
GOT A NAME?
THE BOYS AT THE MORGUE CALLED HER MARIA SALVAJE.
WILD MARIA...SHE IS THE RISEN DEAD!

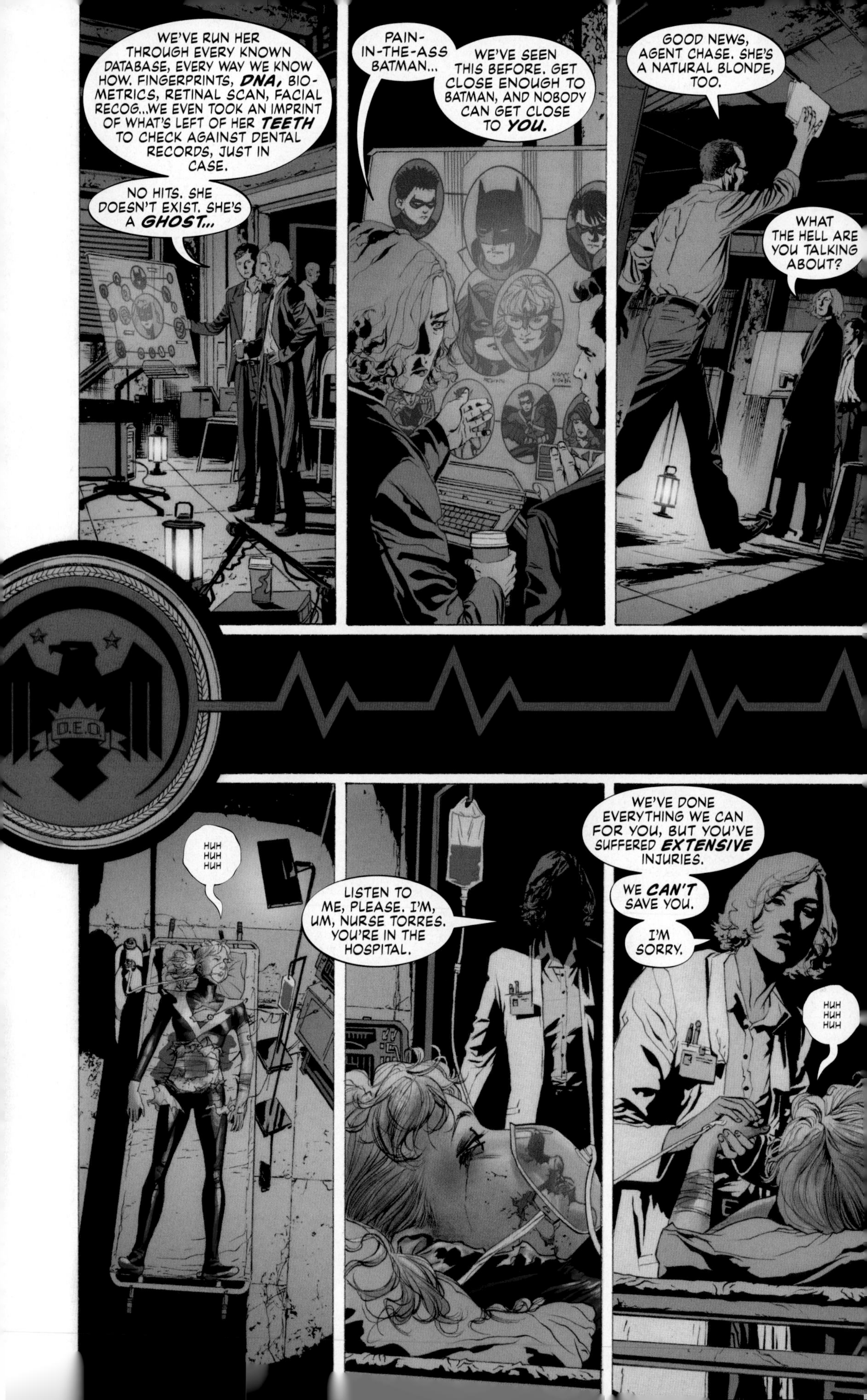

WE'VE RUN HER THROUGH EVERY KNOWN DATABASE, EVERY WAY WE KNOW HOW. FINGERPRINTS, DNA, BIO-METRICS, RETINAL SCAN, FACIAL RECOG...WE EVEN TOOK AN IMPRINT OF WHAT'S LEFT OF HER TEETH TO CHECK AGAINST DENTAL RECORDS, JUST IN CASE.
NO HITS. SHE DOESN'T EXIST. SHE'S A GHOST...
PAIN-IN-THE-ASS BATMAN...
WE'VE SEEN THIS BEFORE. GET CLOSE ENOUGH TO BATMAN, AND NOBODY CAN GET CLOSE TO YOU.
GOOD NEWS, AGENT CHASE. SHE'S A NATURAL BLONDE, TOO.
WHAT THE HELL ARE YOU TALKING ABOUT?
D.E.O.
HUH HUH HUH
LISTEN TO ME, PLEASE. I'M, UM, NURSE TORRES. YOU'RE IN THE HOSPITAL.
WE'VE DONE EVERYTHING WE CAN FOR YOU, BUT YOU'VE SUFFERED EXTENSIVE INJURIES.
WE CAN'T SAVE YOU.
I'M SORRY.
HUH HUH HUH

WE KNOW THAT BATWOMAN HAS A SIDEKICK. THE GIRL IN THAT GRAY UNIFORM WE KEEP CATCHING ON SECURITY CAMERAS? SHE'S A BLONDE.

COULD BE A WIG.

NO. WE COLLECTED BLONDE HAIRS FROM EACH OF THE SIDEKICK'S RECENT FIGHTS. THEY ALL MATCH. THEY ALL BELONG TO HER.

ONCE I REALIZED FLAMEBIRD'S *ALSO* A NATURAL BLONDE, AND ABOUT THE SAME SIZE AND AGE AS THE SIDEKICK, I COMPARED OUR SAMPLES TO HER HAIR.

ANOTHER PERFECT MATCH.

WE MAY NOT KNOW HER REAL *NAME,* BUT--

FLAMEBIRD *IS* THE BATWOMAN'S SIDEKICK.

I NEED TO CALL YOUR PARENTS, YOUR *BOYFRIEND,* ANYONE.

PLEASE, I DON'T WANT YOU TO DIE ALONE. IF YOU CAN HEAR ME, GIVE ME A NAME.

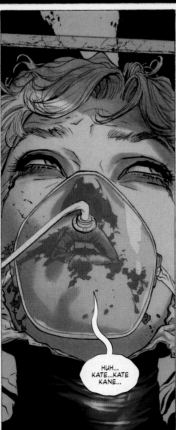

HUH... KATE...KATE KANE...

NOW THAT *CAN'T* BE A COINCIDENCE.

CHANGE HER DRESSINGS, ROLL HER OUT, AND DROP HER AT GOTHAM GENERAL.

SHE WON'T LAST THE NIGHT. NOT *HERE,* ANY-WAY.

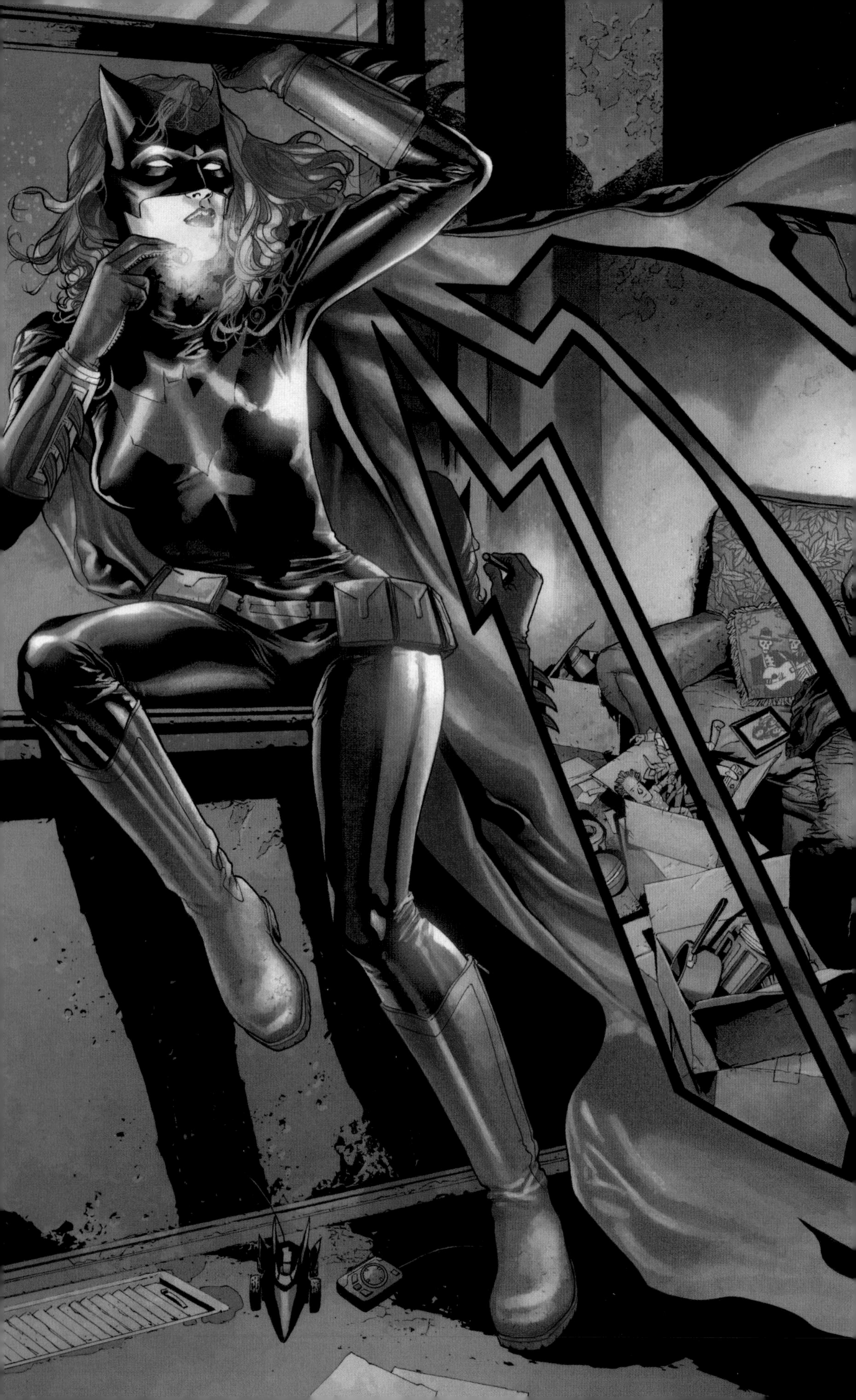

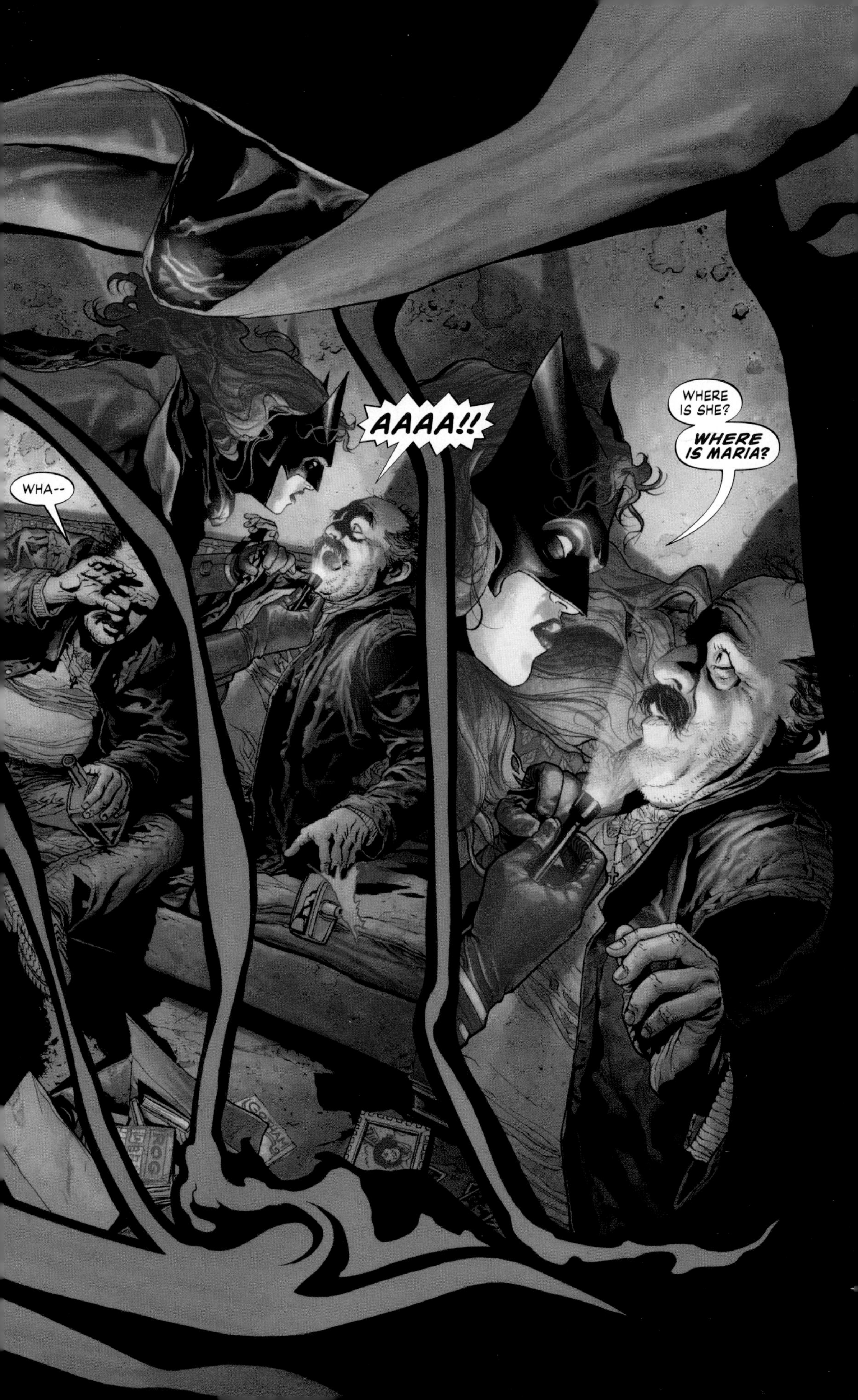
WHA--
AAAA!!
WHERE IS SHE?
WHERE IS MARIA?

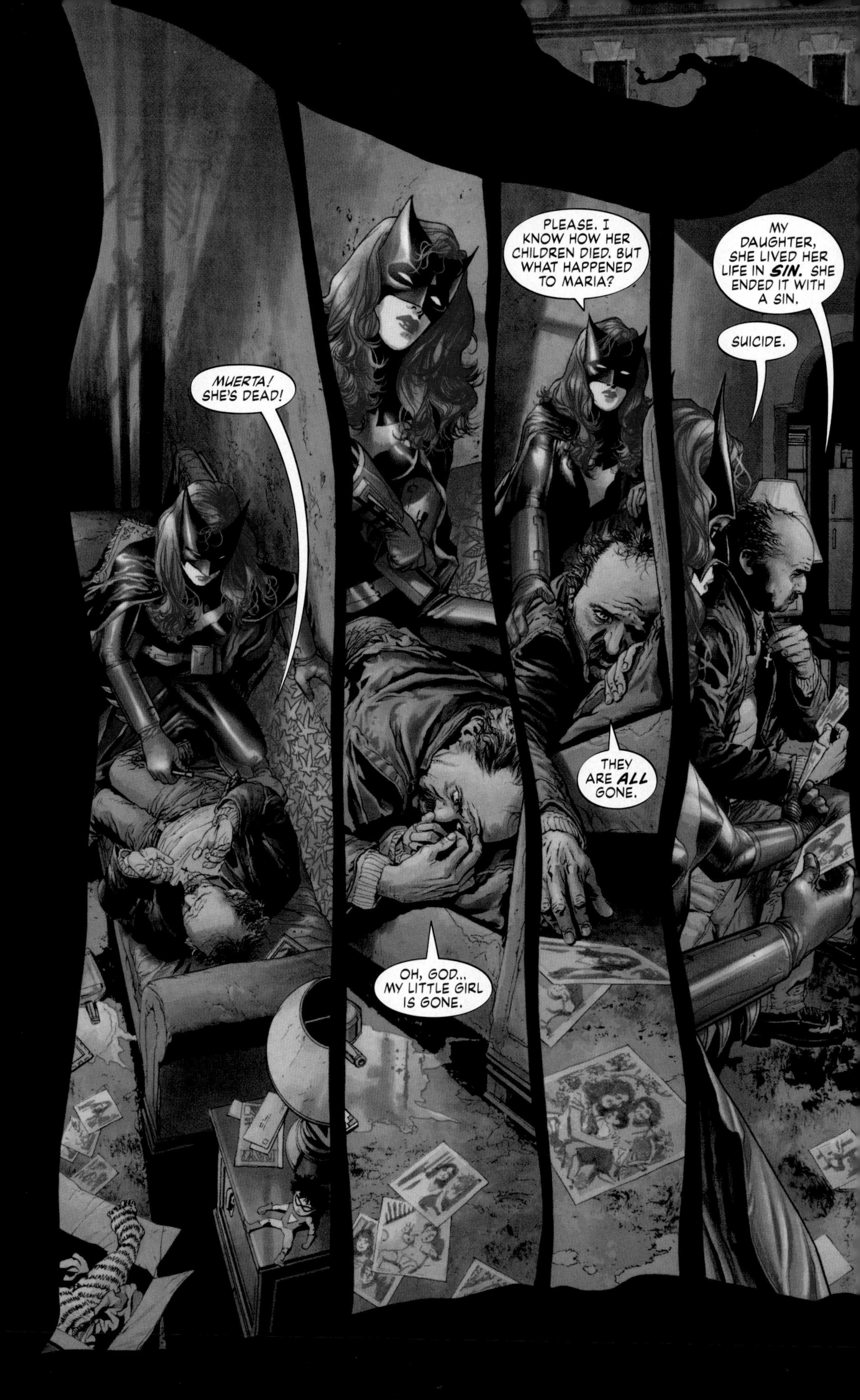
MUERTA! SHE'S DEAD!
OH, GOD... MY LITTLE GIRL IS GONE.
PLEASE. I KNOW HOW HER CHILDREN DIED. BUT WHAT HAPPENED TO MARIA?
THEY ARE ALL GONE.
MY DAUGHTER, SHE LIVED HER LIFE IN SIN. SHE ENDED IT WITH A SIN.
SUICIDE.

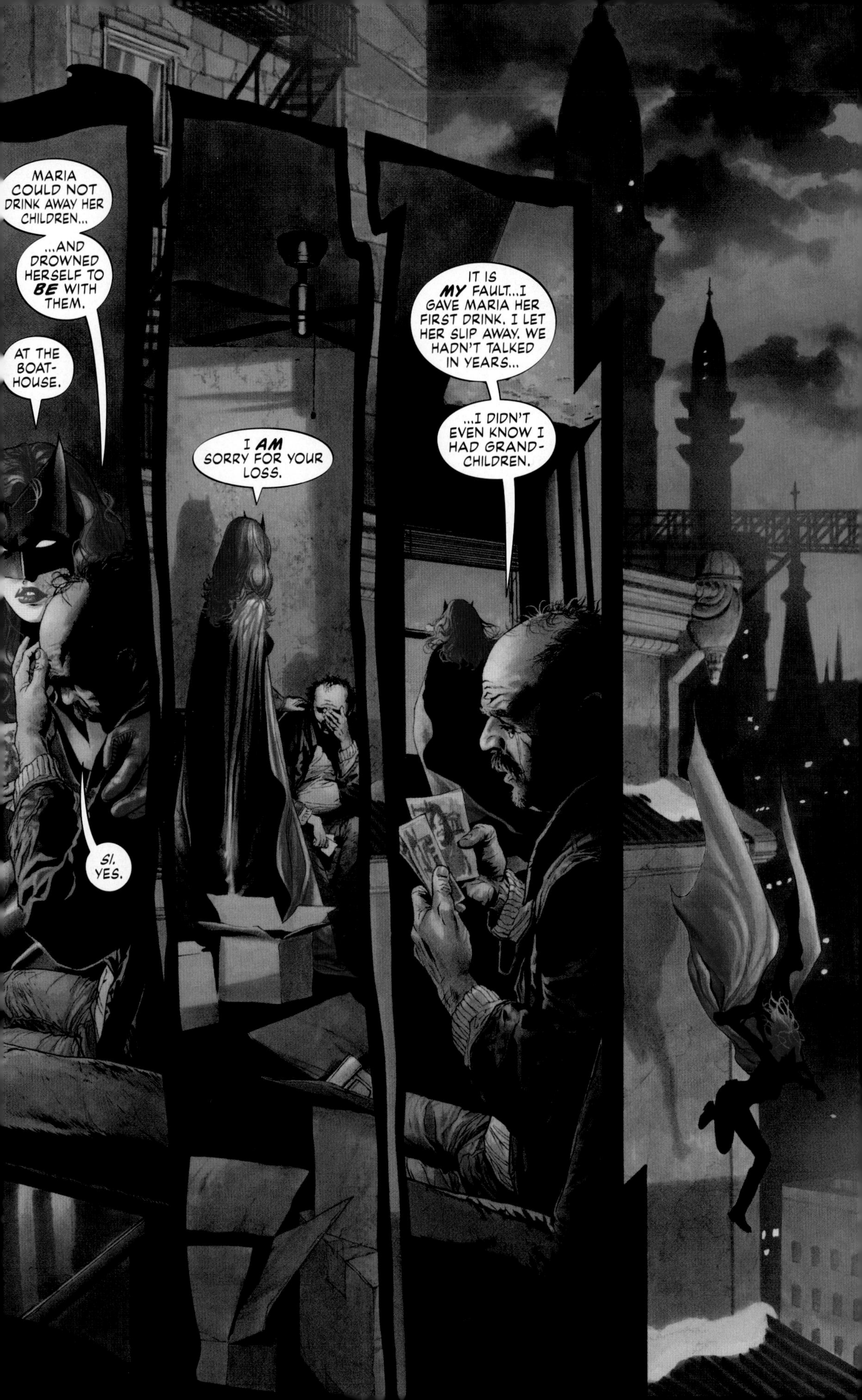
MARIA COULD NOT DRINK AWAY HER CHILDREN...
...AND DROWNED HERSELF TO BE WITH THEM.
AT THE BOAT-HOUSE.
SI. YES.
I AM SORRY FOR YOUR LOSS.
IT IS MY FAULT...I GAVE MARIA HER FIRST DRINK. I LET HER SLIP AWAY. WE HADN'T TALKED IN YEARS...
...I DIDN'T EVEN KNOW I HAD GRAND-CHILDREN.

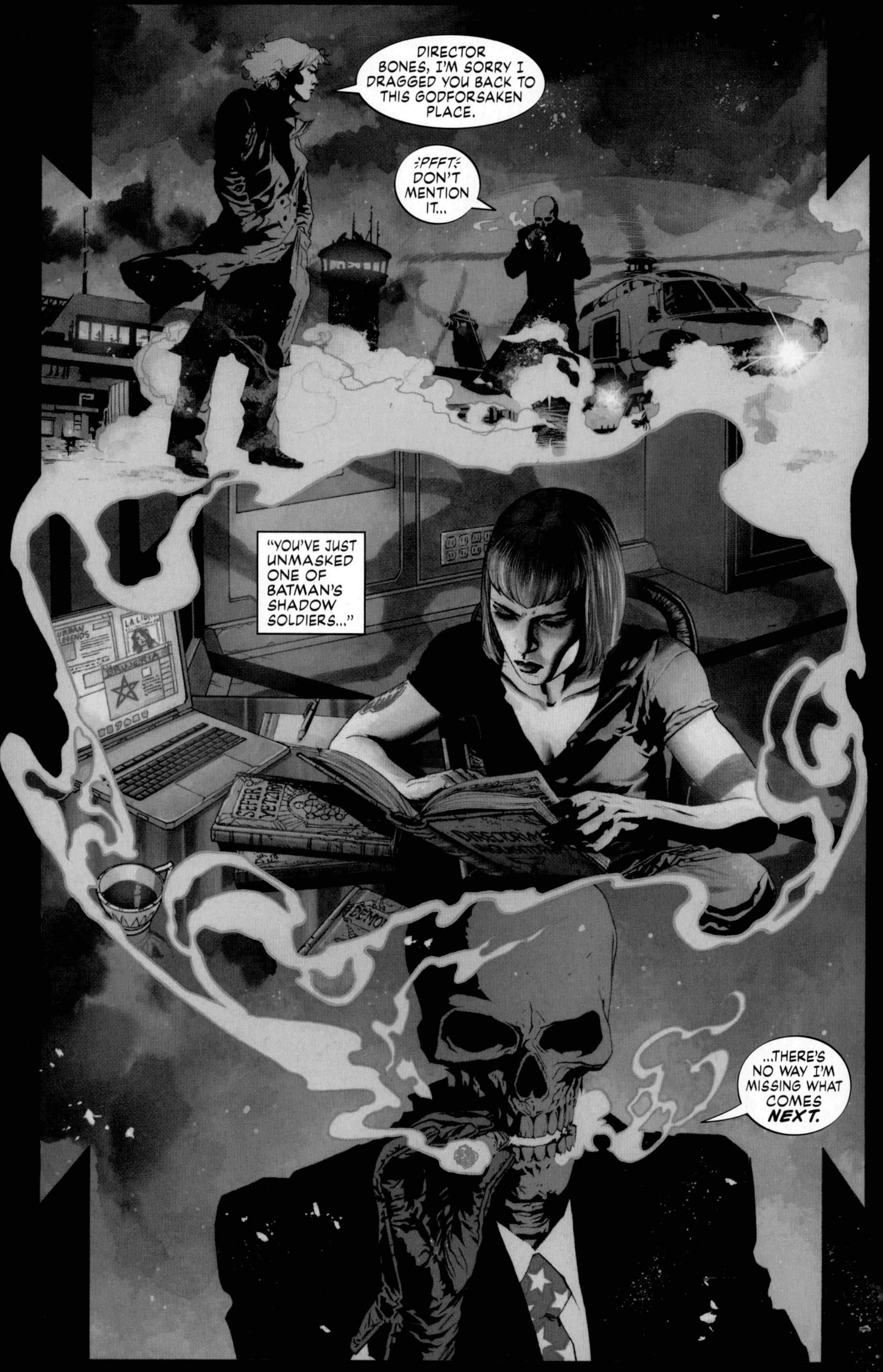
DIRECTOR BONES, I'M SORRY I DRAGGED YOU BACK TO THIS GODFORSAKEN PLACE.
PFFT DON'T MENTION IT...
"YOU'VE JUST UNMASKED ONE OF BATMAN'S SHADOW SOLDIERS..."
...THERE'S NO WAY I'M MISSING WHAT COMES NEXT.

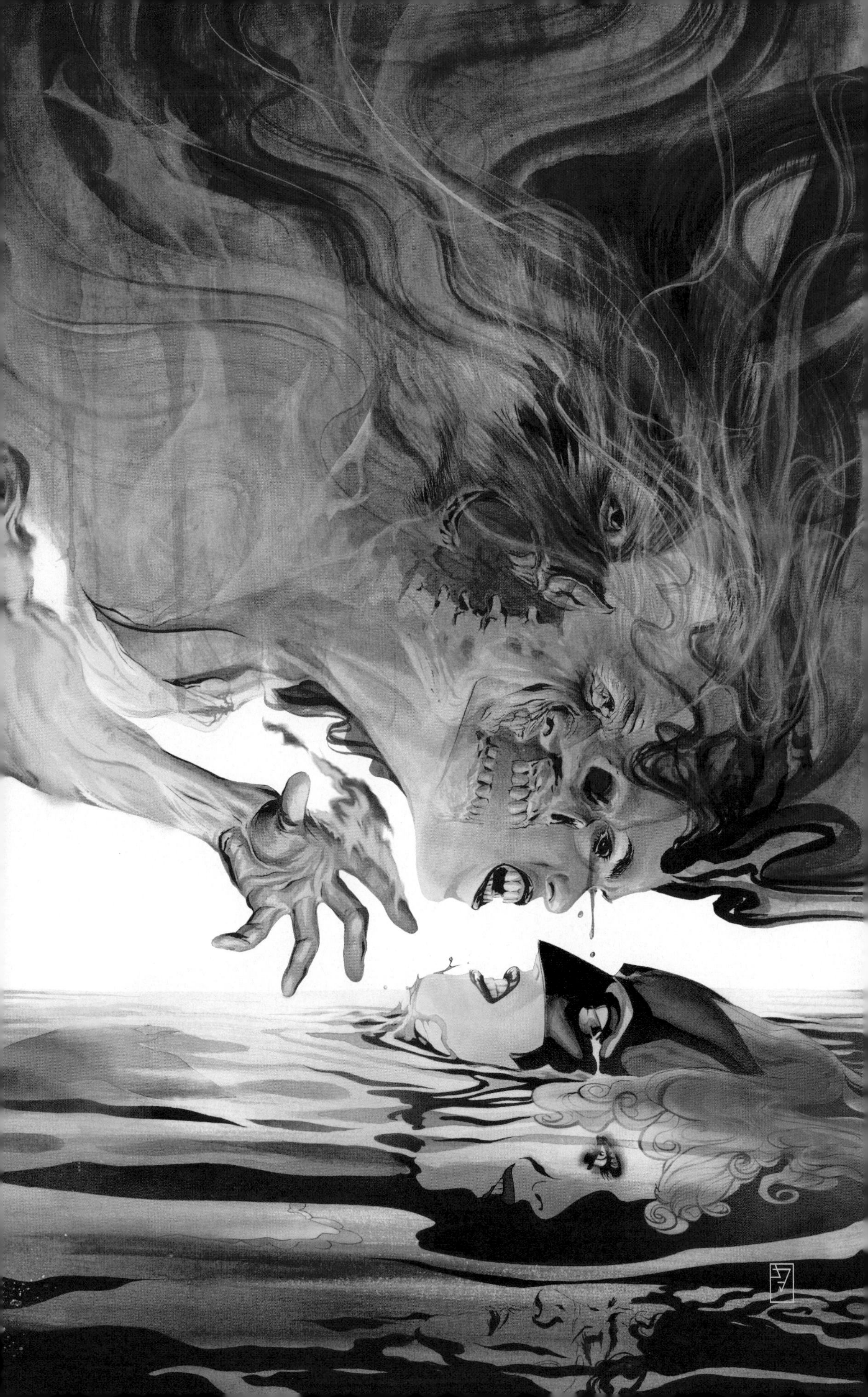

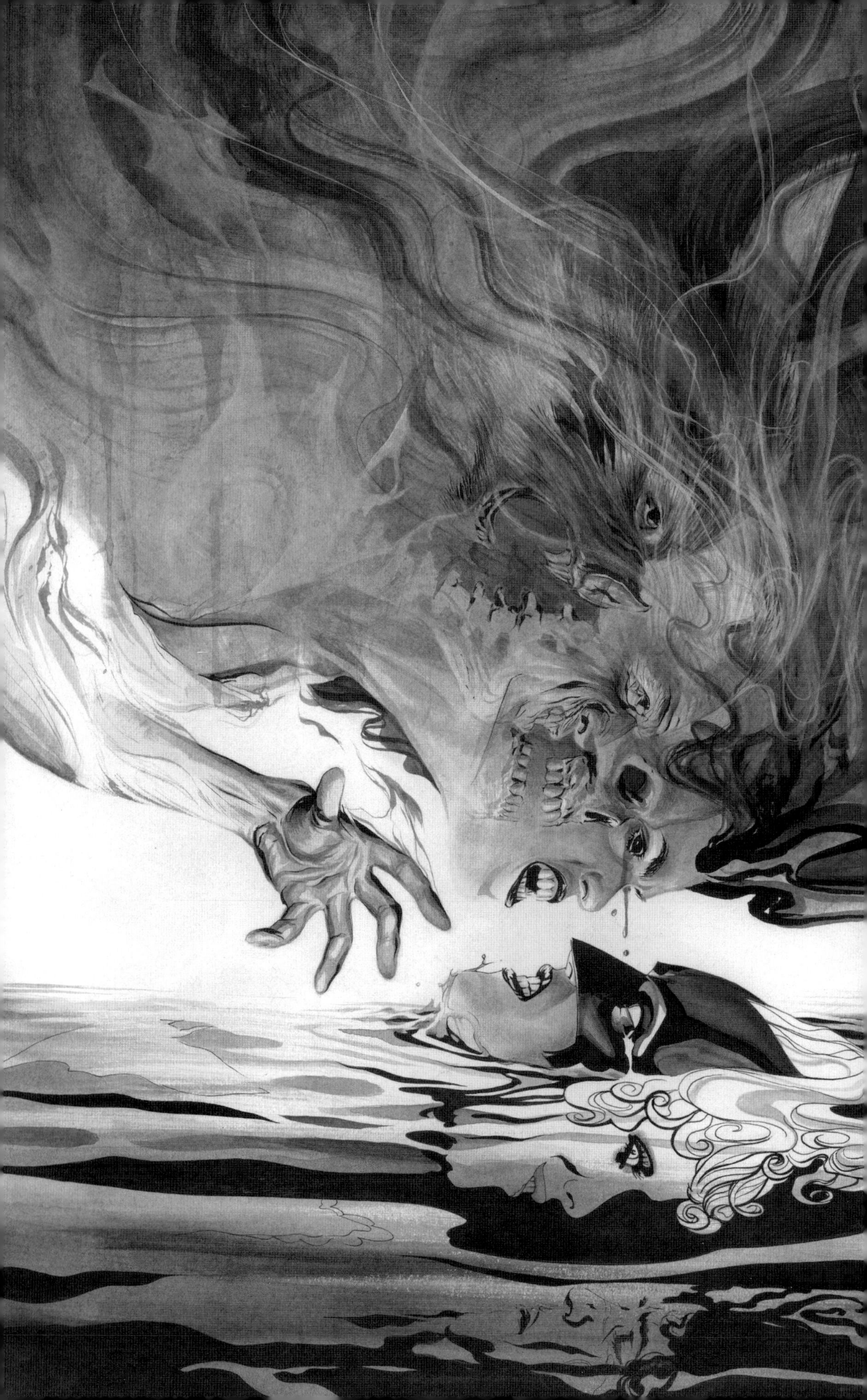

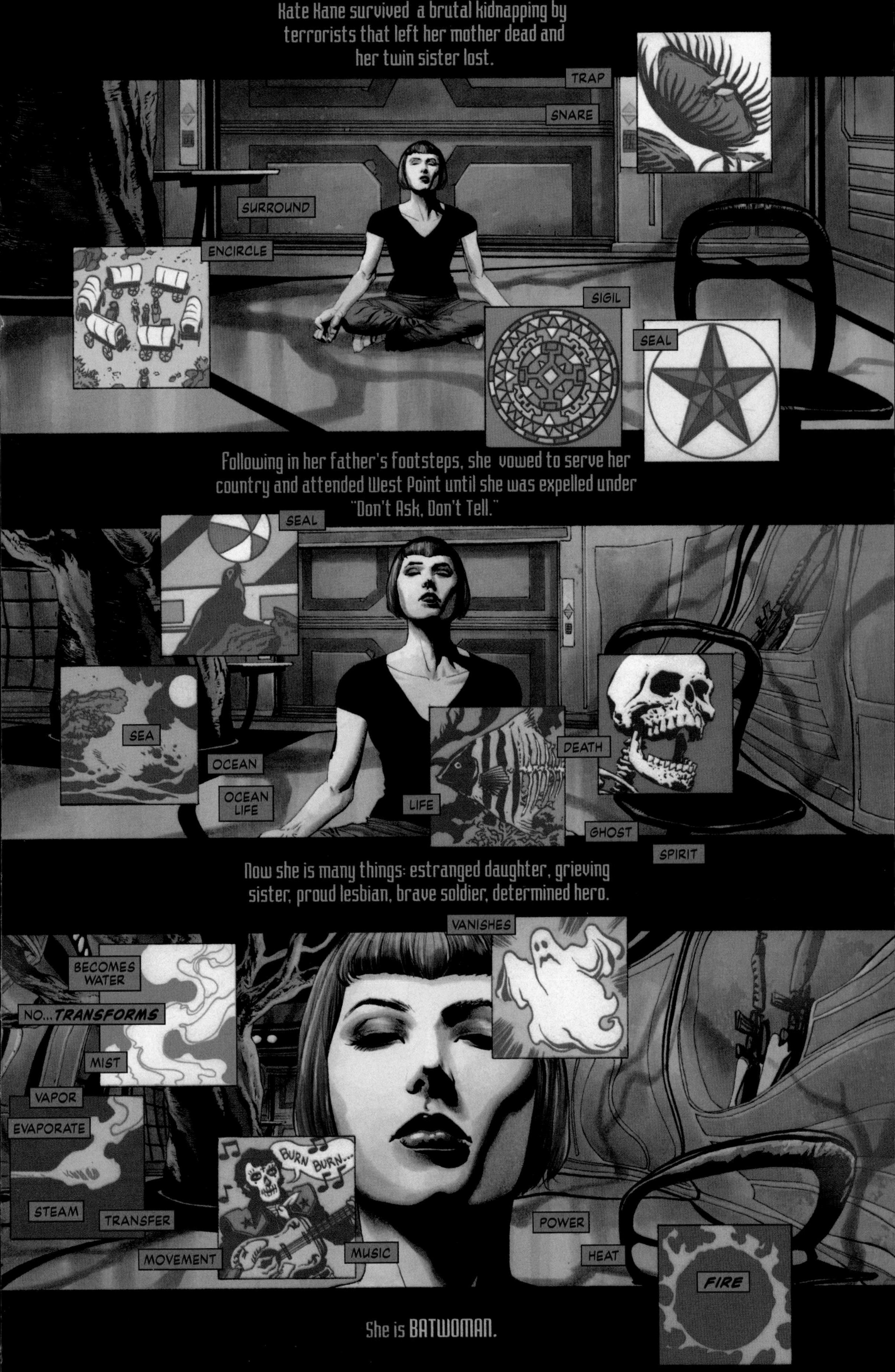

Kate Kane survived a brutal kidnapping by terrorists that left her mother dead and her twin sister lost.
SURROUND
ENCIRCLE
TRAP
SNARE
SIGIL
SEAL
Following in her father's footsteps, she vowed to serve her country and attended West Point until she was expelled under "Don't Ask, Don't Tell."
SEAL
SEA
OCEAN
OCEAN LIFE
LIFE
DEATH
GHOST
SPIRIT
Now she is many things: estranged daughter, grieving sister, proud lesbian, brave soldier, determined hero.
BECOMES WATER
NO...TRANSFORMS
MIST
VAPOR
EVAPORATE
STEAM
TRANSFER
MOVEMENT
BURN BURN...
MUSIC
VANISHES
POWER
HEAT
FIRE
She is BATWOMAN.

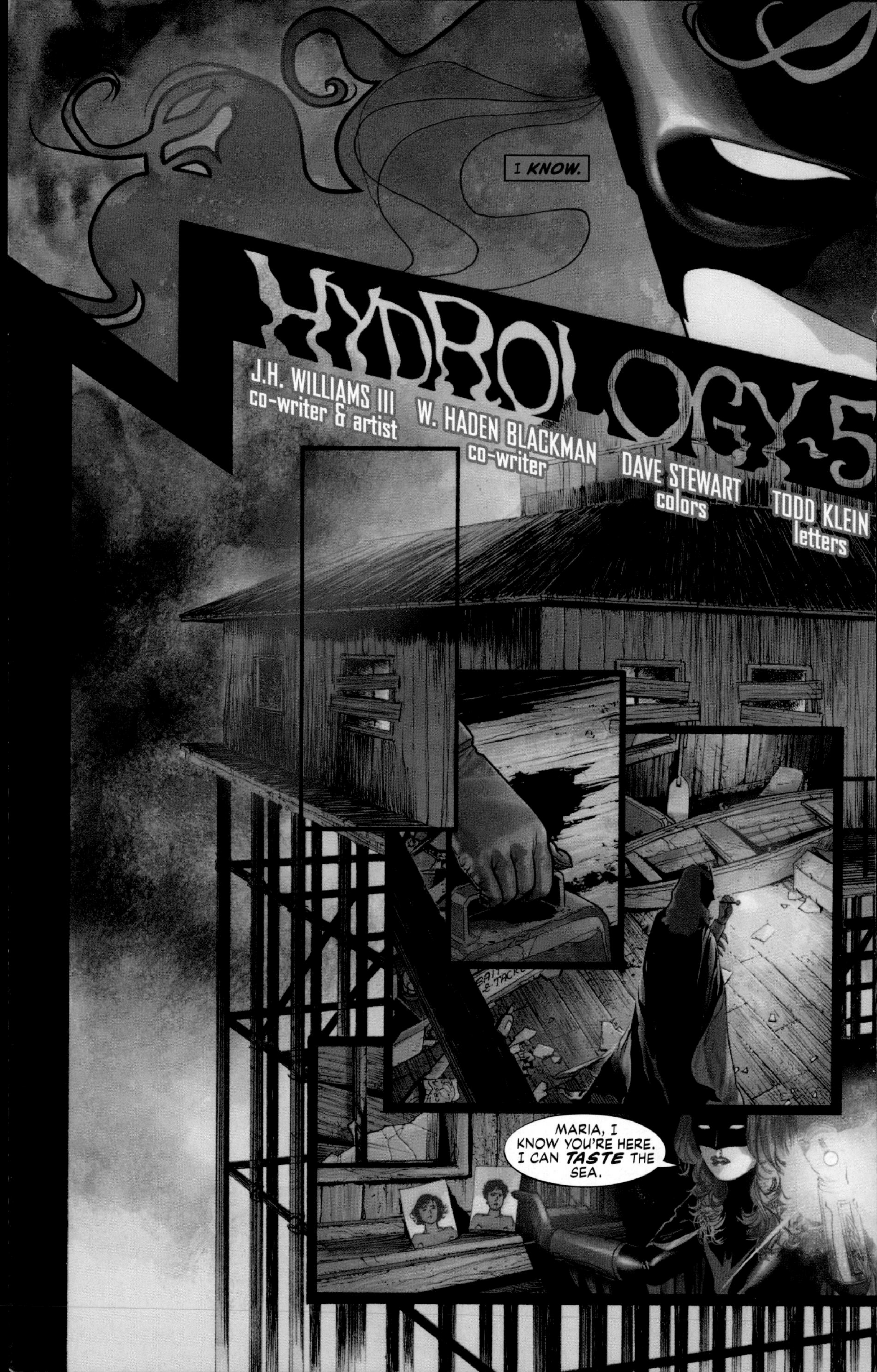

I KNOW.
HYDROLOGY 5
J.H. WILLIAMS III co-writer & artist
W. HADEN BLACKMAN co-writer
DAVE STEWART colors
TODD KLEIN letters
MARIA, I KNOW YOU'RE HERE. I CAN TASTE THE SEA.

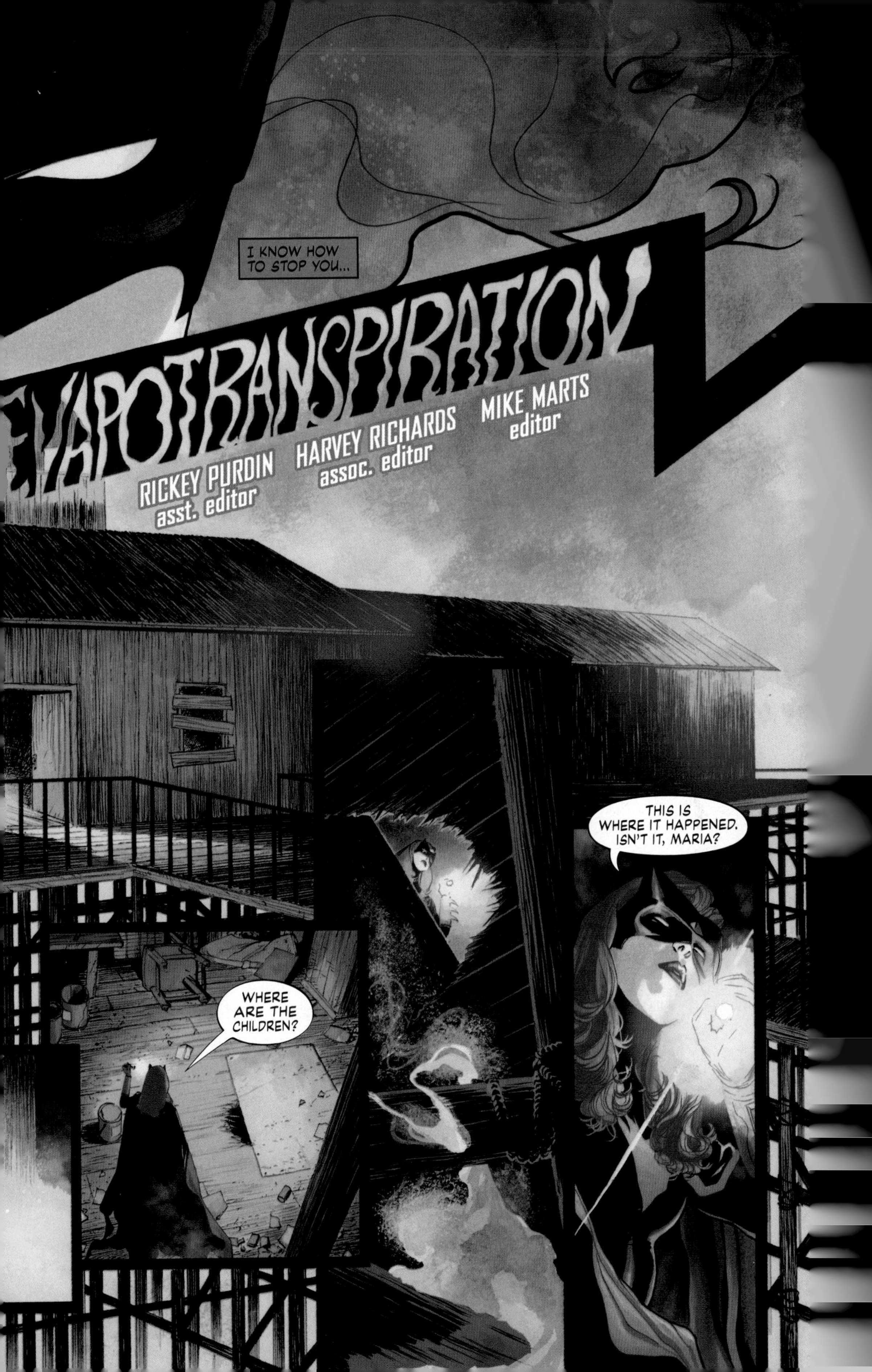

I KNOW HOW TO STOP YOU...
EVAPOTRANSPIRATION
RICKEY PURDIN asst. editor
HARVEY RICHARDS assoc. editor
MIKE MARTS editor
WHERE ARE THE CHILDREN?
THIS IS WHERE IT HAPPENED. ISN'T IT, MARIA?

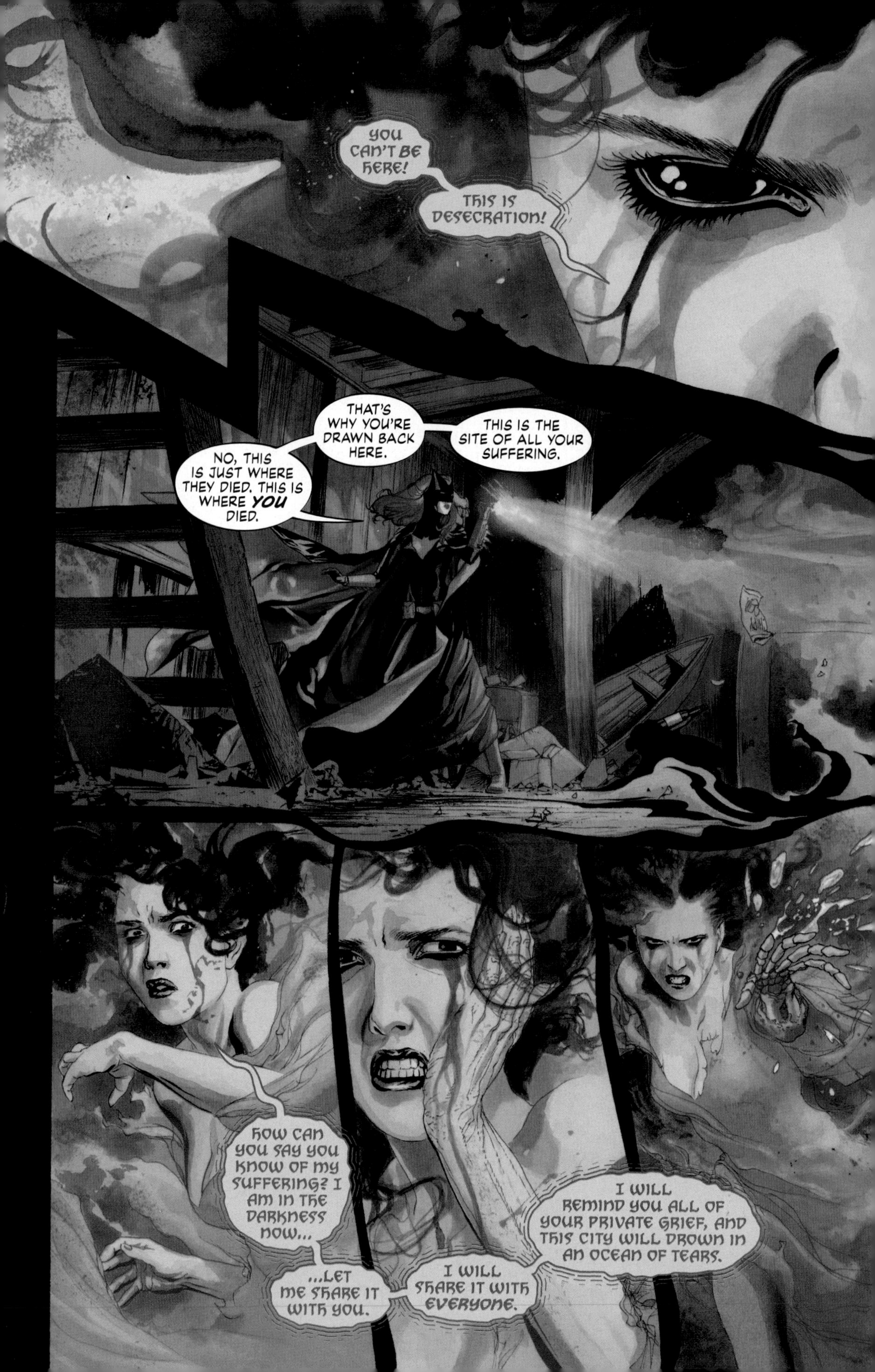
YOU CAN'T BE HERE!
THIS IS DESECRATION!
NO, THIS IS JUST WHERE THEY DIED. THIS IS WHERE YOU DIED.
THAT'S WHY YOU'RE DRAWN BACK HERE.
THIS IS THE SITE OF ALL YOUR SUFFERING.
HOW CAN YOU SAY YOU KNOW OF MY SUFFERING? I AM IN THE DARKNESS NOW...
...LET ME SHARE IT WITH YOU.
I WILL SHARE IT WITH EVERYONE.
I WILL REMIND YOU ALL OF YOUR PRIVATE GRIEF, AND THIS CITY WILL DROWN IN AN OCEAN OF TEARS.

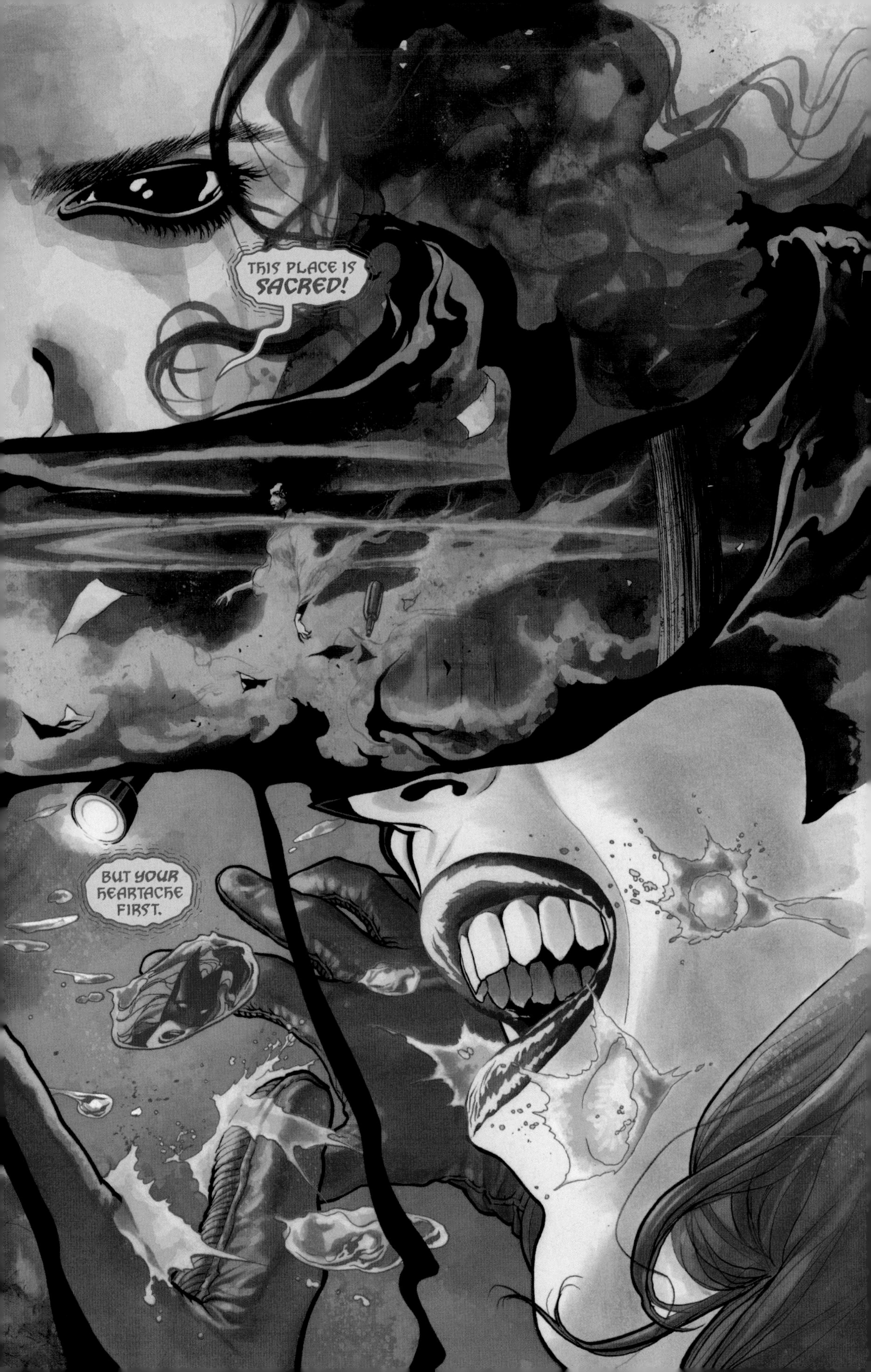
THIS PLACE IS SACRED!
BUT YOUR HEARTACHE FIRST.

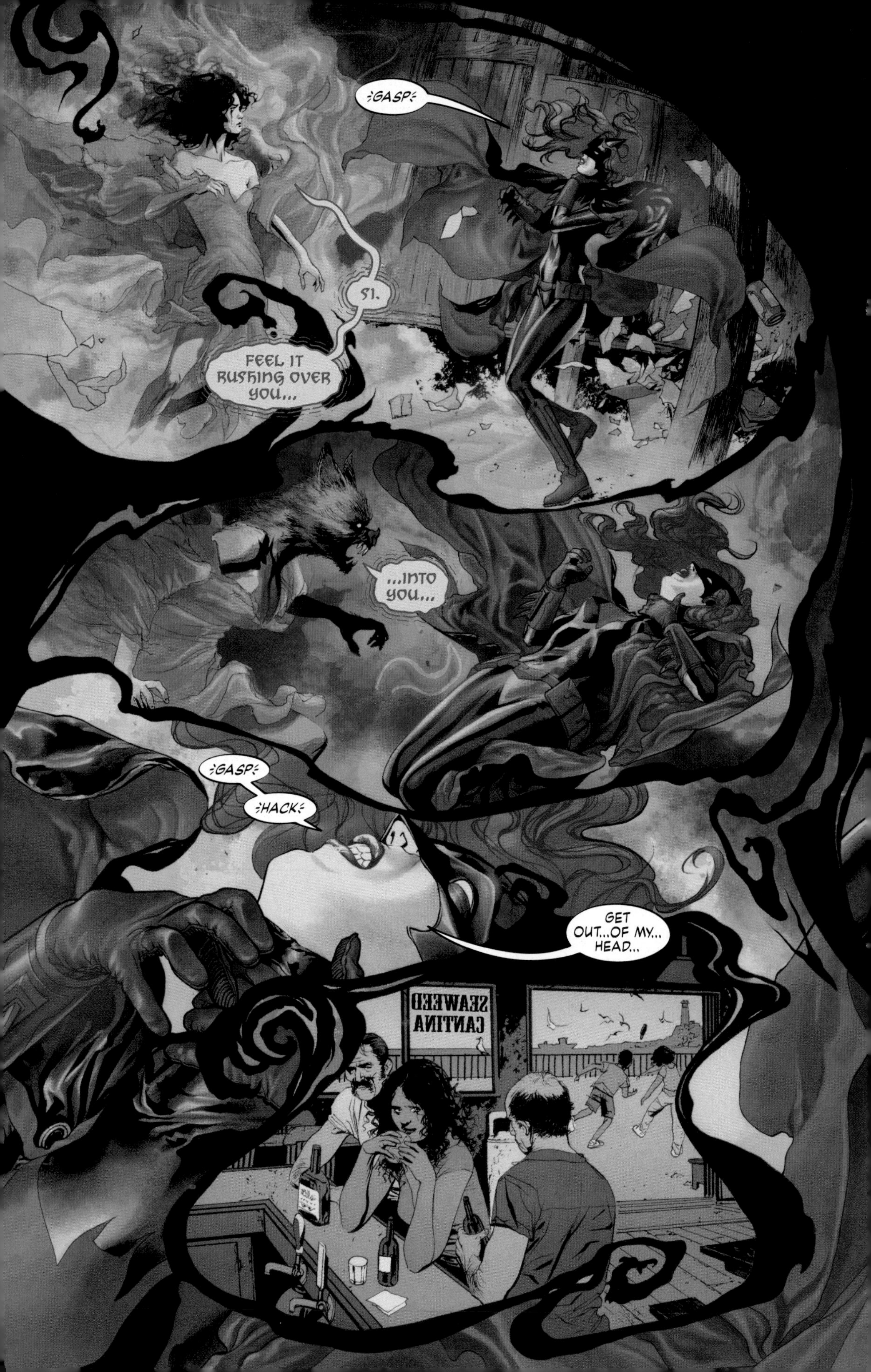
GASP
SI.
FEEL IT RUSHING OVER YOU...
...INTO YOU...
GASP
HACK
GET OUT...OF MY... HEAD...
SEAWEED CANTINA

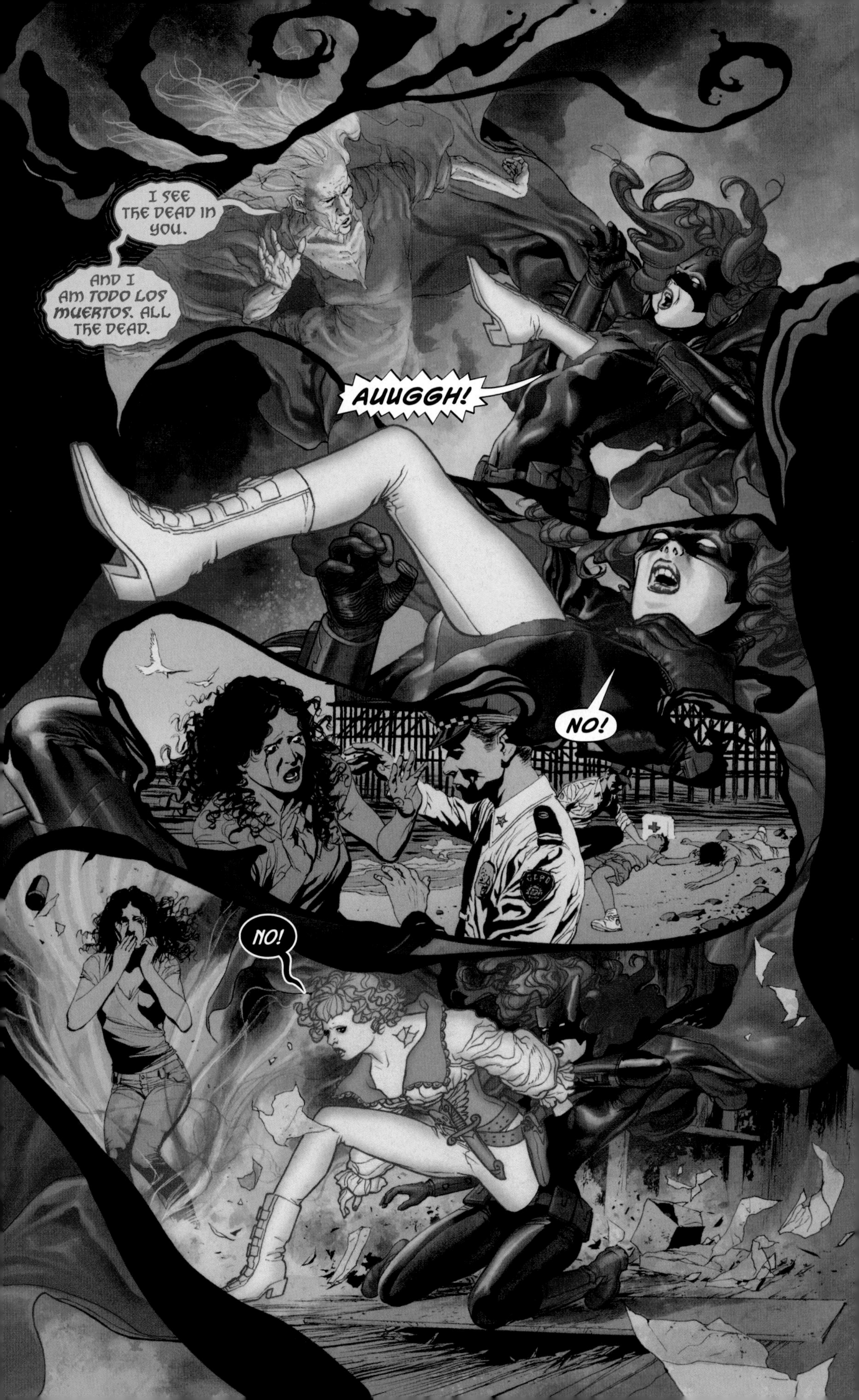
I SEE THE DEAD IN YOU.
AND I AM *TODO LOS MUERTOS.* ALL THE DEAD.
AUUGGH!
NO!
NO!

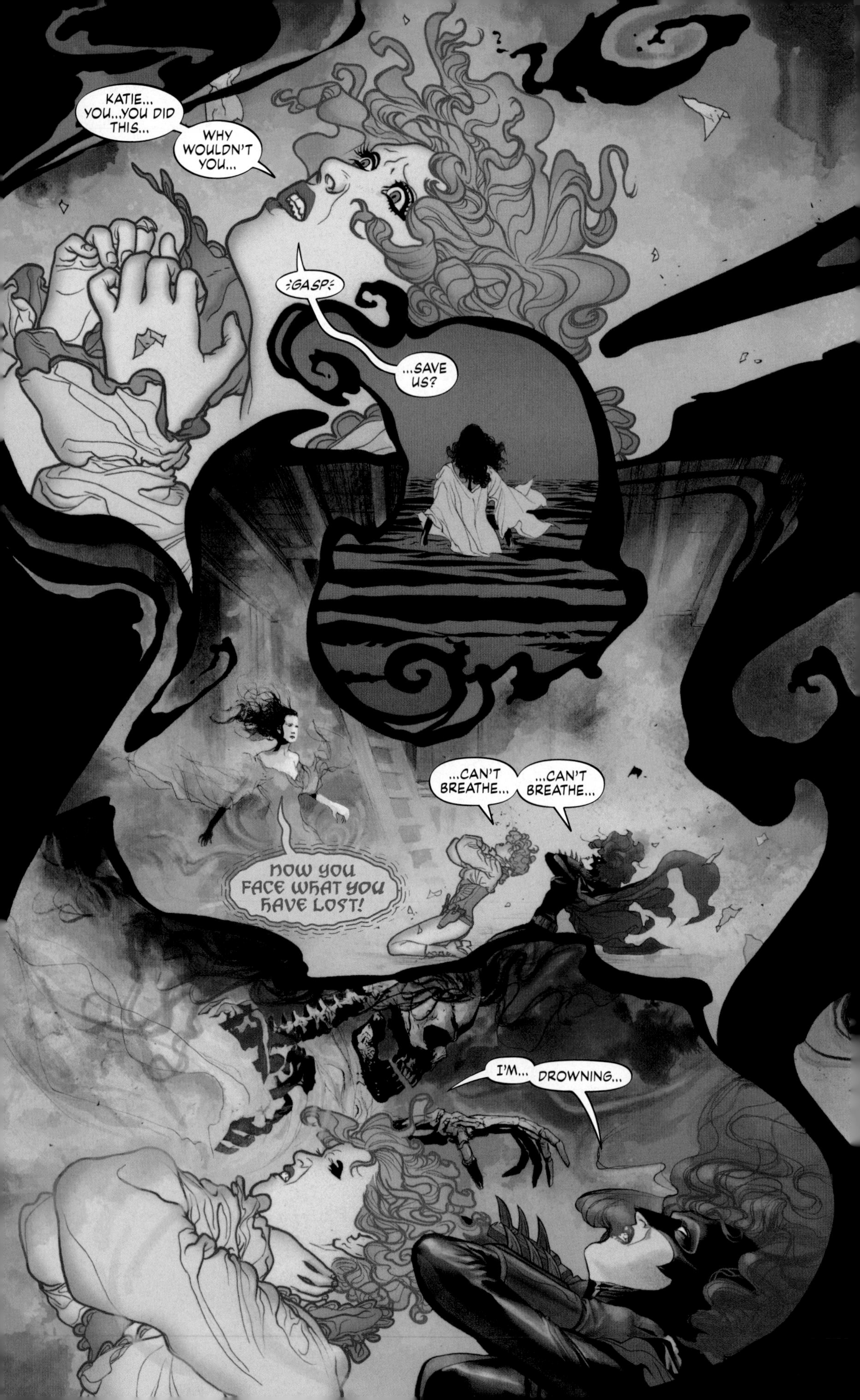
KATIE... YOU...YOU DID THIS...
WHY WOULDN'T YOU...
GASP
...SAVE US?
...CAN'T BREATHE...
...CAN'T BREATHE...
NOW YOU FACE WHAT YOU HAVE LOST!
I'M... DROWNING...

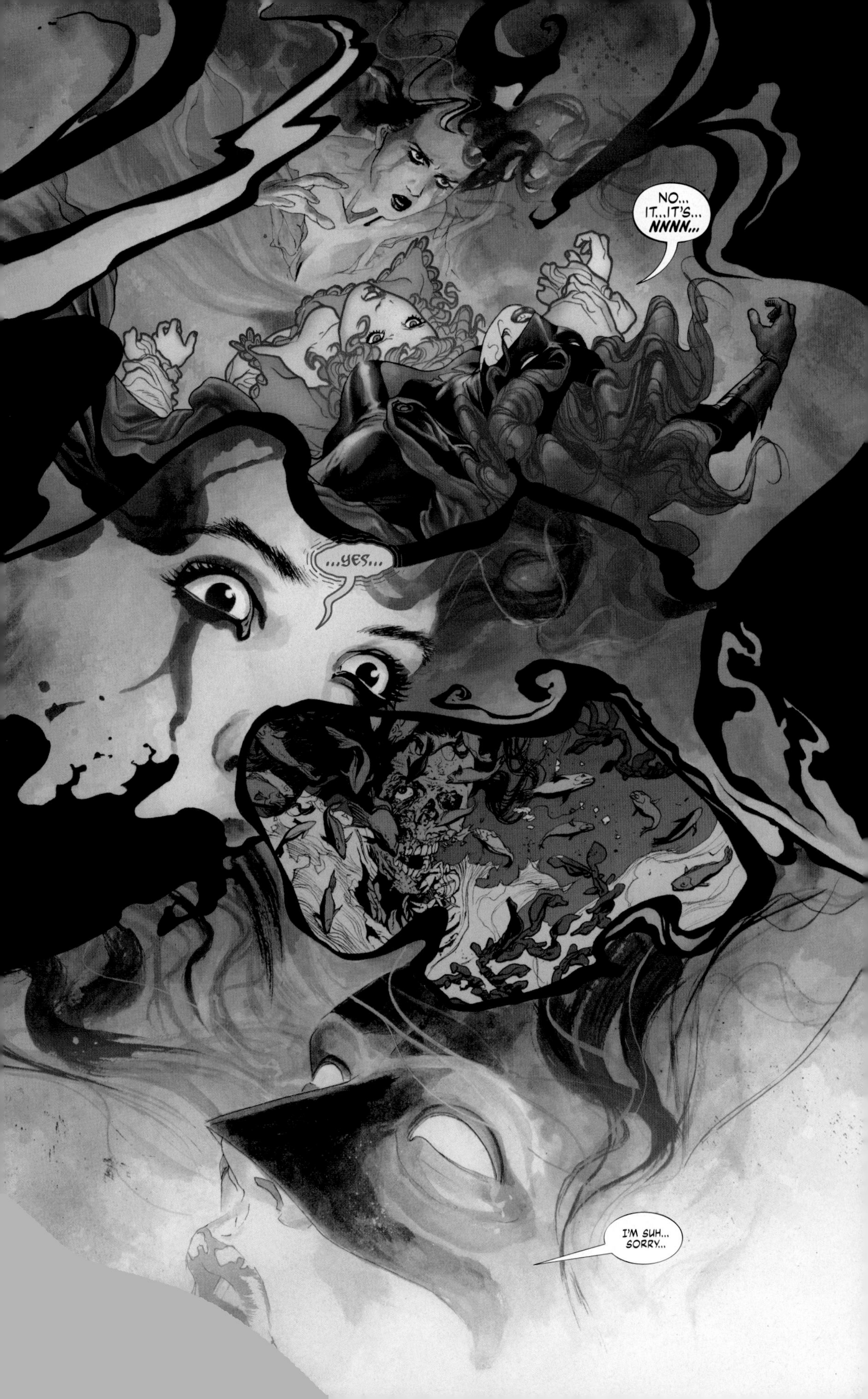
NO... IT...IT'S... NNNN...
...YES...
I'M SUH... SORRY...

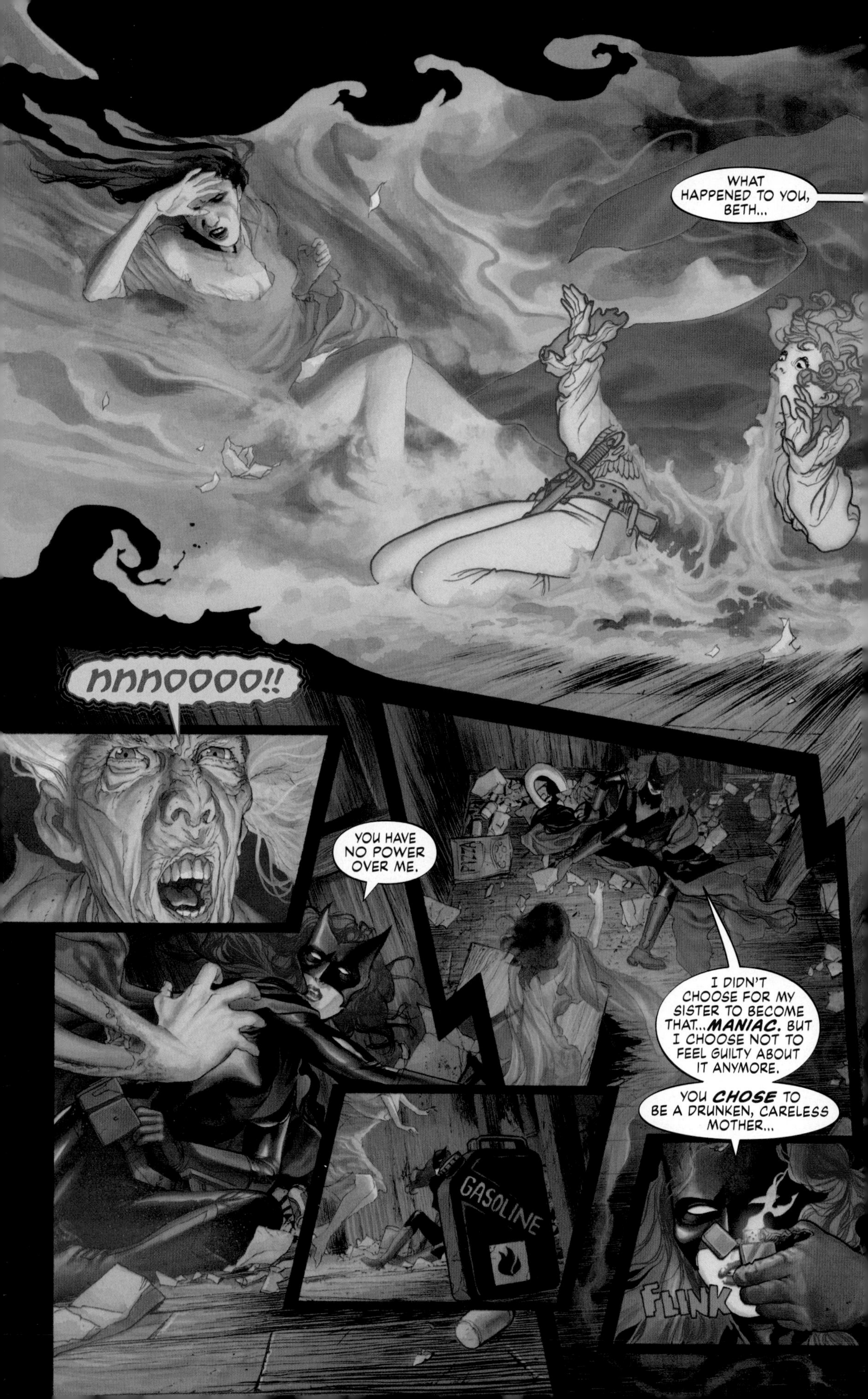
WHAT HAPPENED TO YOU, BETH...
nnnoooo!!
YOU HAVE NO POWER OVER ME.
I DIDN'T CHOOSE FOR MY SISTER TO BECOME THAT...MANIAC. BUT I CHOOSE NOT TO FEEL GUILTY ABOUT IT ANYMORE.
YOU CHOSE TO BE A DRUNKEN, CARELESS MOTHER...
GASOLINE
FLINK

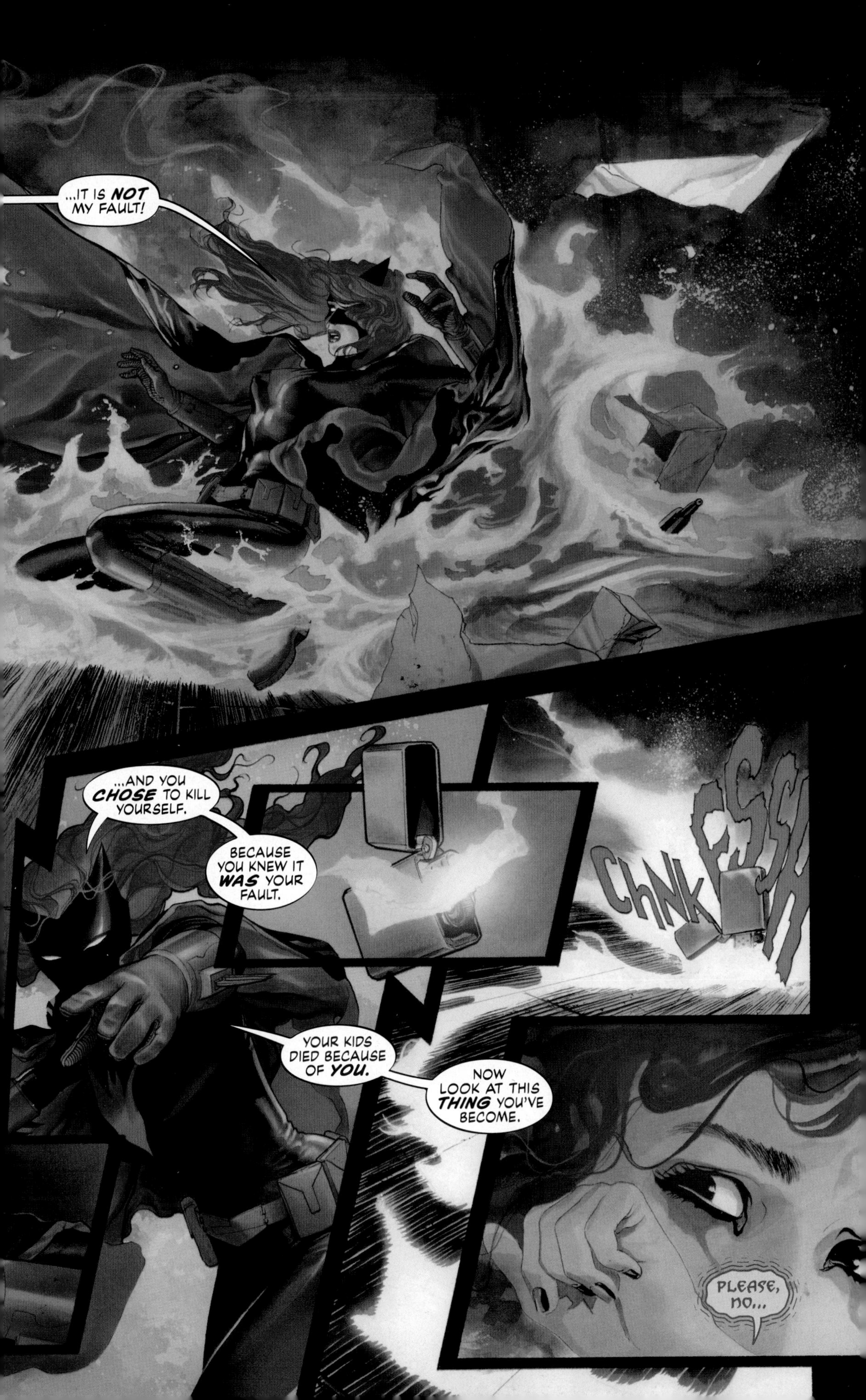
...IT IS NOT MY FAULT!
...AND YOU CHOSE TO KILL YOURSELF.
BECAUSE YOU KNEW IT WAS YOUR FAULT.
ChNK FSSH
YOUR KIDS DIED BECAUSE OF YOU.
NOW LOOK AT THIS THING YOU'VE BECOME.
PLEASE, NO...

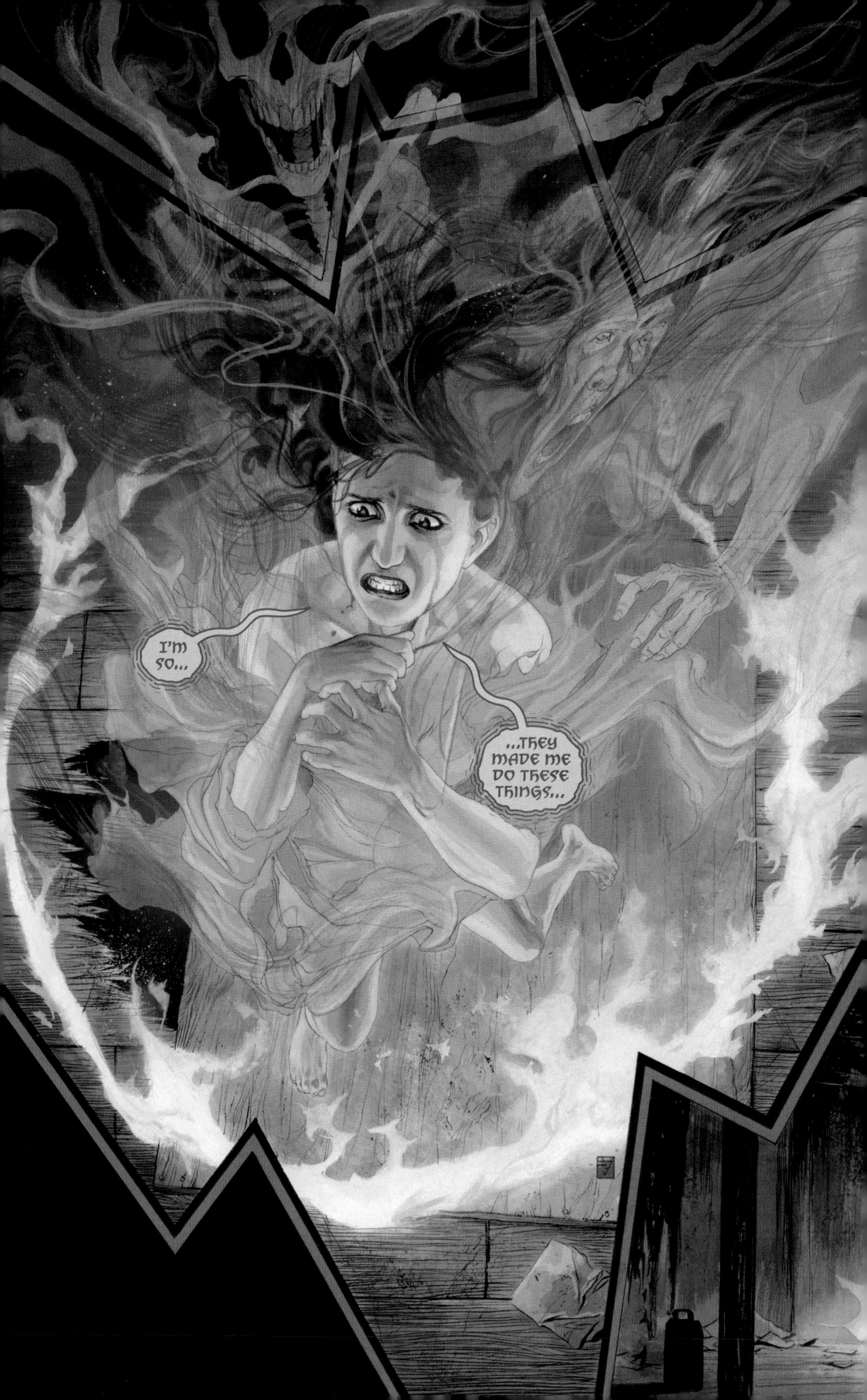
I'M SO...
...THEY MADE ME DO THESE THINGS...

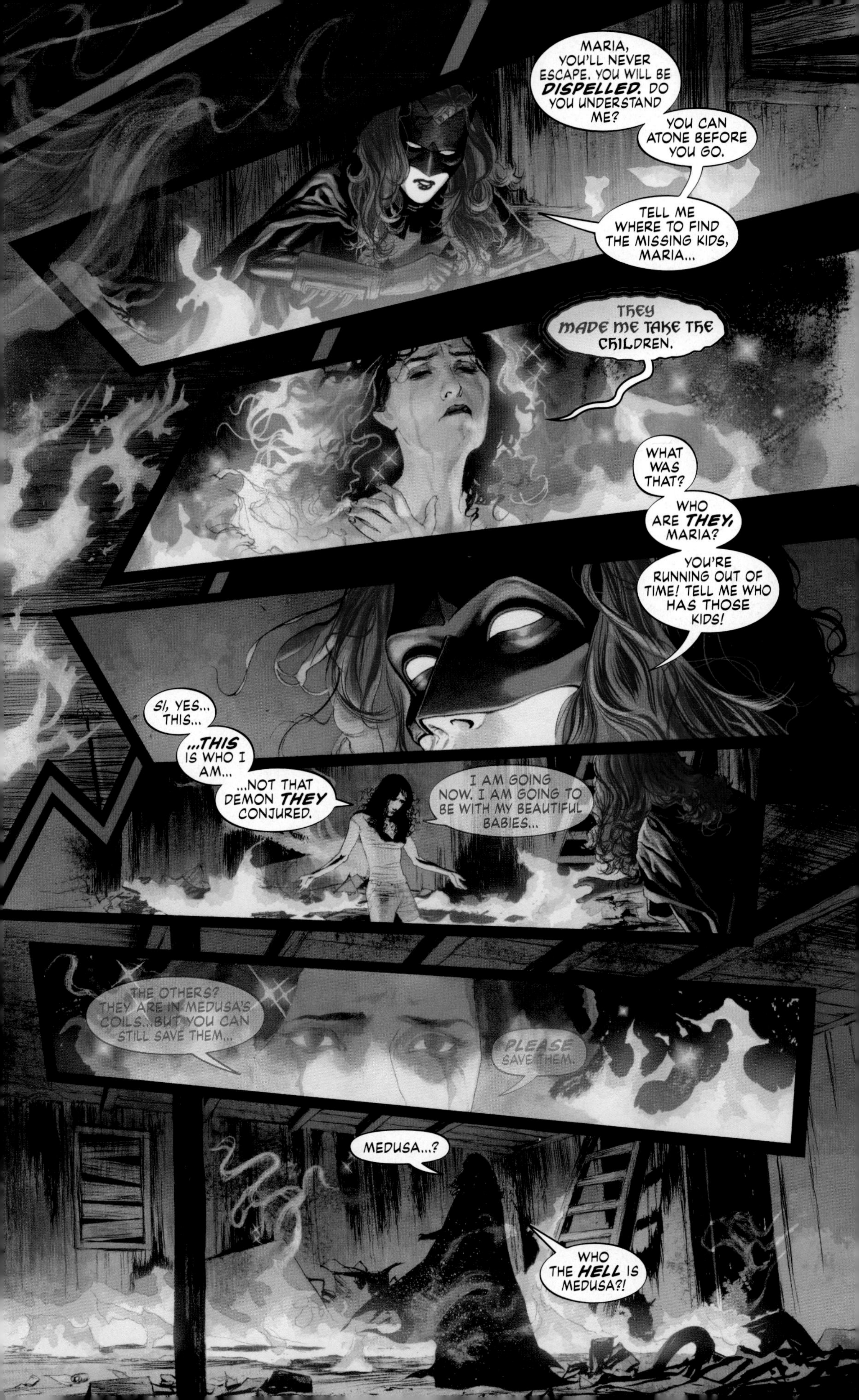
MARIA, YOU'LL NEVER ESCAPE. YOU WILL BE DISPELLED. DO YOU UNDERSTAND ME?
YOU CAN ATONE BEFORE YOU GO.
TELL ME WHERE TO FIND THE MISSING KIDS, MARIA...
THEY MADE ME TAKE THE CHILDREN.
WHAT WAS THAT?
WHO ARE THEY, MARIA?
YOU'RE RUNNING OUT OF TIME! TELL ME WHO HAS THOSE KIDS!
SI, YES... THIS...
...THIS IS WHO I AM...
...NOT THAT DEMON THEY CONJURED.
I AM GOING NOW. I AM GOING TO BE WITH MY BEAUTIFUL BABIES...
THE OTHERS? THEY ARE IN MEDUSA'S COILS...BUT YOU CAN STILL SAVE THEM...
PLEASE SAVE THEM.
MEDUSA...?
WHO THE HELL IS MEDUSA?!

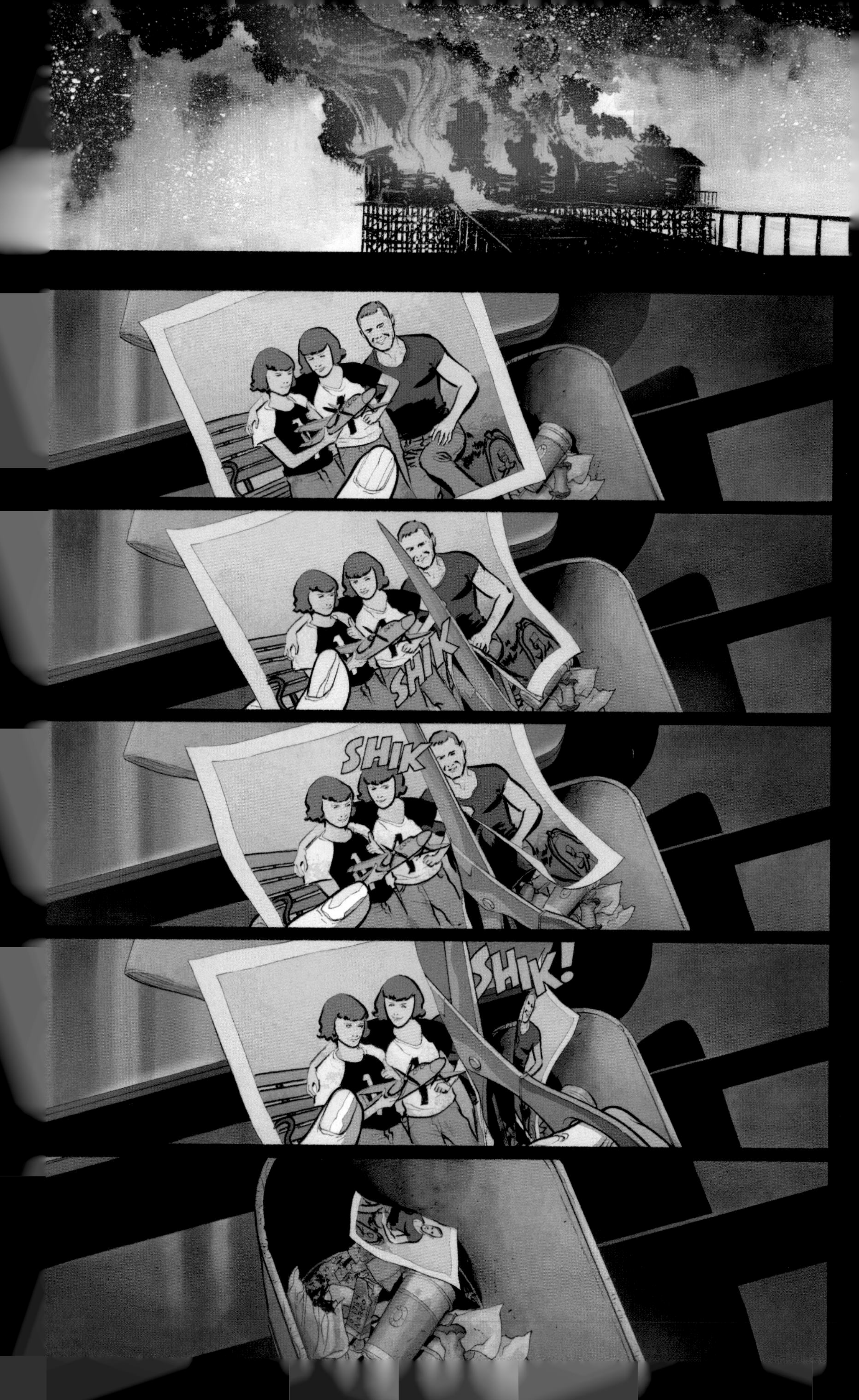
SHIK
SHIK
SHIK!

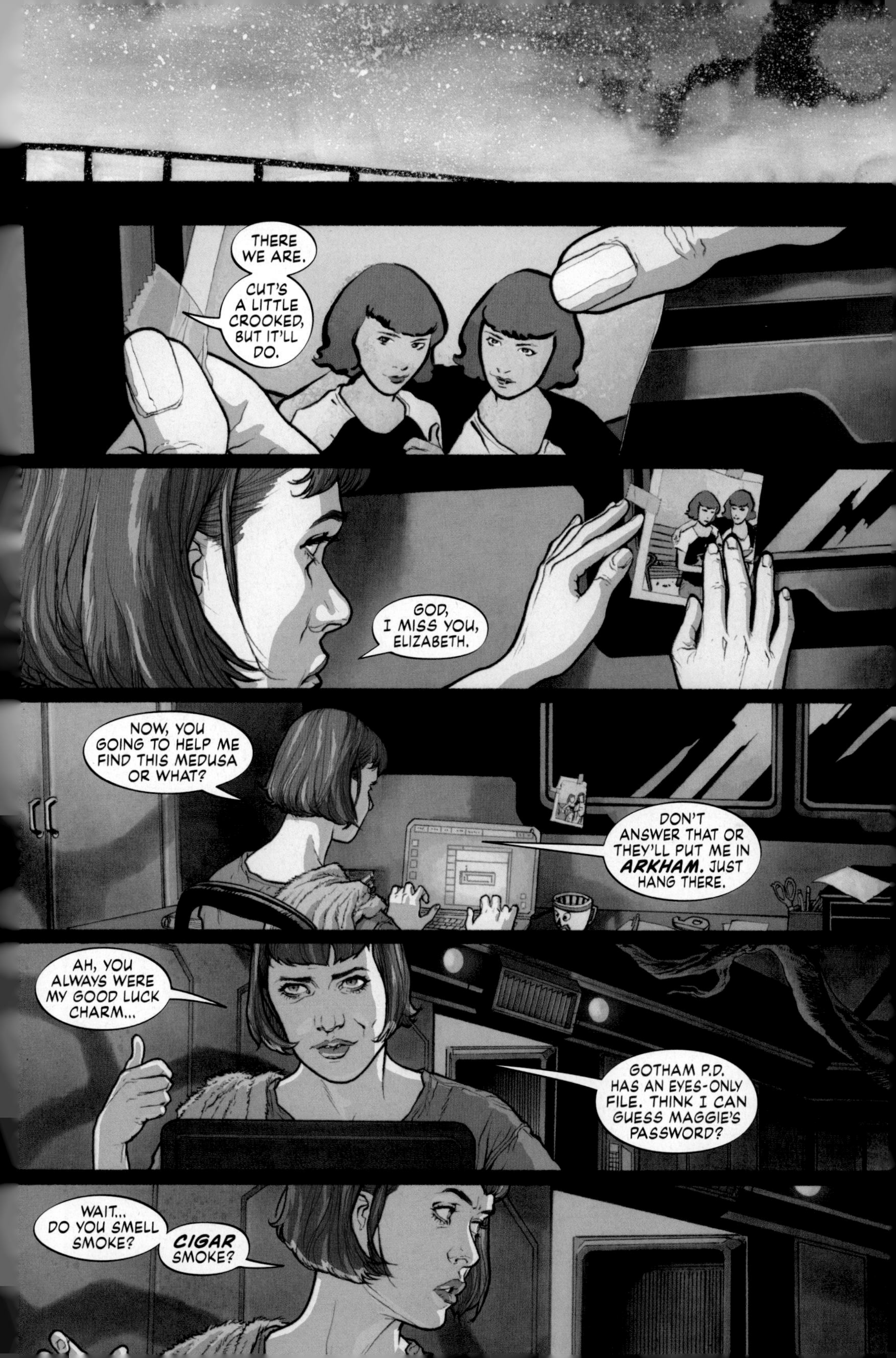
THERE WE ARE.
CUT'S A LITTLE CROOKED, BUT IT'LL DO.
GOD, I MISS YOU, ELIZABETH.
NOW, YOU GOING TO HELP ME FIND THIS MEDUSA OR WHAT?
DON'T ANSWER THAT OR THEY'LL PUT ME IN ARKHAM. JUST HANG THERE.
AH, YOU ALWAYS WERE MY GOOD LUCK CHARM...
GOTHAM P.D. HAS AN EYES-ONLY FILE. THINK I CAN GUESS MAGGIE'S PASSWORD?
WAIT... DO YOU SMELL SMOKE?
CIGAR SMOKE?

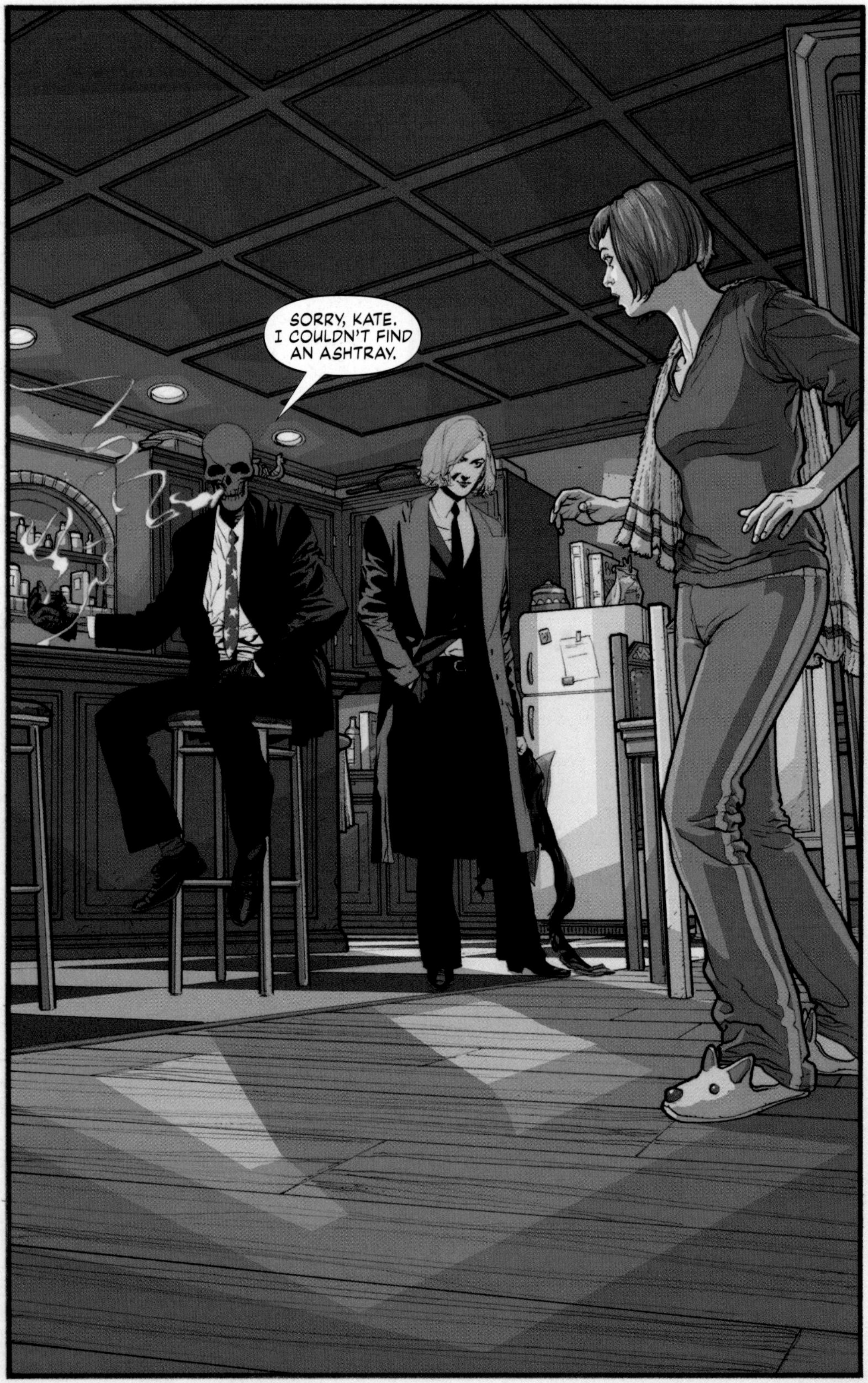
SORRY, KATE. I COULDN'T FIND AN ASHTRAY.

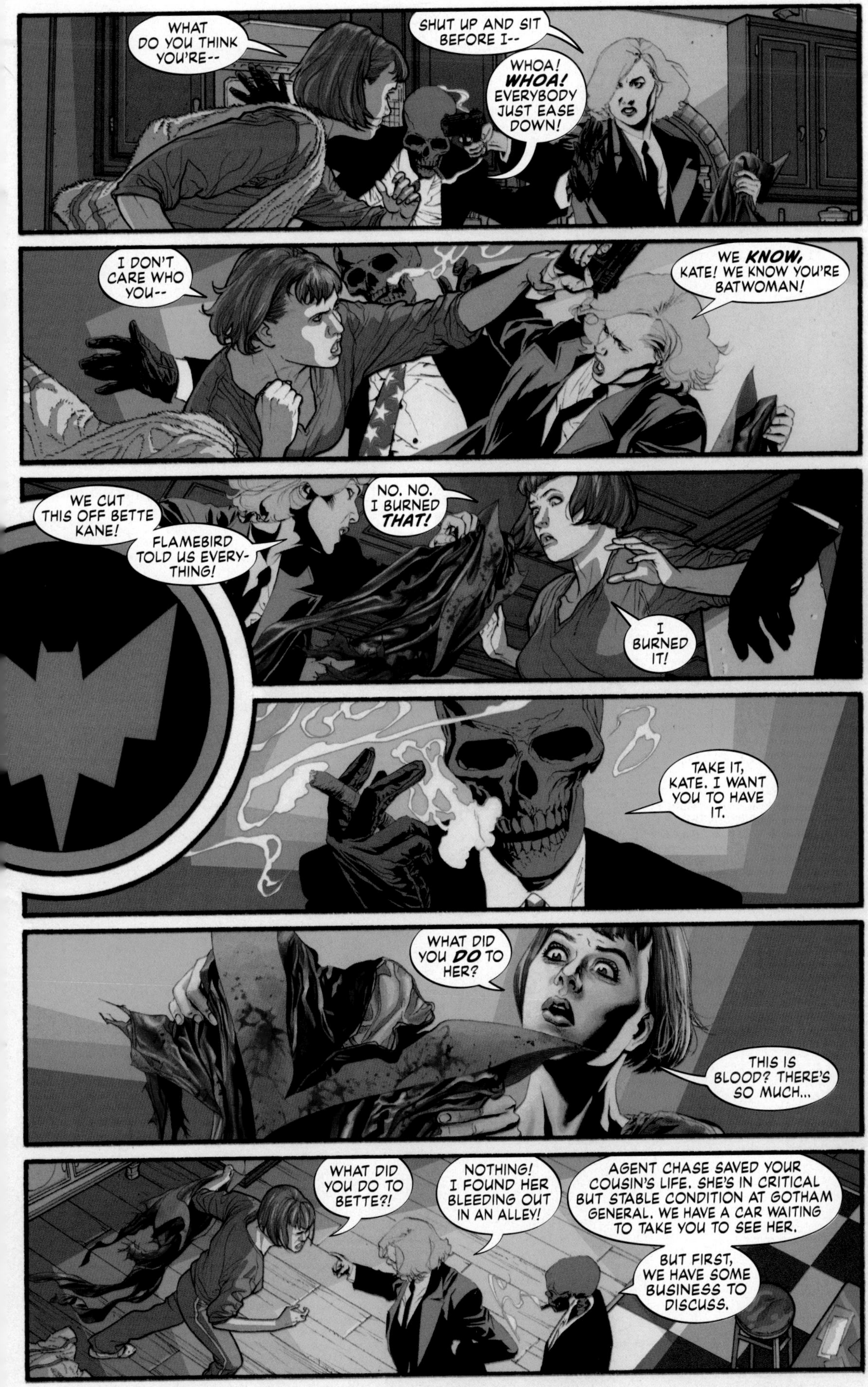
WHAT DO YOU THINK YOU'RE--
SHUT UP AND SIT BEFORE I--
WHOA! **WHOA!** EVERYBODY JUST EASE DOWN!
I DON'T CARE WHO YOU--
WE **KNOW,** KATE! WE KNOW YOU'RE BATWOMAN!
WE CUT THIS OFF BETTE KANE!
FLAMEBIRD TOLD US EVERY-THING!
NO. NO. I BURNED **THAT!**
I BURNED IT!
TAKE IT, KATE. I WANT YOU TO HAVE IT.
WHAT DID YOU **DO** TO HER?
THIS IS BLOOD? THERE'S SO MUCH...
WHAT DID YOU DO TO BETTE?!
NOTHING! I FOUND HER BLEEDING OUT IN AN ALLEY!
AGENT CHASE SAVED YOUR COUSIN'S LIFE. SHE'S IN CRITICAL BUT STABLE CONDITION AT GOTHAM GENERAL. WE HAVE A CAR WAITING TO TAKE YOU TO SEE HER.
BUT FIRST, WE HAVE SOME BUSINESS TO DISCUSS.

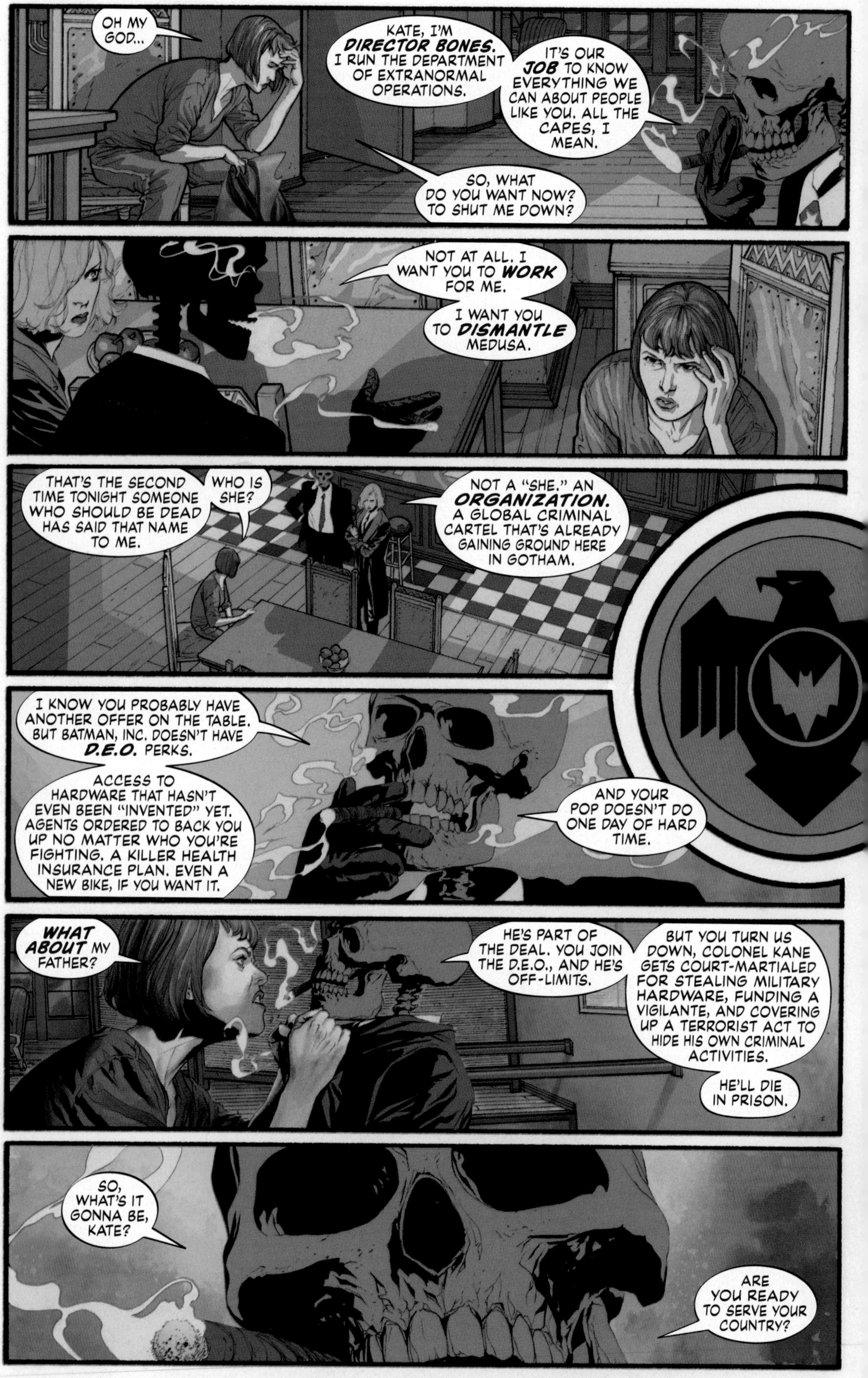
OH MY GOD...
KATE, I'M DIRECTOR BONES. I RUN THE DEPARTMENT OF EXTRANORMAL OPERATIONS.
IT'S OUR JOB TO KNOW EVERYTHING WE CAN ABOUT PEOPLE LIKE YOU. ALL THE CAPES, I MEAN.
SO, WHAT DO YOU WANT NOW? TO SHUT ME DOWN?
NOT AT ALL. I WANT YOU TO WORK FOR ME.
I WANT YOU TO DISMANTLE MEDUSA.
WHO IS SHE?
THAT'S THE SECOND TIME TONIGHT SOMEONE WHO SHOULD BE DEAD HAS SAID THAT NAME TO ME.
NOT A "SHE." AN ORGANIZATION. A GLOBAL CRIMINAL CARTEL THAT'S ALREADY GAINING GROUND HERE IN GOTHAM.
I KNOW YOU PROBABLY HAVE ANOTHER OFFER ON THE TABLE. BUT BATMAN, INC. DOESN'T HAVE D.E.O. PERKS.
ACCESS TO HARDWARE THAT HASN'T EVEN BEEN "INVENTED" YET. AGENTS ORDERED TO BACK YOU UP NO MATTER WHO YOU'RE FIGHTING. A KILLER HEALTH INSURANCE PLAN. EVEN A NEW BIKE, IF YOU WANT IT.
AND YOUR POP DOESN'T DO ONE DAY OF HARD TIME.
WHAT ABOUT MY FATHER?
HE'S PART OF THE DEAL. YOU JOIN THE D.E.O., AND HE'S OFF-LIMITS.
BUT YOU TURN US DOWN, COLONEL KANE GETS COURT-MARTIALED FOR STEALING MILITARY HARDWARE, FUNDING A VIGILANTE, AND COVERING UP A TERRORIST ACT TO HIDE HIS OWN CRIMINAL ACTIVITIES.
HE'LL DIE IN PRISON.
SO, WHAT'S IT GONNA BE, KATE?
ARE YOU READY TO SERVE YOUR COUNTRY?

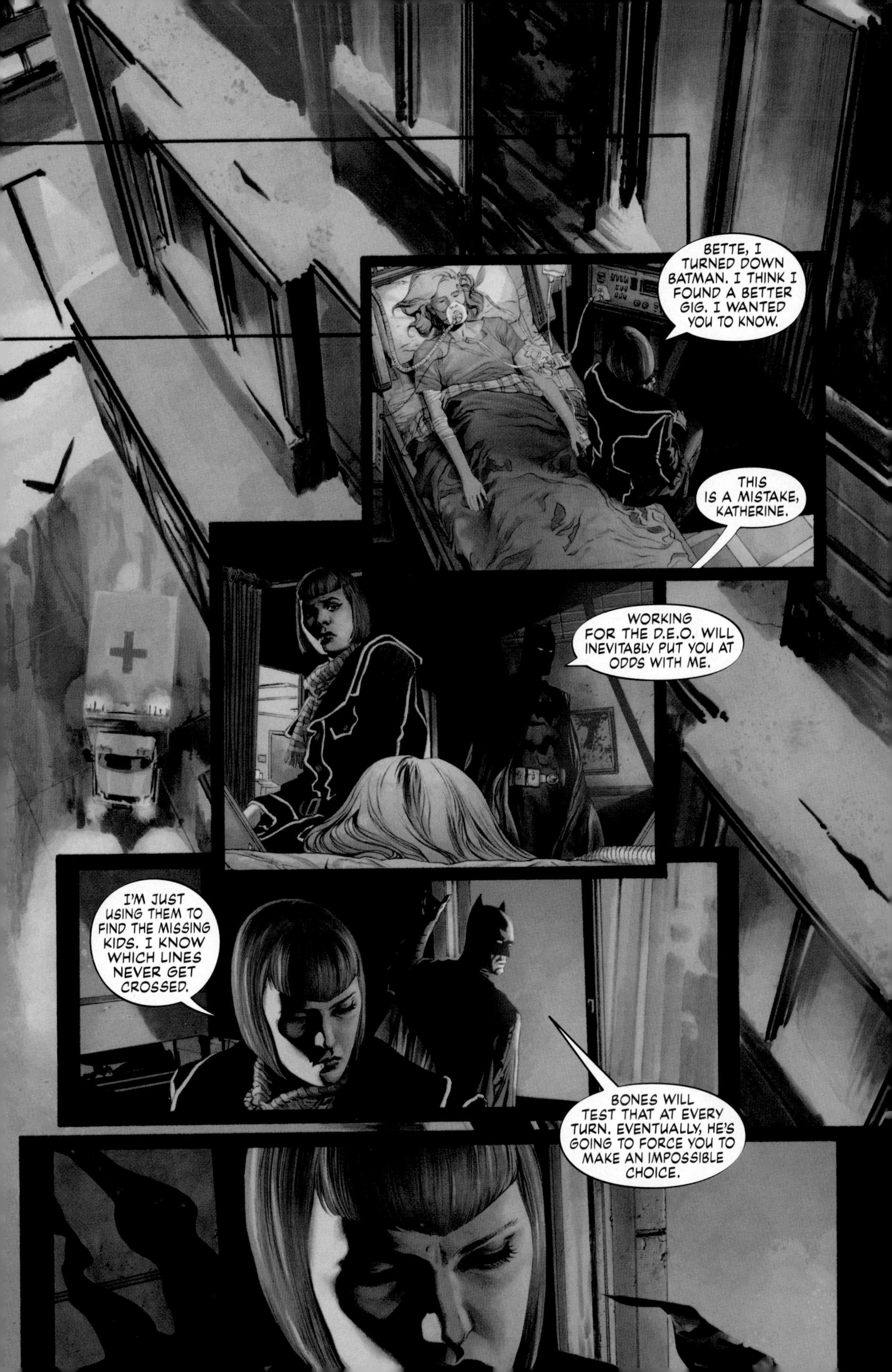
BETTE, I TURNED DOWN BATMAN. I THINK I FOUND A BETTER GIG. I WANTED YOU TO KNOW.
THIS IS A MISTAKE, KATHERINE.
WORKING FOR THE D.E.O. WILL INEVITABLY PUT YOU AT ODDS WITH ME.
I'M JUST USING THEM TO FIND THE MISSING KIDS. I KNOW WHICH LINES NEVER GET CROSSED.
BONES WILL TEST THAT AT EVERY TURN. EVENTUALLY, HE'S GOING TO FORCE YOU TO MAKE AN IMPOSSIBLE CHOICE.

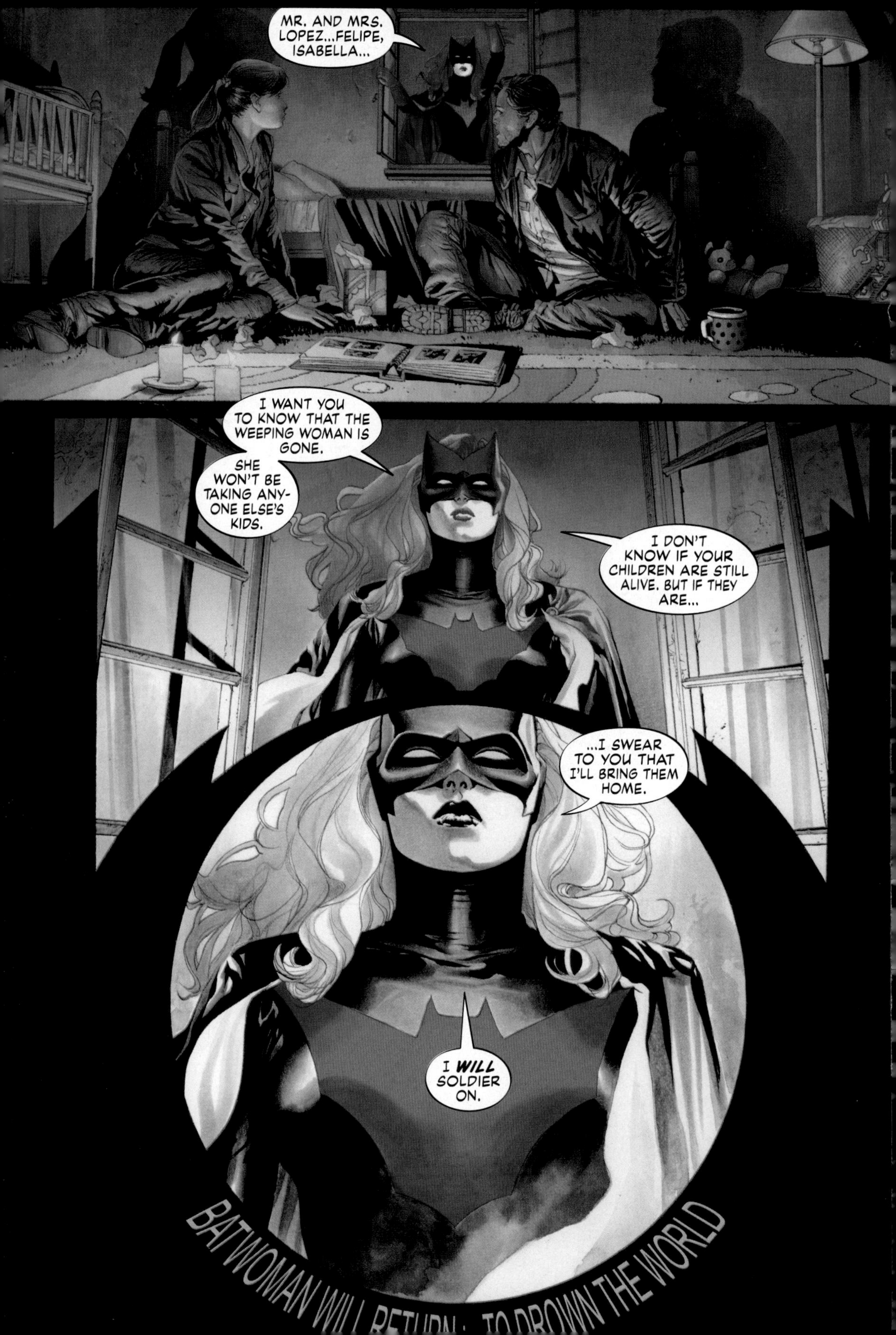
MR. AND MRS. LOPEZ...FELIPE, ISABELLA...
I WANT YOU TO KNOW THAT THE WEEPING WOMAN IS GONE.
SHE WON'T BE TAKING ANY-ONE ELSE'S KIDS.
I DON'T KNOW IF YOUR CHILDREN ARE STILL ALIVE. BUT IF THEY ARE...
...I SWEAR TO YOU THAT I'LL BRING THEM HOME.
I ***WILL*** SOLDIER ON.
BATWOMAN WILL RETURN... TO DROWN THE WORLD

BATWOMAN

ART BY J.H. WILLIAMS III SCRIPT BY J.H. WILLIAMS III & W. HADEN BLACKMAN

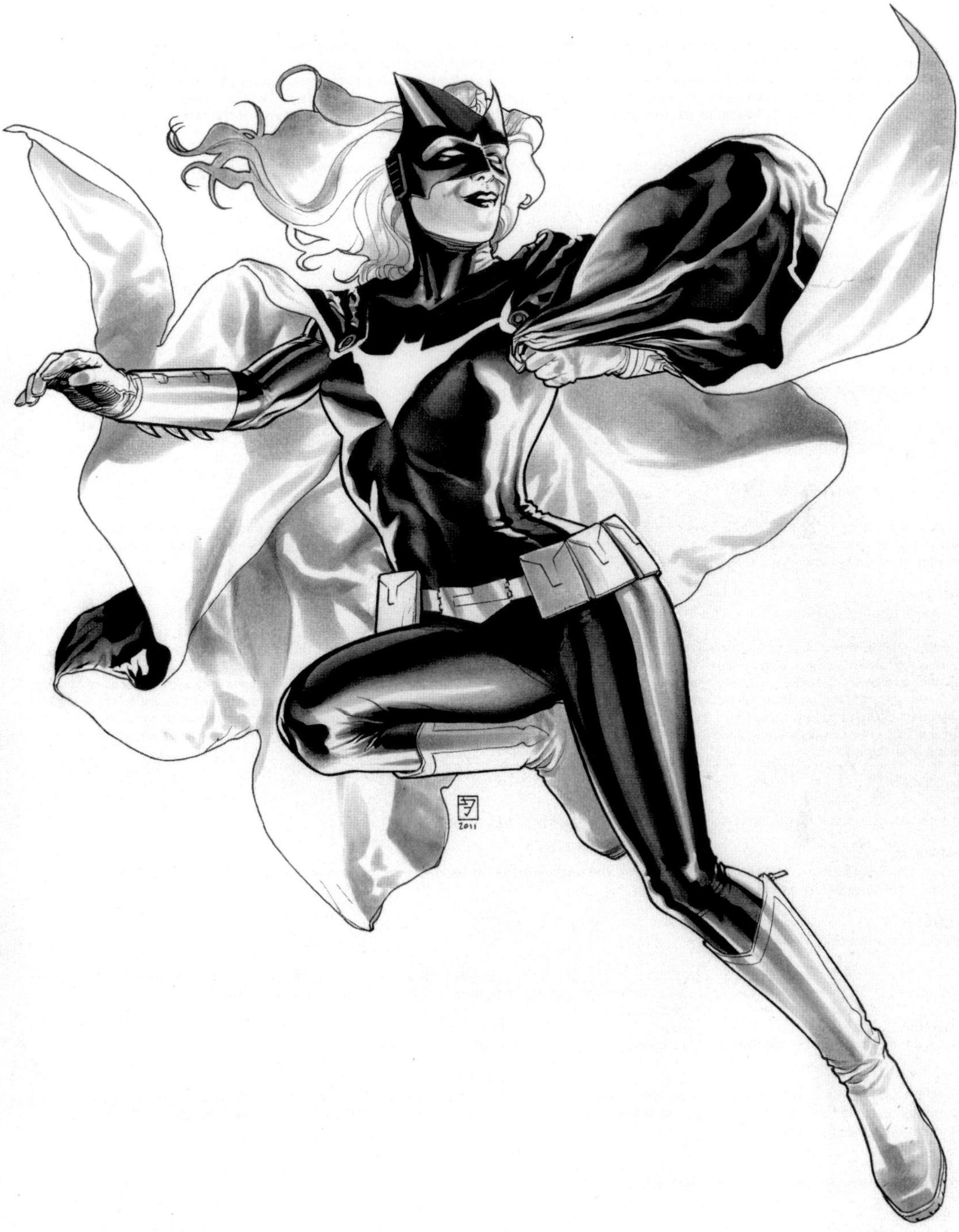

This image of Batwoman, illustrated by J.H. Williams III, was used for a DC Universe mural which is displayed in the DC Entertainment offices.

Script excerpt from BATWOMAN #2 by W. Haden Blackman and J.H. Williams III.

PAGE FOURTEEN/FIFTEEN (9 Panels)

The art here is more in style of the Batwoman look with shadows and textures.

Panel 5 is a central image across both pages, with the conversations happening in other panels surrounding it. So the main image of the entire scene runs through the middle of the spread from left to right. Panels 1, 2, and 3 are placed along the left side. Panel 5 is the largest panel on the page, in the middle of the spread, and silent, with two inset panels, these being panels 4 and 6. Panels 7, 8 and 9 run down the right side of the spread. So when Maggie's first line in panel 6 is read, it becomes two things: response to Chase, and a comment on the scene which this panel is inset, the full shot of all the dead.

Panel 5 is also the establishing shot of the location. Guttersnipe Gardens is basically a homeless encampment in the ruins of an old enclosed arboretum or giant greenhouse, perhaps something built for a World's Fair long ago. Now, it's just a rusting skeletal structure, with only a third of its windows still intact (but enough that it provides some shelter from the elements if you put up your tent or cardboard box in the right place). It's overgrown with leafless trees, mosses, and dead hanging plants. We can see it's still winter — there's snow on the ground, but only in patches and drifts (again to suggest that whatever remains of the windows and other parts of the structure offer some barest form of shelter).

Panel 1. Close-up of a puddle of blood in dirty looking snow, with spent bullet shell casings everywhere. We can see Chase's shoes as her feet barely touch the bloodied area of snow.

1-CHASE (OP):
Is there anywhere in Gotham that *doesn't* have bloodstains?

Panel 2. Semi-close on Chase, Bullock, and Maggie. We can't see what they're looking at yet, but we can see their expressions: Chase is annoyed; Bullock is his usual grumpy self; and Maggie is professional, keeping any emotions she might be feeling in check.

2-CHASE:
It's going to take days for my agents to collect all the shell casings.

3-BULLOCK:
At least no one got *snatched*, huh?

Panel 3. Chase, holding up a severed hand in an evidence bag, showing this to Bullock. Her body language and expression are a little aggressive, sarcastic — as if she's irritated with Bullock for not thinking things through a bit more.

4-CHASE:
Oh really? Well, *this* doesn't belong to any of the victims.

Panel 4. Inset into the giant panel 5. One of the DEO agents is kneeling next to a were-beast. We can't see the details of the were-beast here — just an arm or a tentacle. We can see the agent is taking tissue samples from the creature's appendage. The camera is low angled, looking up at Chase and Maggie as they look down at the agent. Chase is gesturing towards the corpse.

5-CHASE:
You know about these things?

Panel 5. Establishing shot of Guttersnipe Gardens (see above). In addition to the physical location described above, we can now see that there's a makeshift camp in the arboretum made up of tents, trash barrels for fires, and other signs of derelicts squatting. Some of the barrels have been knocked over, and there should be lots of evidence of a big fight having recently occurred here. The corpses of several were-beasts and Medusa thugs are strewn about. DEO agents are everywhere — they've clearly taken control of the crime scene. They are collecting clues, studying the bodies, taking photographs and notes. Chase, Maggie, and Bullock are in the center of the action. If we can see this from this angle Bullock is pissed, maybe arms crossed, defensive. Batwoman can be seen mixing into the details of the scene, hiding and spying.

NO COPY

Panel 6. Inset into the giant panel 4. The focus is on Maggie with Chase behind her.

6-MAGGIE:
In Gotham, there's the underworld and then there's the *underworld*. The were-beasts belong to the latter. They're an offshoot of the Religion of Crime led by a fanatic named Abbott.

7-CHASE:
I could have read that on-line.

Panel 7. Focus on Chase as she responds further to Maggie, Bullock in the Background with his arms crossed, clearly annoyed with the DEO stepping on their turf. In the shadowy structure we can see indications of Batwoman's cape as she spies.

8-CHASE:
I'll do you one better. Our snitches say this legion of freaks is at war with a rival gang.

Panel 8. Now Maggie is kneeling next to another body — one of the Medusa thugs, his stomach has been ripped open violently. We should be able to clearly see the Medusa symbol — a snake crest of some kind. Possibly Chase is nearby. Maggie is pointing/ indicating towards the symbol.

9-MAGGIE:
Well, it *is* Gotham. So, yeah, that's probably accurate.

10-MAGGIE:
But these uniforms... *these* I don't recognize.

Panel 9. Close on Maggie, still kneeling next to the body, but looking grim, the weight of everything hitting her. Chase and Bullock dark in the background.

11-MAGGIE:
Just what we need... *another* new gang.

12-CHASE:
You think you know what happened here?

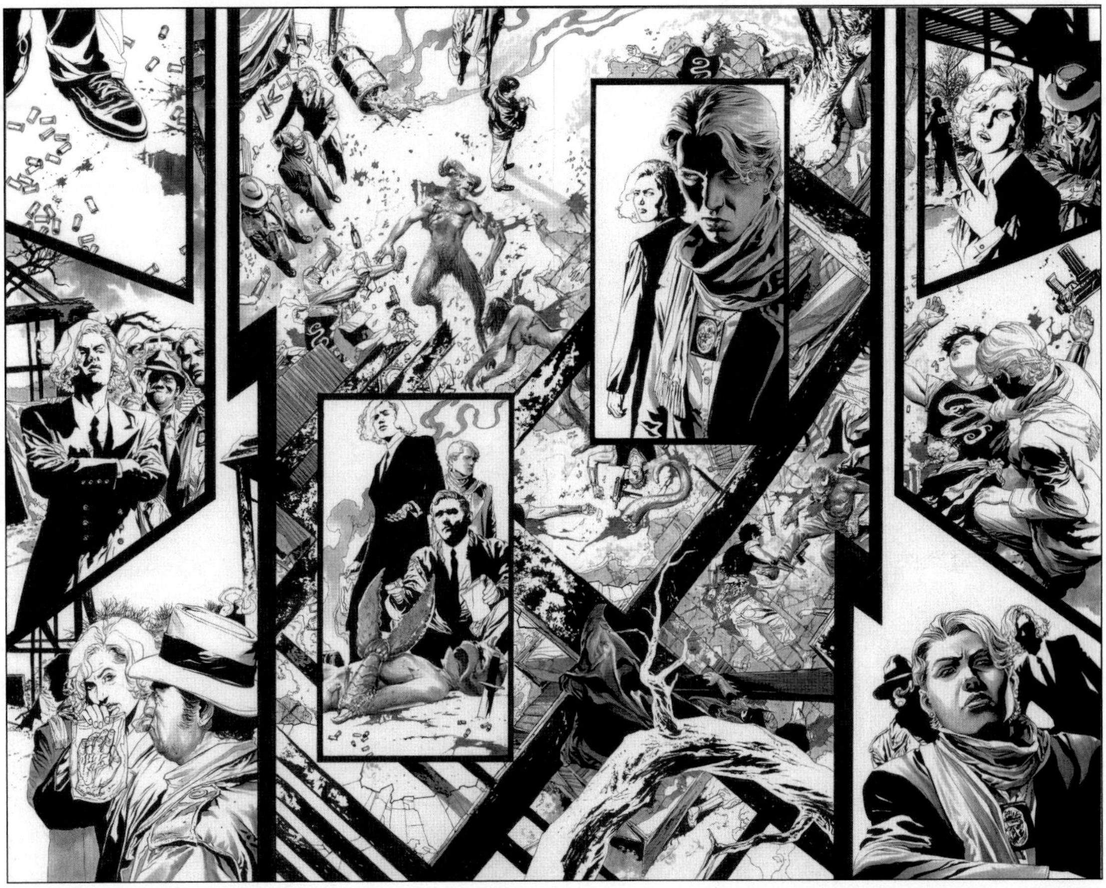

Black and white art by J.H. Williams III from BATWOMAN #2 pages 14-15 (above) and pages 16-17 (below).

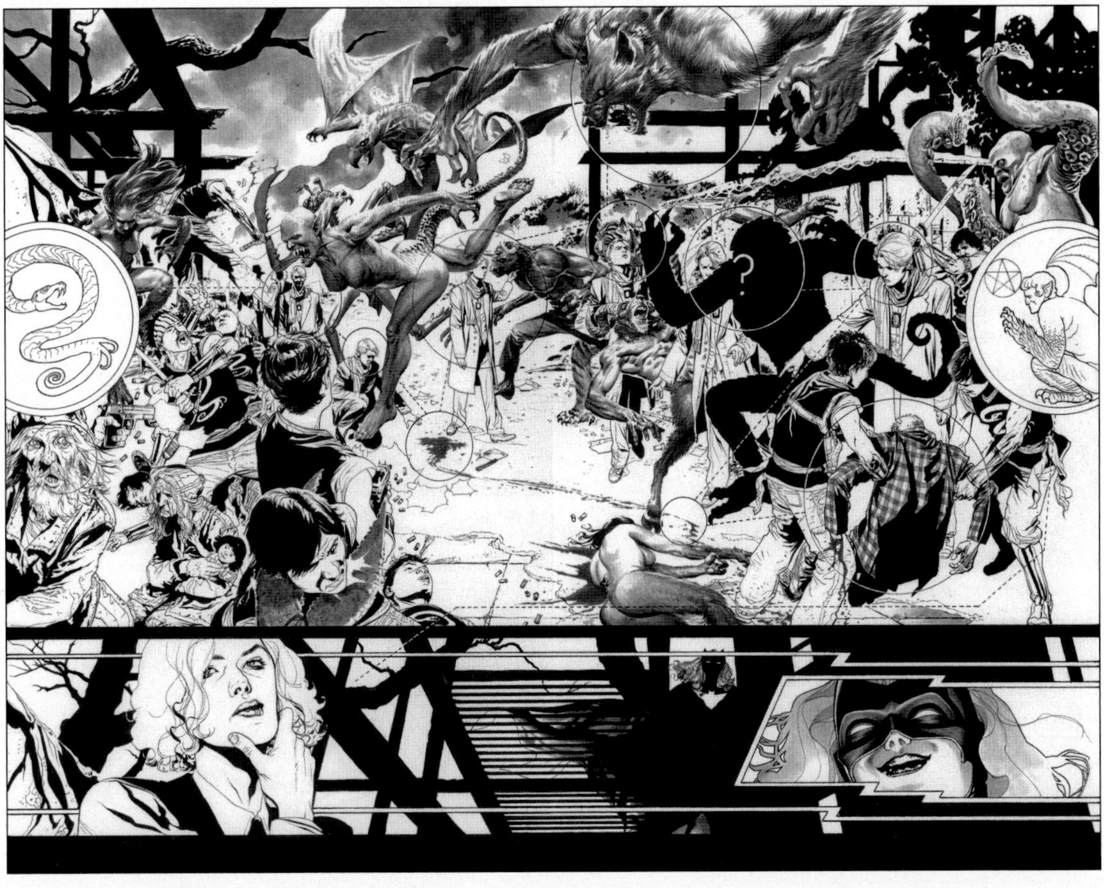

Script excerpt from BATWOMAN #2 by W. Haden Blackman and J.H. Williams III.

PAGE SIXTEEN/SEVENTEEN (8 Panels)

The were-beast cultists here will be drawn and rendered like we've shown them before in Detective Comics (Batwoman: Elegy).

Most of this page is a big widescreen spread running across 2/3rds of the pages. It shows the fight between the were-beasts and Medusa's thugs, all happening at once, as if frozen in time. The Medusa thugs are mostly arranged in the middle and left side of the spread. Some were-beasts are crashing through windows on the right side of the spread, while another group is dropping into the center of the spread from above. Throughout the spread, Medusa thugs are gunning down were-beasts. In the center of the spread, the were-beasts are ripping into the thugs. We can also see two Medusa thugs, their backs largely to us, dragging a mysterious figure towards the bottom of the panel. The figure is a mentally ill homeless guy who has lost his left hand (chopped off), and who will eventually become the Hook. This man is actually Rush from all the way back in Detective Comics 854 page 1. But all of these details are somewhat unknown to us right now and we can't see much about him here, his back to us as Medusa things drag him towards us and about to go off panel... trailing blood from his wound. Finally, standing between the retreating Medusa thugs dragging the soon-to-be-Hook and the weres is a massive shadowy figure (Killer Croc, but we don't want the reader to know that because Chase and Maggie don't know yet — he should just be a huge shadow). His back is to us, and he's ripping apart one of the weres. He's surrounded by were corpses.

Maggie is walking through the scene like it's a big diorama, calling out specific moments in the fight (again, all seeming to happen at once in this panel, even though they might have occurred at different points in time during the actual fight). She's starting at the top left of the panel, making her way across towards the bottom right. Panels 1-5 call out what Maggie is saying and doing, but again these are just multiple images of Maggie moving through the bigger spread (if absolutely necessary, these can be insets).

The remaining space is taken up by a panel of Chase, oblivious to Batwoman hiding somewhere above her, and an inset showing Batwoman more clearly for the reader.

Panel 1. Maggie, starting at the top-left of the spread, looking around at the crime scene, which is now filled with images of the were-beasts and the Medusa thugs, as if drawn from Maggie's imagination.

(Again, note that the "panel" is really just Maggie's placement in the bigger spread — not a discrete panel on its own.)

1-MAGGIE:
Pretty routine ambush.

Panel 2. Maggie is kneeling near a pool of blood, only a few paces from where she started in "panel" 1. On the left side of the pool are armed Medusa thugs; on the right side, a group of were-beasts charging forward, some getting gunned down, others making it through and lashing out at the thugs. Members of both crews are already falling to the ground. We can see a trail of blood leading from the pool on the ground to the Medusa thugs dragging away their victim.

2-MAGGIE:
Unsubs attacked our missing victim here, but only managed to lop off his **hand** before Abbott's crew arrived.

NOTE: "Unsub" is jargon for "unidentified subject."

Panel 3. Maggie has moved a few paces towards the right of the panel, where the were-beasts are coming through the windows or over the makeshift rooftops. She's pointing towards the right, sort of directing our attention.

3-MAGGIE:
Based on the position of the bodies and the **debris** pattern, a first wave of weres came in from the east.

Panel 4. Maggie has moved further right, across the center of the spread, right where the were-beasts are dropping in from above, and in the middle of the conflict. She's looking up, pointing above.

4-MAGGIE:
But that was just a distraction. The second wave came in from **above**.

Panel 5. Maggie is standing right next to the Killer Croc silhouette stand-in. She's looking at the ground, where dead and dying weres have collected, looking at the evidence rather than the figure itself.

5-MAGGIE:
Something went wrong... Several weres look like they've been torn apart.

6-MAGGIE:
The unsubs had a **meta** with them. A big one.

Panel 6. Maggie has moved nearly to the bottom right now. She's pointing towards the blood trail left behind by the soon-to-be-Hook as he is being dragged away. It's imperative that we show his left hand missing from his body, dripping blood.

7-MAGGIE:
Unsure who won, but someone dragged the original victim away.

Panel 7. Low shot and close Chase, maybe hands on hips if we see that much of her. We're looking up at her, and can see past her, over her shoulder. A shadowy figure (Batwoman) lurks on top of one of the steel girders that forms the "roof" of the rotting arboretum, kneeling or standing and watching the scene unfold below.

Note: I may decide to combine 7 and 8 into a single image but use a panel box around Batwoman to isolate her from the shot of Chase.

8-CHASE:
Yeah, that's pretty much how we see it too.

Panel 8 (inset to panel 7). Zoom in on Batwoman atop the arboretum, hiding in the shadows, well out of view. She's looking down at the scene, though, and smiling.

9-BATWOMAN (whisper):
Nice work, babe.

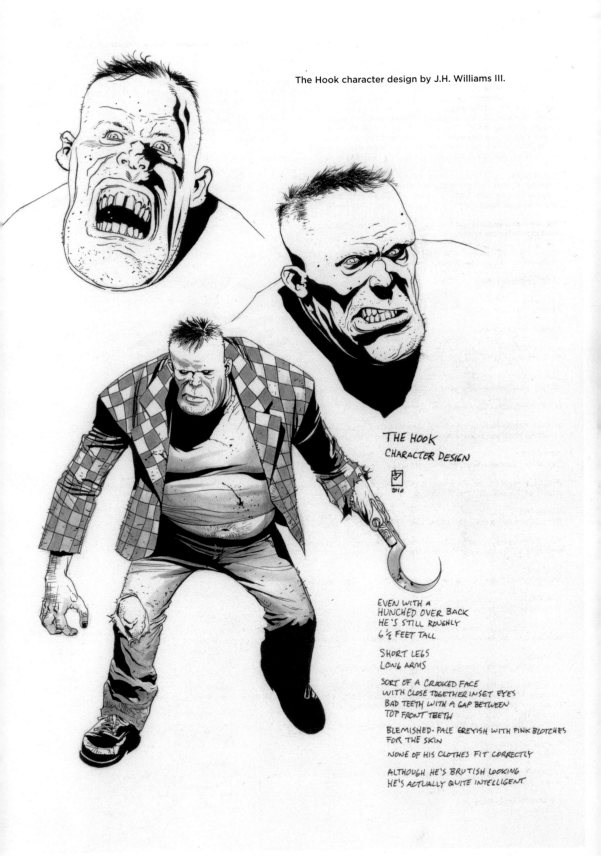

The Hook character design by J.H. Williams III.

THE HOOK
CHARACTER DESIGN

2010

EVEN WITH A
HUNCHED OVER BACK
HE'S STILL ROUGHLY
6 ½ FEET TALL

SHORT LEGS
LONG ARMS

SORT OF A CROOKED FACE
WITH CLOSE TOGETHER INSET EYES
BAD TEETH WITH A GAP BETWEEN
TOP FRONT TEETH

BLEMISHED- PALE GREYISH WITH PINK BLOTCHES
FOR THE SKIN

NONE OF HIS CLOTHES FIT CORRECTLY

ALTHOUGH HE'S BRUTISH LOOKING
HE'S ACTUALLY QUITE INTELLIGENT

Design by J.H. Williams III for the Boathouse used in the first two story arcs of BATWOMAN.

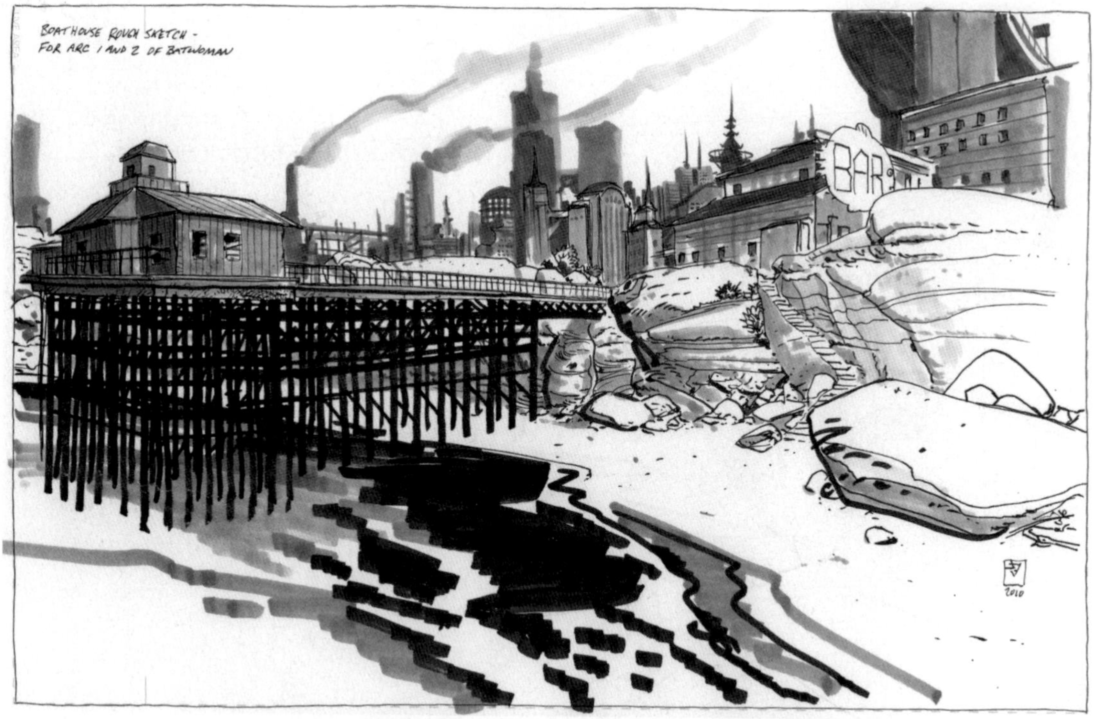
BOATHOUSE ROUGH SKETCH -
FOR ARC 1 AND 2 OF BATWOMAN
BAR
2010

Cover sketches by J.H. Williams III for BATWOMAN issues #0, 1, 4 and 5.

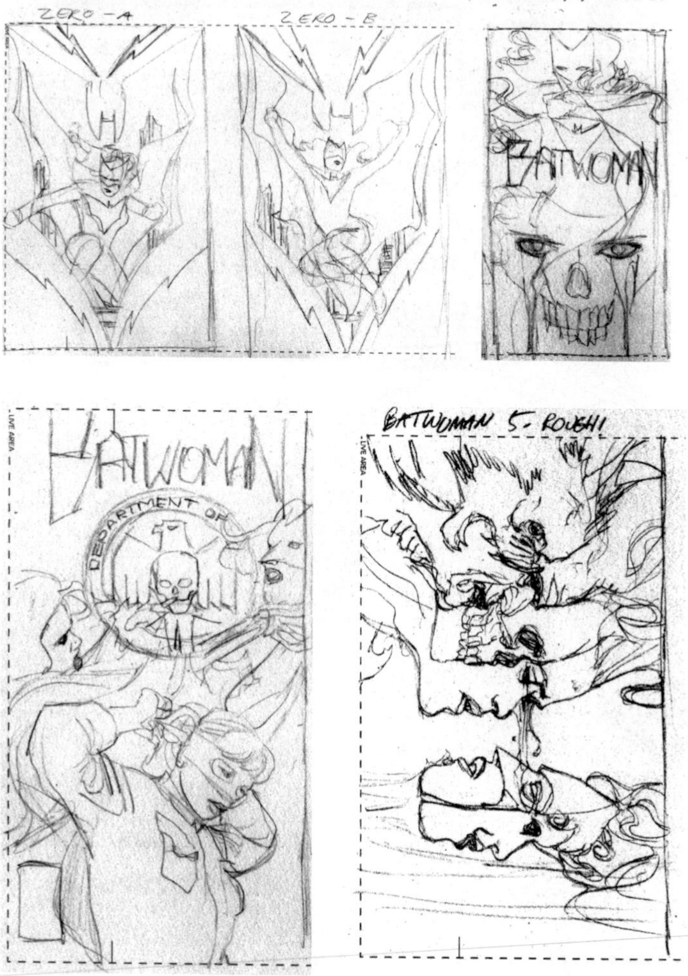
ZERO - A
ZERO - B
BATWOMAN
BATWOMAN
DEPARTMENT OF
BATWOMAN 5 - ROUGH